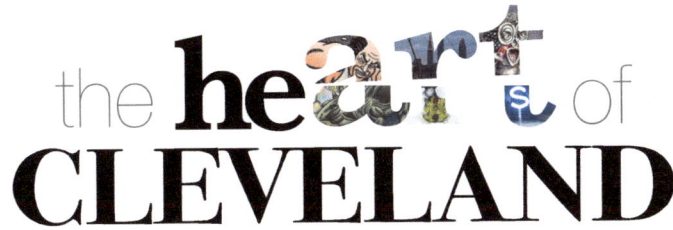

the heART**s** of CLEVELAND

BY SCOTT KRAYNAK

INTRODUCTION BY HENRY ADAMS

ESSAYS BY DOUGLAS MAX UTTER,
WILLIAM G. SCHEELE, RA WASHINGTON
AND MIKE HUDSON

COVER DESIGN AND INTERIOR LAYOUT
BY BRANDON WEIL
brandonweil.com

FOR CLEVELAND.....

FIRST EDITION, 2018
ISBN 978-0-9968717-8-5
PRINTED IN THE UNITED STATES BY:
INGRAMSPARK

FOR MORE "HEART OF CLEVELAND" NEWS, EVENTS OR INFORMATION PLEASE CONTACT SCOTT KRAYNAK AT CLEVELANDRANGER@HOTMAIL.COM

RED GIANT BOOKS
3117 HUNTINGTON RD., SHAKER HTS, OH 44120

10 9 8 7 6 5 4 3 2 1

PRINTED IN THE UNITED STATES OF AMERICA.
WWW.REDGIANTBOOKS.COM

I've said from the beginning that this is not MY book, it is OUR book. It is the City of Cleveland's book. I may have come up with the idea and concept, but without so many people helping, offering advice and guidance, this book would never have come to fruition. I would first like to thank all of the artists who supported and were excited about this idea from day one. Thank you for taking the time to communicate with me over such a long period. Thank you for your patience. And thank you for submitting art that truly embodies what Cleveland has meant to you and your work. There is no book without all of you.

The biggest thank you of all goes to Brandon Weil for taking so much time out of your busy schedule as a husband, father of two girls, and professional graphic designer to create the entire design and layout of this book. This would truly look like shit without you, and honestly, I don't think this would have been possible without you. By the way, Brandon and I were roommates at Kent State. After graduation and working in the area, Cleveland found a special place in Brandon's soul. That happens a lot to people.

Much thanks to Bill Scheele, Douglas Max Utter, RA Washington and Henry Adams for giving your extraordinary talents and valuable time to this project.

The essays they contributed to this book are as vital and important as the art. I thank each of you from the bottom of my heart for all the time you spent researching, gathering, contemplating, and organizing your words and art to make this book a truly educational and informative collection of Cleveland Art, its vast history, and lasting legacy. Cleveland is very fortunate to have all of you as ambassadors of the city and its art.

Thank you to Ms. Katie Steiner and the Volunteer Lawyers for the Arts for your advice and expertise. I cannot put into words how much your guidance is appreciated. You truly provide a great service for the artistic community.

To Dave Megenhardt and Red Giant Books for believing in this book and deciding to partner with me to bring this to publication. Having you behind me helped reinforce the idea that I was on the right path and that this was something that MUST be done.

Thanks to the Cleveland Museum of Art, especially James Kohler, for your help and guidance in providing me with images from the great Cleveland School artists. It is my hope that this book will continue to keep their legacy alive and garner new interest.

Much thanks to R!ch, Billy, and Christina at e11even2 Gallery for not only supporting the book, but more importantly, for fully believing in the significance of what is IN the book to host its release and exhibit during one of the most important times for art the city of Cleveland has ever seen.

RIP - Mike Hudson. Thank you for your essay, and pouring your heart out about growing up in Cleveland, the punk days, and The Pagans. Your music will never die.

Thank you to my brother Jeff for doing so much editing, re-writing, and proofreading. He is definitely the writer in our family!

And last but not least, thank you Cleveland. It's weird thanking an inanimate object such as a city, designated by man-made boundaries, taking up a piece of land that is just a piece of a much greater being called Earth. But I'll tell you, there is something about our city that just brings enormous pride, strength, and fortitude for those of us lucky to be from here. Maybe we know something the rest of the world doesn't, and I think we do, and that has been the case for many, many years. Words can't express my pride of being a Clevelander, so I'll leave it at this: I love you Cleveland; you are my heart and soul.

SCOTT KRAYNAK

FOREWORD

"Something in the water?!"

I came up with the idea for this book around four years ago while park rangering at Grand Canyon National Park. I've been fortunate in this profession to have lived and worked in some of the most beautiful and pristine areas of the United States. But no matter where I have found myself, Cleveland has never left my heart and soul. I could be at the rim of the Grand Canyon or the middle of the Everglades, and Cleveland would always pulse through my veins and be on my mind.

It's not that Cleveland is perfect or some sort of utopia, it just seems that if you are born and raised in a place, you can't help but feel a sense of pride and affection for it that the rest of the world may not quite understand or appreciate.

While I have extremely fond memories and feelings toward Cleveland, it has had its dark days, and there is always more work to do. Perhaps best illustrating its darker times, the great Robert Crumb has this recollection of his time there back in the 1960's:

I actually don't have fond memories of Cleveland. I remember Cleveland as a harsh, brutal city, a place which was rapidly being wasted and destroyed, and whatever there once was that was nice about the city being flattened, wiped off the map, by the venal, greedy, racist bastards who ran it strictly for their own benefit and didn't give two shits about the general population. I remember Cleveland as a city divided into bitter ethnic enclaves who all feared and despised each other, a city where everyone I knew who was sensitive or visionary either committed suicide, became a severe alcoholic, ended in a mental hospital or on narcotic drugs, or left town. Only Pekar stayed and persisted and stuck it out through the decades, by the skin of his teeth, 'til cancer got him.

I used to ride the Euclid Avenue bus, or the Cedar Avenue bus, all the way from downtown, from Public Square, out to where I lived near University Circle, instead of taking the rapid transit sometimes to get home from work (at American Greetings) just to gaze out the window and observe the vast bleakness of the streets, on and on for miles… It was appalling to behold.

This is not a pleasant or joyous rememberence of Cleveland, but it's true and it's real. But as any hard-nosed, strong-bodied, good-hearted, proud Clevelander would hopefully attest to, we aren't afraid of hard work and sweat to make things better and to improve our city. And I would like to think that we have done so in many ways.

I am not a good writer, and I have a hard time putting my heart-felt thoughts into words even in normal conversations. Maybe that's why I am a visual artist. Not all of us can master BOTH the visual and verbal like our friend Crumb. I guess what I hope to convey in this foreward is that after taking in all of the art submitted for this book (the different mediums, styles, methods, fields, and subject matter), that the reader will have an even greater understanding of the incredible power that this city has; that it's touched so many different artists in so many different ways, and has motivated them to turn this inspiration into a celebration of where they come from. Not only is this book meant to be visually stimulating, but reading the essays will educate the long, proud history that Cleveland has with its artists.

Of course we are not the only city that has this inspiration or diversity of aritsts. But hey, along with so many other inventions (the electric streetcar and traffic light, golf ball, Superman, medical scanner, gas engine, gas mask, rock n roll, etc.) let this book celebrate the wide variety of ALL artists in ALL fields and mediums birthed from ONE city; our city! As always, Cleveland Rocks.

It is my simple hope that after going through this book, people will look at the city of Cleveland as not only a beautiful place with plenty of extraordinary things to offer, including one of the largest sources of freshwater in the world, Lake Erie, but also as a breeding ground for world-class artists who have sprung from this fertile ground.

But again, maybe Cleveland does have some mystic powers (perhaps it's in the water). Again, here is Crumb:

[I came across] a gypsy lady in a shop at 105th and Euclid. I was 19 at the time and still a virgin, feeling very depressed about my prospects, especially with GURLS. The gypsy lady read my palm and told me, "Your luck's gonna change." She got that right. Eventually, I got EVERYTHING I EVER WANTED! But you know the old proverb, be careful what you wish for. You might GET IT!!

Maybe we've already got it and just don't know it!

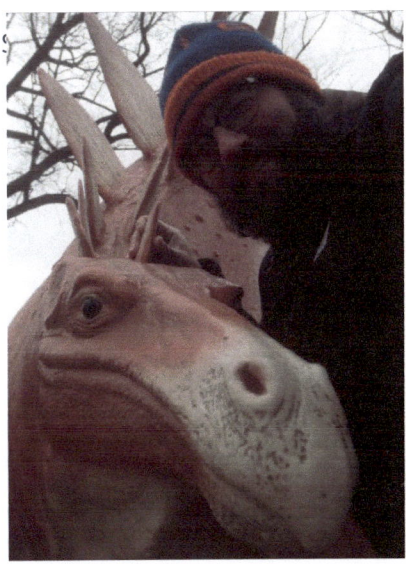

CAN GREAT ART BE PRODUCED IN CLEVELAND?

When I first came to Cleveland for some reason I had just developed a passion for Art Deco, and in reading about American art deco one object struck me as particularly remarkable, a large punch bowl known as The Jazz Bowl which was reproduced in just about every book on Art Deco that I came across. Indeed, one book, The Look of the Century, reproduced it twice. At some point, someone mentioned to me that the man who designed the Jazz Bowl was named Viktor Schreckengost, and that he lived right here in Cleveland. On a whim I decided to call him up. There were not very many Schreckengosts in the phone book (it was still the age of phone books), and only one Viktor. I was then a curator at the Cleveland Museum of Art, and he agreed to come down to talk to me. We met in the lobby. After half an hour of conversation I was struck that he had interesting stories to tell, I decided that it would be interesting to do some interviews with him, and I enlisted a graduate student to help me transcribe them.

I must confess that a good deal of what led me to do this is that Viktor had known many of the notable American artists of the early 20th century, such as Charles Burchfield and Rockwell Kent, and I thought it would be interesting to get his reminiscences of them. But as he talked about his life, I realized that he had done quite a bit himself, that there was a story about his work that had never been fully written up. Not only had he designed the Jazz Bowl, but he had done monumental sculptures, had exhibited paintings around the country, had done stage and costume design, and had produced a fantastic amount of industrial design, including the first modern mass-produced American dinnerware, and the first cab-over-engine truck. Indeed, some 100 million bicycles had been made to his designs.

In fact, it turned out that he had designed the very bicycle my student had owned as a child, one of those "Kooky bikes" with a huge rear wheel and a tiny front wheel, designed to do wheelies and acrobatic tricks. Bright magenta in color, it had pretzel handlebars, a banana seat, a gigantic gearshift, and a sissy bar on the back. She had carefully picked it out herself and it had been a fixture of her childhood. Viktor was well into his 90s at the time, and I was rather curious what sort of impression he had made on a youngster of today with his tales of things that happened in the days of Franklin and Eleanor Roosevelt. I need not have worried. As we left the house, Shannon turned to me and commented: "You know, Viktor is wicked cool."

In the end this set of interviews with Viktor ended up leading to an exhibition of his work at the Cleveland Museum of Art, which proved a great popular success and also provided full documentation of his career and achievements for the first time. I always like to end an exhibition with a "surprise," rather like what you get when you open a Faberge egg. In most cases the "surprise" is the most stunning and expensive work of art in the show, but in this instance it was exactly the reverse. The last room of the show featured bicycles, electric fans, lawn furniture and pedal cars that Viktor had designed, which many of them designs that visitors recognized because they had grown up with them, or even still had them at home. They had never stopped to think about who might have designed these objects, or about the fact that they were, in fact, remarkable works of art.

When we're asking whether great art can exist in Cleveland, I think the career of Viktor Schreckengost shows that it can. But at the same time, we need to be willing to recognize that great art often appears in unexpected guises, and often doesn't fit into the categories we're accustomed to. Viktor Schreckengost's career provides a good example of that. The irony is that a figure like Viktor who worked largely anonymously affected the lives of millions of people, far more than most draftsmen, printmakers or painters.

If you look through surveys of American art, there's little made in Cleveland that's featured, but that, I think reflect a number of biases. Surveys of art history usually focus principally on oil paintings, and much of what's been made in Cleveland has fit into other categories, such as metalwork, pottery, and industrial design, which get less attention than they deserve. Indeed, even when they made paintings, Cleveland artists generally did their best work in watercolor—often classes as a "minor" medium—rather than in oil. What's more, Cleveland art draws on sources of inspiration different from that of many other American centers such as Boston or New York. Those places drew largely on influences from Paris, whereas Cleveland, which was largely settled by figures from Eastern Europe, drew inspiration largely from Germany, Austria, and central European countries. Viktor Schreckengost, for example, after graduating from the Cleveland School of Art, studied in Vienna, at the Kunstegerbeschule, where he worked with some of the great pioneers of modern design, such as the architect Josef Hofmann. In the last few decades, art historians have become more interested in the artistic centers of Germany and central Europe, such as Berlin, Vienna, and Prague, and surely in time this will lead to a reassessment of Cleveland art as well.

The first artist from Cleveland to produce work that was noteworthy on the national stage was Archibald Willard, who was largely self-taught, and who began his career as a carriage painter and then moved into making designs for popular prints, often of comic subjects. In 1875 he moved from Wellington, Ohio, to Cleveland, to be closer to his publisher, James F. Ryder, and in that year he produced a painting that became a huge popular success, The Spirit of '76, showing three rag-tag revolutionary soldiers, of different ages and in mismatched costumes, proudly marching together, to fife and drum. With its mix of patriotism and humor, the painting captured something deep-rooted in American society, a spirit of good-humored improvisation, and the ability to set aside differences to work together. It's still an iconic emblem of the spirit of America, even today.

What might be termed the "golden age" of Cleveland art, however, came just a little later, and coincided with the extraordinary growth in the city at the turn of the century, as a hub for railroads and shipping on the Great Lakes, and as a center of steel-making, oil refining, and manufacturing of all sorts. Notably, Cleveland became the center of operations for John D. Rockefeller, who astutely recognized that the key to controlling the Pennsylvania oil industry was not pumping oil from the ground but refining it and shipping it to market. Cleveland made the ideal place for this, since it had three competing railroad lines, and if their rates were too high, one could circumvent all three and send the oil by boat over the Great Lakes. By making secret deals with the railroads for low rates, and quietly buying up refineries, Rockefeller came close to establishing a monopoly on the sale of oil, and became the richest person in human history up to that point.

What's been largely forgotten is that during this period Cleveland was also the center of many art-focused businesses, such as furniture-making, clothing manufacture, wallpaper production, the printing of posters, and sheet-music publishing. These all required designers and artists. Sheet music covers, for example, are a rich and still largely-unexplored area of illustration. Even the manufacture of things such as radiators and automobiles often required artistic skills. Consequently, during this period Cleveland supported some five or six thousand commercial artists, among whom were two or three hundred painters who supported themselves through the exhibition and sale of their work.

Several newly formed organizations provided a support network for this group. The Kokoon Klub, which started as a place where artists from Otis Lithograph, and other commercial printers, could draw from the nude model, quickly became a center of modernists ferment, as well as the staging place for the annual Kokoon Klub Ball, an annual carnival which for a night each year overturned the staid traditions of Cleveland with its risqué entertainment and wacky decorations and costumes. More sedate was the Cleveland School of Art, which interestingly was founded by a group of wealthy women with grand homes on Euclid Avenue. It came into the world as a school of art for women, intended to provide a profession for women other than prostitution or domestic service which could earn them a living wage. While eventually it accepted male students as well—in the early years, men snuck into classes by agreeing to serve as "janitors"—the school has always had a strong emphasis on professional training for women, and has also differed from many art schools in its emphasis on industrial design and handicrafts as well as painting. Finally, there was the Cleveland Museum of Art, which from 1919 to 1993 staged The May Show, an annual exhibition of the work of Cleveland art in different categories, with awards and prizes, which drew huge crowds, stirred up local interest, and generated sales. On a smaller, more informal level, was a colorful local hangout, Laukhauf's bookstore, in the downtown Arcade, which carried adventurous writing on modern art, and where you could even buy copies of banned books, like James Joyce's Ulysses, under the table. It provided an informal meeting place for a group of modern-minded figures in various creative fields, many of whom went on to great achievement, such as the painter William Sommer, the architect William Lescaze, and the poet Hart Crane.

Determining who was a "Cleveland artist" is a little complicated, since some artists spent their entire careers in Cleveland and others just a few years here before moving on to other parts. But during this period Cleveland served as both a training ground and a home for a surprising number of notable artists. During this period Cleveland was one of the nation's major centers of printing, due partly to its location, which made distribution on a national basis relatively swift, and partly to the fact that it was home to Harris Printing, the nation's major manufacturer of printings presses. It's often forgotten, for example, that when Henry Luce established Time, Life, and Fortune magazines, he established his headquarters in Cleveland, because of its preeminence in handling print runs of massive scale.

Loosely speaking the notable artists of Cleveland might be divided between those who flourished in fields of commercial art and those who taught at art schools. Interestingly, many of the key modernists—the painter William Sommer (who stayed in Cleveland), and the sculptors William Zorach and Hugo Robus (who moved on) all worked at Otis Lithograph. The great photographer Margaret Bourke-White, who started as a commercial photographer in Cleveland, worked with Henry Luce at Fortune and Life magazines. An unusual highlight of this period is the work of Paul Feher at Rose Ironworks, who produced the best Art Deco ironwork in the United States, notably a remarkable fireplace screen, featuring an image of Josephine Baker, which is generally considered the greatest American masterpiece in this genre. Interestingly, along with his artistic accomplishments William Zorach was an important innovator in art education. He was the first person in the United States to teach art classes for small children which stressed bringing out their inner creative impulses rather than drilling them into copying by rote.

Other important figures studied at or taught at the Cleveland School of Art. One of the earliest graduates of the school, for example, was Clara Driscoll, one of the greatest artists of the age, who went on to design most of Louis Tiffany's lamps, and also headed "The Tiffany Girls," a group of female glassworkers who produced much of the Tiffany firm's best work. By the 1920s and 1930s the school had a good number of quite gifted painters on its faculty, including Henry Keller, Paul Travis, and Frank Wilcox, all of whom produced very good work, particularly in watercolor. Aside from Viktor Schreckengost, who established this country's first program in modern industrial design, probably the school's most illustrious graduate in this period was Charles Burchfield, who eventually settled in Buffalo, but whose work clearly reflected the teachings and viewpoint of "The Cleveland school." In addition, several other painters also achieved a national reputation, among them Clarence Carter, many of whose paintings landed in major museums, including the Museum of Modern Art. As noted, a key factor in energizing Cleveland art was the May Show at the Cleveland Museum of Art, supervised by William Milliken, who first came to the museum as curator of decorative arts in 1919, was promoted to Chief Curator in 1925, and served as director from 1930 to 1958.

Sadly, while there were bursts of notable achievement, the "golden age" of Cleveland art sputtered to an end in the years after World War II, in part due to the demise of many of the industries that had supported Cleveland artists, such as the publishing of hand-drawn lithographic posters, or sheet music covers. By the late 1930s, a diaspora of Cleveland artists began to take place, with many of them moving first to New York, and later to Hollywood. In addition, with the retirement of William Milliken in 1958, the May Show lost its energy and life. Ironically, in 1957, Leonard Hanna of Cleveland left a bequest to the Cleveland Museum of Art which made it the richest museum with regard to funds for the purchase of works of art, but Milliken's successor, Sherman Lee, took a perverse pride in disdaining support of local or regional art and preferred to focus on "masterpieces" produced elsewhere. This was also the period when Cleveland industry went through a drastic decline, the urban population dropped by 50%, and urban problems multiplied, culminating in the Hough riots of 1966, in which four people were killed, hundreds of buildings were set on fire, and twenty blocks of the commercial strip on Hough Avenue was completely destroyed. Despite the devastation of this period, however, Cleveland artists continued to produce significant work. Most notably, it became a leading center of Op Art, including Ed Mieckowski, Richard Anuskiewicz and Julian Stanzcak.

I wish Cleveland did more for its living artists. It's a shame that the May Show was extinguished. One of the most positive developments of the last few years has been the magazine CAN--edited and directed by Michael Gill. The unusual name of the magazine stands for Cleveland Arts Network, a collection which now includes over 100 different Ohio arts organizations, both for profit and non-profit. I must confess, that while my business is to know about art, before CAN I had no idea of the number of arts organizations and art galleries in the area, and of the resources available in Cleveland for paper-making, print-making, glass-blowing, and other creative activities. CAN has made the activities of these organizations available and accessible in a new way.

The magic of the magazine is that it's both elitist and populist. It's been the vehicle for some of the deepest, most probing, most thoughtful art-writing we've seen in Cleveland for a long time, by people like William Busta and Douglas Utter, and also a place where individual artists and small arts organizations can have a voice, can say their two bits, and can contribute to the larger arts community. I think CAN has played a significant role in some of the popular surges of interest in the arts that we've seen lately, as a popular phenomenon, such as the enormous attendance on Friday evenings at the 78th Street Studios.

Along with the magazine itself, Michael has also played an active role in other activities, notably the CAN Triennial, which will add a local and regional component to the FRONT Triennial, which is devoted almost exclusively to the work of artist from elsewhere.

Can Cleveland produce great art today? The answer of course is "Yes." My own involvement with living Cleveland artists has been somewhat haphazard, and not the result of any clearly organized program, but I've had the good fortune of working with two Cleveland artists whose work I think is very good, indeed: Chris Pekoc and Dexter Davis. Chris produces remarkable work with pieces sewn together, in a way which suggests wounds inflicted on a body, and deals with issues of damage and healing. Dexter produces multi-media extravaganzas, which explore, in a poetic and almost religious way, the challenges of growing up African-American in a very tough neighborhood in Cleveland. His work is at once disturbing and inspiring and has an amazing rhythmic pulse. Dexter supports himself as a guard at the Cleveland Museum of Art, which has purchased one of his best multi-media creations, and thus, rather amusingly, often has been assigned the job of guarding his own work. What I like about both these artists is their willingness to take on tough subject matter, and to deal with it an authentic way. While their work isn't parochial, it grows in large part out of their experiences in Cleveland.

In singling out their work, I don't wish to imply that there aren't other artists in Cleveland of powerful talent as well. Surely one of these is Douglas Utter, who's not only a painter of probing, perhaps somewhat neurotic intelligence, but a writer of remarkable skill, insight, and interpretive depth. Of course there are dozens of other very gifted artists, although though it becomes boring to start making long lists and trying to mention everyone. This book does a wonderful job of bringing together the work of some really remarkable talents, including figures whose work I didn't know.

To speak only of "great art," however, to my mind is to do the community a disservice. I think for example of the artist Jose Ruiz Blasco (1883-1913) who was an art teacher in Malaga Spain and specialized in paintings of pigeons. Art historians have not been gracious in what they've said about this work: they view his paintings as repetitive and unimpressive. But he was the father and the first teacher of an artist they regard more highly Pablo Picasso, who developed his amazing technical skills as a child under his father's tutelage. Surely, in a healthy art community, the art-making impulse is spread more widely than to a few geniuses. Teachers, amateurs, and artists who never become famous are important as well. That's what enables art-making to grow and flourish. It's important, I think, that we all become more aware of the range and diversity of art-making taking place around us, and this book is a very positive step towards that goal.

HENRY ADAMS

Ruth Coulter Heede Professor of Art History
Case Western Reserve University, Cleveland

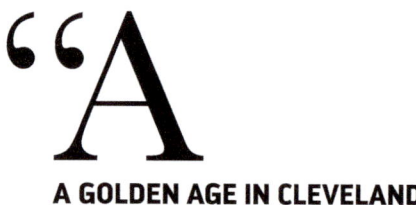

A GOLDEN AGE IN CLEVELAND

THE CLEVELAND SCHOOL ARTISTS

I first heard of the "Cleveland School Artists" from my parents, both artists from a generation who had art teachers Jean and Paul Ulen at West Tech High School, along with Henry Keller, Frank Wilcox, Paul Travis and Carl Gaertner at the Cleveland School of Art. My mother and father revered their art teachers and honored them throughout their lives.

My father's early interest in art and nature came from his love of early American artists Alexander Wilson and John James Audubon. The interest in nature was fueled by frequent family excursions in the surrounding countryside observing wildlife, while collecting rocks, fossils and Indian artifacts. The family home in Cleveland's Old Brooklyn neighborhood still houses the museum they developed, complete with built-in display cases.

Jean and Paul Ulen taught for decades at West Tech High School, promoting strong drawing and tight watercolor skills learned at London's Slade School of Art. My mother Joann, gravitated to portraiture. My father William, honed his nature study skills under their tutelage in the late 1930s. When my parents moved on to the Cleveland School of Art, their abilities were broadened by the combination of traditional and modern art training from an incredible faculty of artists.

Here is some background history on how Cleveland's art scene evolved to such a high level during the first half of the twentieth century.

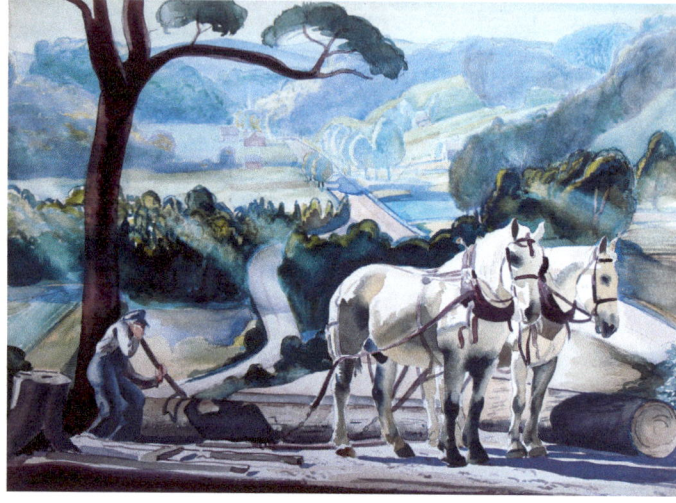
Fig.1 Ulen, Paul "Horses in Field"

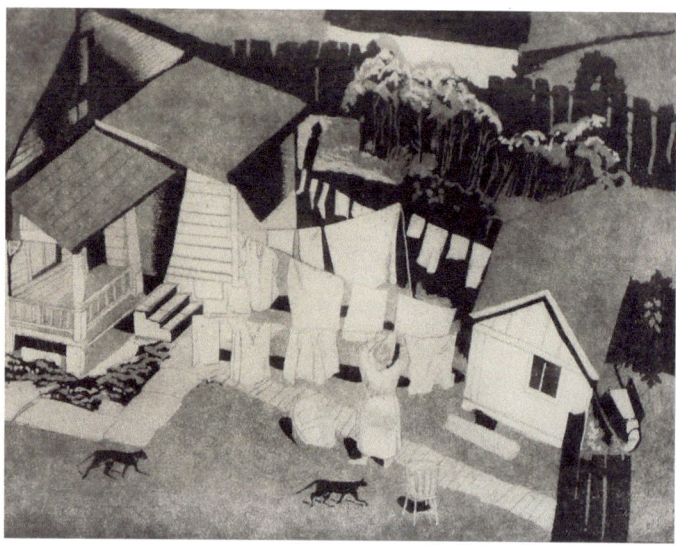
Fig.2 Ulen, Jean "Washday"

LATE 19TH CENTURY

From the time of the Civil War through the Turn of the Century, Cleveland's population exploded from 40,000 to 400,000 people. The development of oil refining, steel and other manufacturing work attracted immigrant workers from all over Europe. A group of new, wealthy businessmen built elaborate mansions that utilized skilled wood and stone craftsmen, and painters provided decorative motifs, landscapes and family portraits. Creative work was nurtured in the growing city.

Archibald Willard was a leader of the earliest group of Cleveland artists, known as the "Old Bohemians." They included Adam Lehr, Allen Smith, Louis Loeb, John Semon, Otto Bacher, R. Way Smith, Max Bohm, Frederick Gottwald and others. Willard's painting of The Spirit of '76 is one of the most recognizable images of early American Patriotism. After it was originally created in 1876, its popularity required several other versions to be produced. Classical subjects were the primary focus of these early painters, producing beautiful portraits, still life works and landscapes. This group also formed the first Cleveland Art Club in 1875 and provided instructors for the emerging art school.

CLEVELAND SCHOOL OF ART

The Western Reserve School of Design for Women was established in 1882. Despite its name, the school also had male students, and one, Henry Keller, would go on to teach there for 42 years. By 1888, the school became associated with Western Reserve University, but had its own charter as the School of Art. By 1891, the school and university separated and the Cleveland School of Art emerged under the leadership of Georgie Leighton Norton, with the intention of providing a balanced education in fine and applied arts.

Many local artists made a living teaching at the Cleveland School of Art, primarily following a traditional European structure, focused on basic drawing, painting, sculpture and design. Frederick Gottwald, Henry Turner Bailey, Herman Matzen, Walter Sinz, Louis Rorimer and Henry Keller were the established Elders, followed by George Adomeit, Frank Wilcox, William Eastman, Rolf Stoll, Paul Travis, Carl Gaertner, Grace Kelly, William Grauer and others.

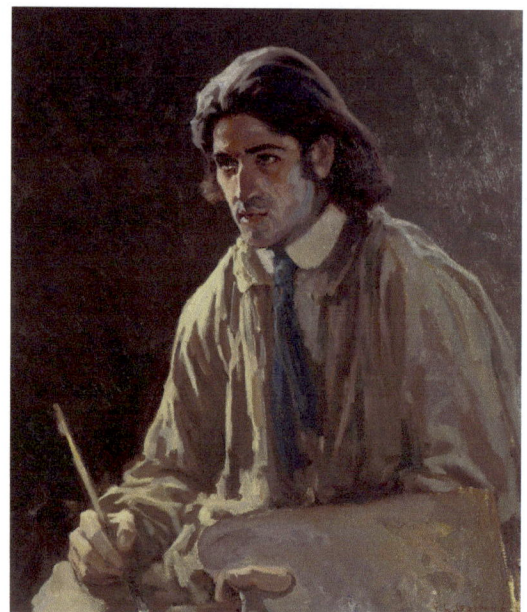

Fig.3 Gottwald, Frederick "The Dremaer"

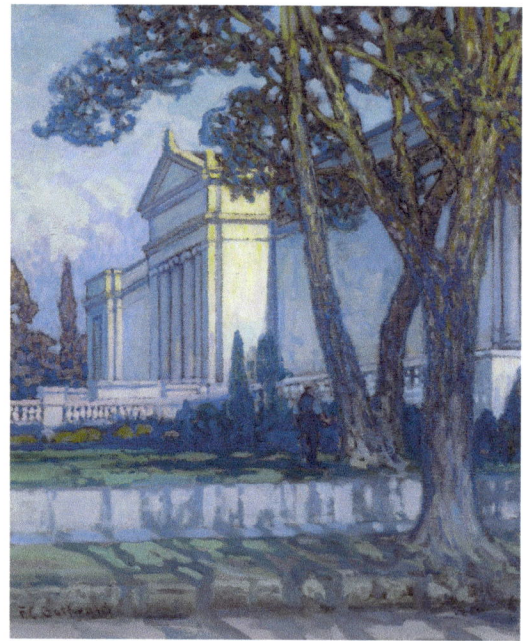

Fig.4 Gottwald, Frederick "View of CMA"
©Cleveland Museum of Art

Frederick Gottwald (1858-1941) was one of the first local artists to study in Europe. He spent four years at the Royal Academy in Munich, followed by work with William M. Chase in New York, prior to his return to teaching in Cleveland. Gottwald was a drawing and painting teacher who greatly influenced many of the school's early students until his retirement in 1926. His summer travels in Italy influenced new, colorful landscapes in sharp contrast to older, darker works. He was awarded the Penton Medal at the 1919 May Show for his powerful self portrait, titled The Dreamer.

Henry Keller (1869-1949) was a beloved teacher who exerted major influence on many early Cleveland School artists like Frank Wilcox, Paul Travis and Charles Burchfield. He taught at the Cleveland School of Art and the Carnegie Institute for over 40 years. Keller's interest in impressionism and "en plein air" painting inspired him to teach summertime classes outdoors in Berlin Heights, Ohio (1903-1920s) with Grace Kelly, Frank Wilcox, Clara Deike, August Biehle and William Eastman. From 1910 to 1913, he collaborated with John MacCleod (Western Reserve Medical School) on color theories, which found academic painting to be dull and unimaginative, favoring the brighter, inventive colors of the post-impressionists and fauves. Keller promoted Cezanne as the pioneer of new pictorial design, unifying compositions through abstract structural rhythms and surrounding forms with intense blue to create dimensional volume. He lectured publicly on the modern art movements and urged artists to be creators, instead of copyists.

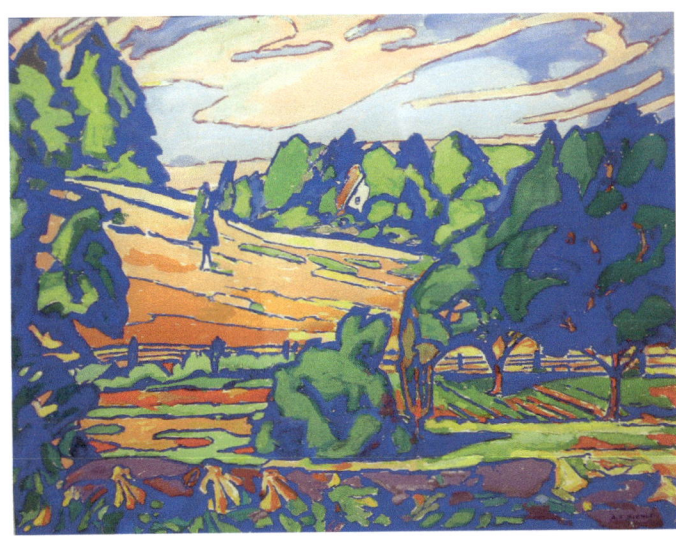

Fig.5 Biehle,August "Hillside in Berlin Heights"

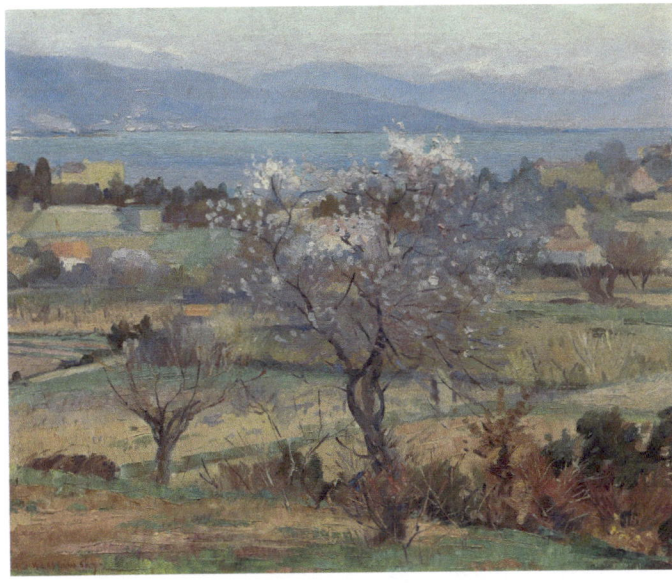

Fig.6 Warshawsky, Abel "Springtime"

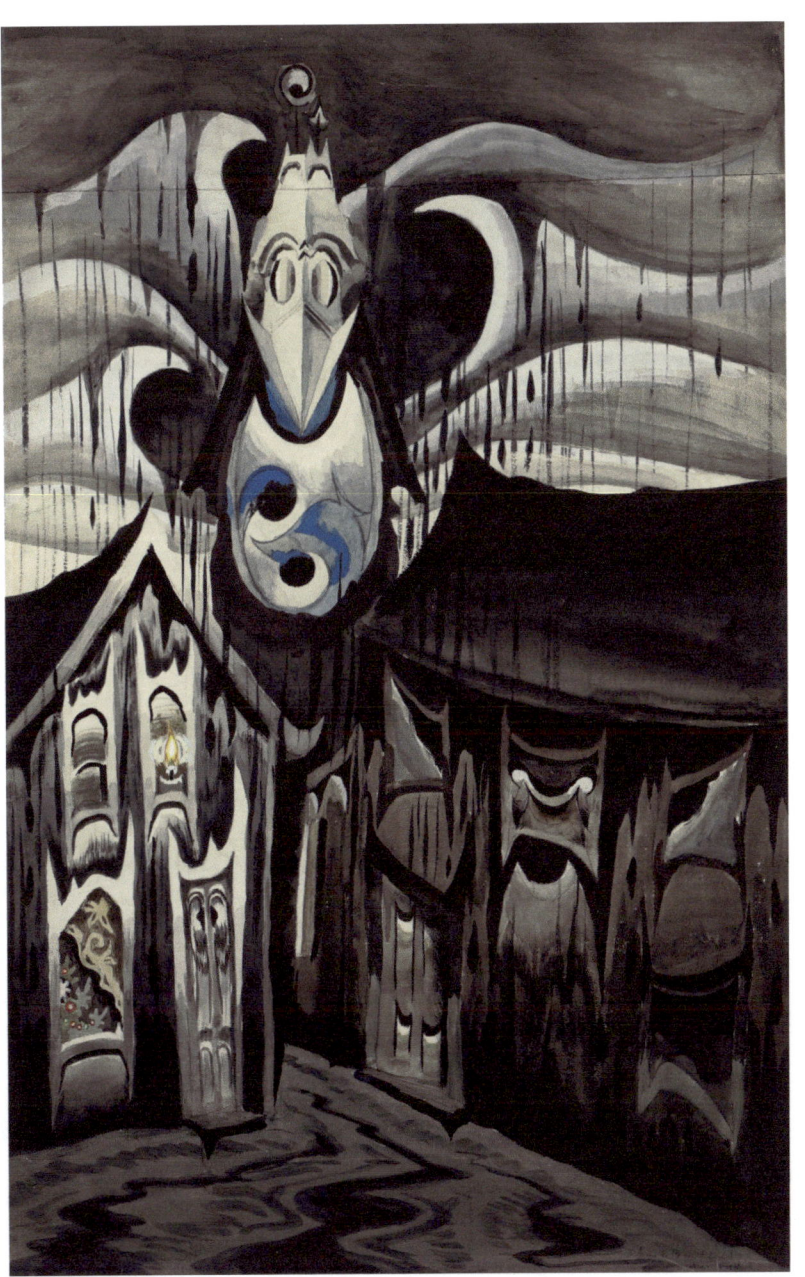

Fig.7 Burchfield, Charles "Church Bells Ringing"
©Cleveland Museum of Art

EARLY 1900S

By 1910, Cleveland's population had doubled to 800,000, making it the country's 6th largest city. The city's growth enabled the art community to grow... first with the art school's evolutionary growth and second with the creation of the art museum.

Several local artists traveled to Europe to experience the Modernist Movement in the early 1900s and came back with new and different attitudes, seeking more individuality and freedom from conventional standards. By 1909, Henry Keller and Louis Rorimer established a Design Department open to non-Western art, color theory and decorative ornament. Earlier, Rorimer had opened a studio producing handmade furniture to counter the mass production and commercialism that was sweeping America. In 1910, he championed Modernism in Cleveland exhibiting new, brilliantly colored paintings by Abel Warshawsky, who had been working in France for three years. By 1911, Keller, Warshawsky, Sommer and others exhibited as the "Secessionists," offering an alternative to the art school's juried exhibitions. In March of 1912, William Zorach had his first solo exhibition at Taylor Gallery. By the Fall, Biehle exhibits paintings at Rorimer-Brooks Studios influenced by the Blue Rider group he encountered in Germany. All of this activity preceded the famous Armory Show of 1913 in New York City, in which Henry Keller exhibited his Wisdom & Destiny painting.

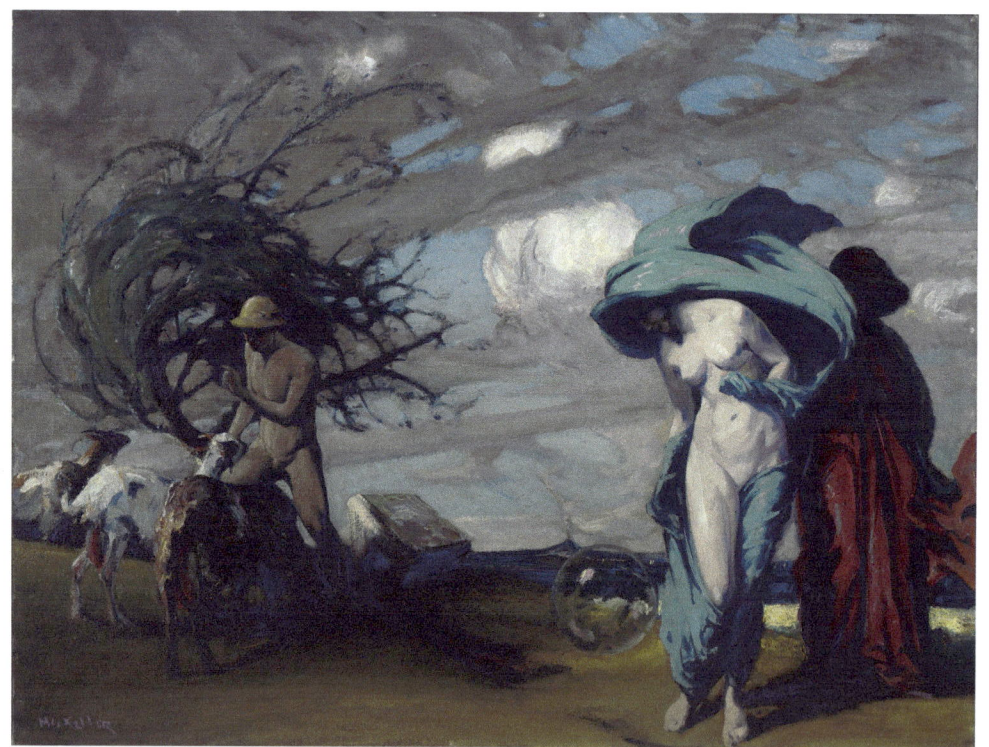

Fig.8 Keller, Henry "Wisdom & Destiny"
©Cleveland Museum of Art

Also in 1911, William Sommer and
Carl Moellman established the
Kokoon Arts Club, along with fellow
artists who worked professionally
as commercial lithographers.
Cleveland had several lithographic
printing companies that employed
artists, providing an alternative
to teaching at the art school.
Before photography took over, the
artist's drawing skills were highly
regarded in the production of

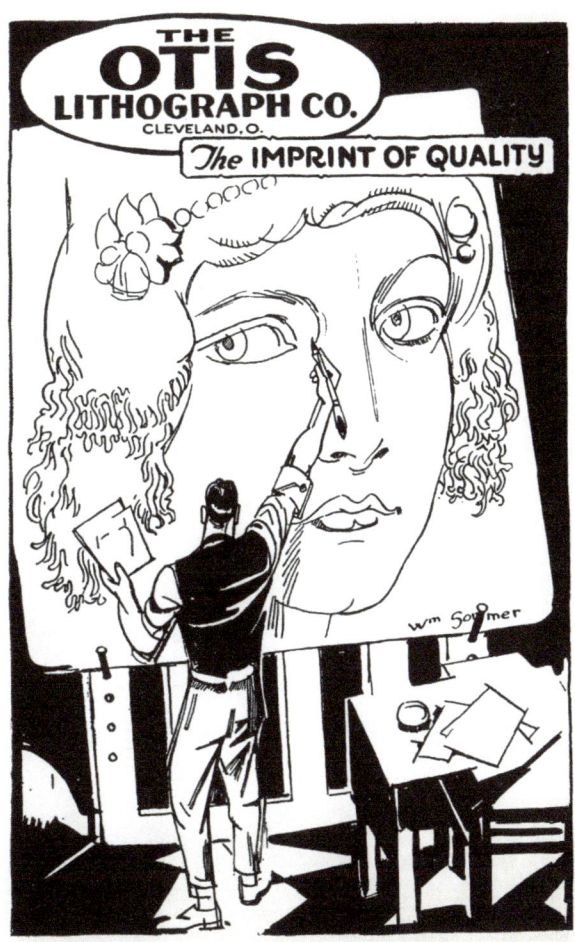

Fig.10 Sommer, William

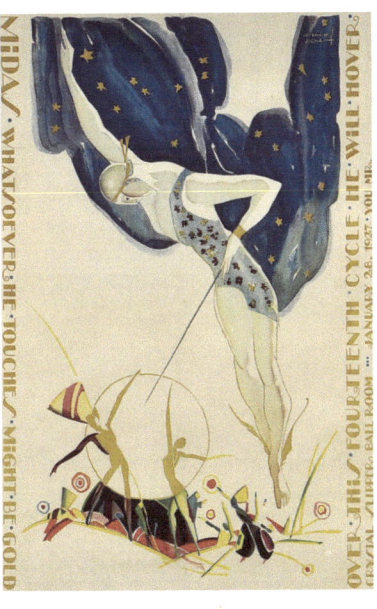

Fig.11 Jicha, Joseph

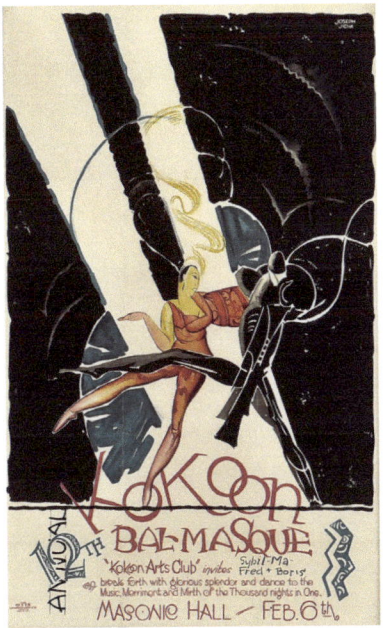

Fig,9 Jicha,Joseph

graphic advertising. Other members included Henry Keller, Joseph Jicha and August Biehle. Within a few years, they devised an event to raise funds for the club. Their costumed Bal Masque parties became a unique entertainment highlight of Cleveland society. The invitations they produced were beautiful graphic works that are now prized collectibles.

William Sommer (1867-1949) came to Cleveland via Detroit and New York to bolster the growing Cleveland printing industry. His drawing skills enabled him to stylize black & white compositions and his interest in modernist trends helped visualize more colorful designs for advertising purposes. But he ultimately believed in an artistic idealism that rejected commercial art, in favor of a true pursuit of creativity. Sommer greatly admired the work

of Kandinsky, Matisse and the Blue Rider group, and their experiments in the distortion of form and color. As he worked more from his rural, Brandywine studio in the mid-teens, he applied these new techniques to the farms, animals and children around him.

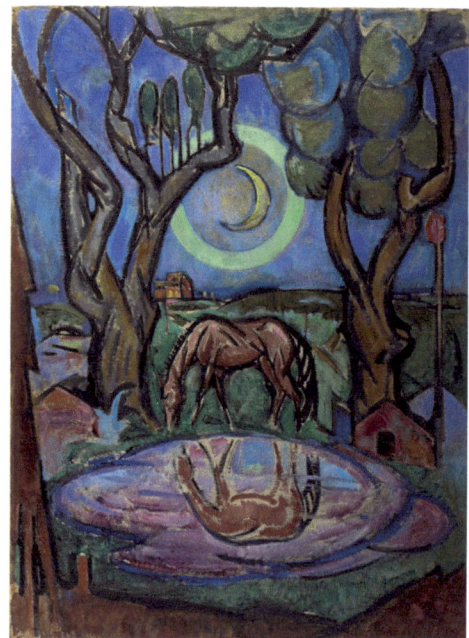

Fig.12 Sommer,William "The Pool"
©Cleveland Museum of Art

The Playhouse Settlement (later Karamu House) was founded in 1915 for social purposes and evolved as an arts center. It promoted "Democracy in Art" in celebration of the city's diverse cultures. The Cleveland Play House was established in 1916 as a workshop for music, poetry, dance and experimental art. In 1918, Sommer took the lead in designing the set, costumes and program for a production of Everyman. Art exhibitions there brought more attention to the work of Sommer, Warshawsky, Zorach, Keller, Deike, Burchfield and Robus.

Another art element emerged in 1912 with the establishment of the Women's Art Club of Cleveland with 24 charter members. Their purpose was to augment the predominantly male-oriented art groups in existence and make significant contributions to the city's art scene. Many had ties to the Cleveland

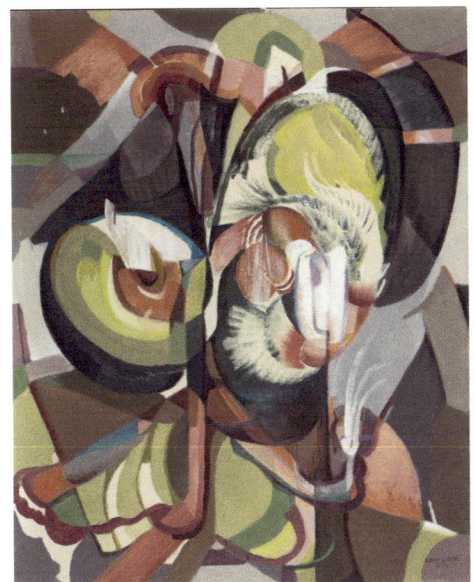

Fig.13 Deike, Clara "Rhythmic Movement"
°Cleveland Museum of Art

School of Art and exhibited regularly in the annual art museum May Show. A majority of these talented women worked in various media, bridging the gap between fine art and crafts, and adding depth to regional art. Belle Hoffman, an illustrator and fashion designer, encouraged her fellow artists to take their art seriously and work hard for success as professional artists.

Workmates William Sommer and William Zorach became the most radical followers of the Modernist Movement and participated with others in local exhibitions at Rorimer-Brooks Studio and Laukhuff's Bookstore. Richard Laukhuff was a German immigrant who opened a bookstore (1916) in the Taylor Arcade. It became a hangout for Sommer and others interested in European avant-garde magazines, left-wing periodicals (The Masses), New York's The Dial, and books by Ezra Pound and James Joyce. He also displayed modernist paintings and hosted visiting writers, like Langston Hughes and Sherwood Anderson. It was Laukhuff's gift of Anderson's Winesburg, Ohio to Charles Burchfield that influenced the painter to abandon his modernist painting for his own interpretation of the American scene. Sommer befriended Hart

Crane during this period and the two shared creative principles and the growing feelings of despair in a country moving rapidly towards mass production without artistic sensitivity.

Elmer Brubeck, August Biehle and Zorach were a few of the artists who lived and studied in France for periods of time. The Modernists were driven by an intuitive, emotional and spontaneous approach to art that contrasted greatly with the entrenched conservative artists approach, and eventually led to harsh ridicule and public rejection.

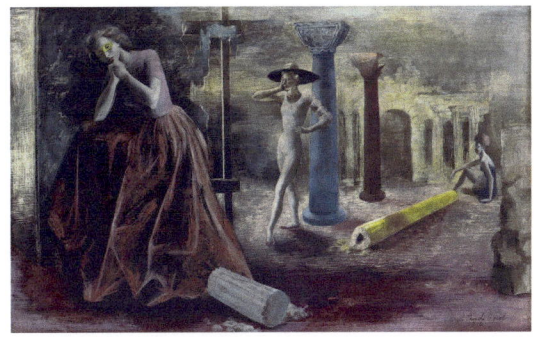

Fig. 14 Janicki, Hazel "Contemplation"

As World War I loomed, the Modernist ties to Europe were viewed by many as dangerous to the traditional values of American standards. In 1913, Frederick Gottwald, Ora Coltman, George Adomeit and others formed the Cleveland Society of Artists as a conservative rival to the modernist Kokoon Arts Club. Henry Keller was one of the most outspoken defenders of the Modernists, the Armory Show, the Cubists and the new, innovative methods of reconstructing visual imagery. But World War I brought more controversy and the Modernists were now referred to as the "Lunatic Fringe" and not allowed to participate in the first May Show in 1919. Violent riots broke out on Public Square on May Day. The war cry became the need for a return to normalcy, denying the experimental European influences.

AMERICAN REGIONALISM

After the tremendous amount of negativity generated in response to the Modernist Movement, many of our painters and printmakers moved on and gained recognition for what would become known as "Regionalism" or "American Scene" subject matter. Henry T. Bailey and Frederic Whiting, heads of the art school and art museum, both urged artists to embrace the beauty of Northeast Ohio, with its agrarian and industrial subject matter. The Cuyahoga River, with its numerous bridges and industrial operations, provided artists with ample subject matter. August Biehle, Frank Wilcox and Carl Gaertner often painted scenes of Cleveland's industrial Flats, comparing favorably to the Group of Eight and George Bellow's best works. Margaret Bourke-White photographed the area, creating new, close-up visuals using black &

white techniques. Louis Rosenberg was commissioned by the Van Sweringen brothers to produce a portfolio of 22 etchings depicting the stages of construction of the Terminal Tower complex from 1927-32. In 1921, Max Kalish created a series of bronze sculptures depicting laborers, honoring the reality of industrial America.

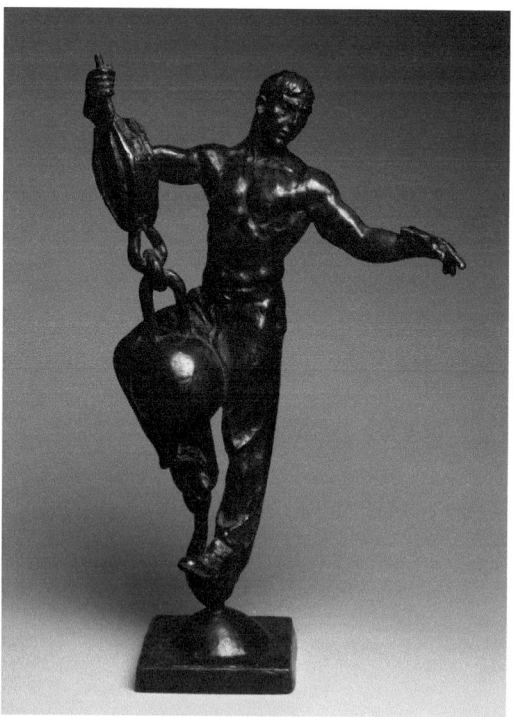

Fig.15 Kalish, Max "Riding the Crane"
©Cleveland Museum of Art

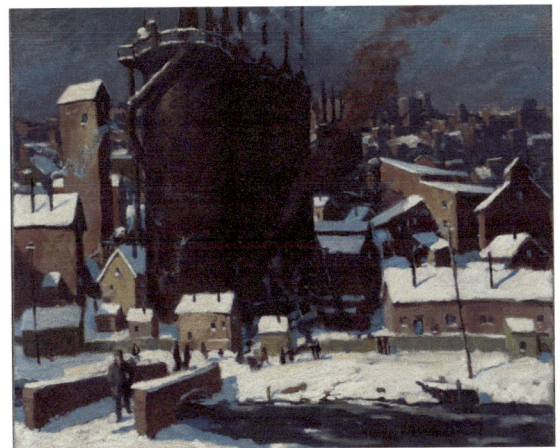

Fig.16 Gaertner, Carl "The Furnace"
©Cleveland Museum of Art

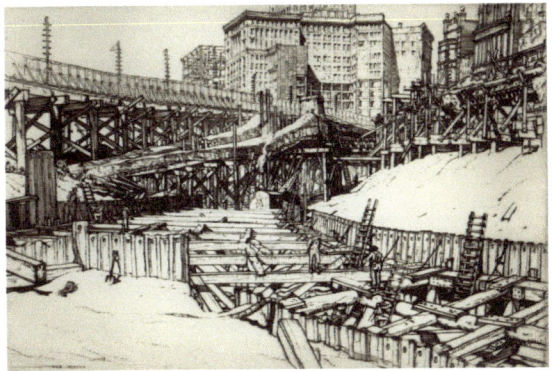

Fig.17 Rosenberg, Louis "Terminal Tower 6"

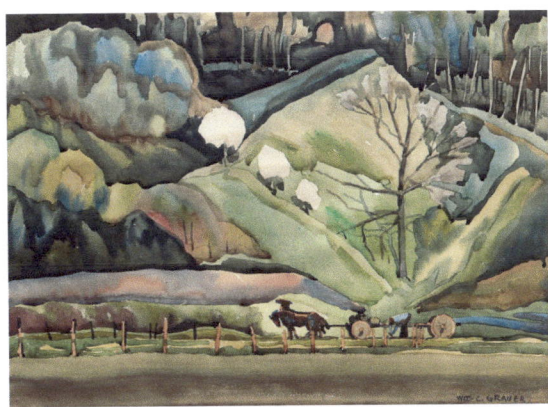

Fig.18 Grauer, William "Farm Scene in Hills"

Rural northeast Ohio also provided beautiful landscape subjects, populated with the ever-growing farming ventures. Frank Wilcox, Charles Burchfield and William Grauer all depicted activities outside city limits, honoring agrarian efforts. National contemporaries working in similar veins included Thomas Hart Benton, Grant Wood, John Stewart Curry and others.

Oil painting was always one of the most popular art mediums in the early 1900s, but by the 1930s, Cleveland had become the leader in American watercolor painting. Many Cleveland School artists exhibited their work locally and in National exhibitions, these included Henry Keller, William Sommer, August Biehle, Frank Wilcox, Abel Warshawsky, William Zorach, Grace Kelly, Ora Coltman, William Eastman, Clara Deike, Charles Burchfield, Paul Travis,

William Grauer and Carl Gaertner. The medium echoed the modernists love of the swift and spontaneous ability to translate subject matter faster than the slower oil approach. August Biehle, Clara Deike and William Sommer certainly utilized the modernist tweaking of forms, interpreting colorful rural scenery as never before. Charles Burchfield developed a magical watercolor style that visualized the Vibrations of Life... in wind and storms, fields and forests, insects and birds.

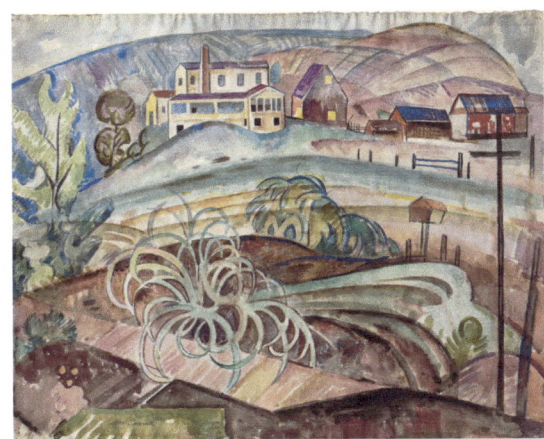

Fig.19 Sommer, William "Farm on Northfield Road"
©Cleveland Museum of Art

CLEVELAND MUSEUM OF ART

The Cleveland Museum of Art opened to the public in 1916, providing the region with the beginnings of a world-class art museum. By 1919, William Milliken presented the first May Show, which eventually grew into the region's premier, competitive annual art exhibition. A strong statement defined it... "the duty of a city museum is to foster the creative elements of it's community by holding such an exhibition, by building a representative collection of local artists, showing their work with peers at all times and by developing a public to support them by purchase."

The May Show provided artists and craftsmen with a regular opportunity to compete for the highest honor in numerous artistic categories, as well as a platform to sell their work. Along with painting, printing, pottery and sculpture, other categories included architectural rendering, basketry, book binding, commercial design, furniture, jewelry, and several others. Important, nationally known artists were brought in as Jurors, like George Bellows, Edward Hopper and Rockwell Kent. There was even an oil painting category called "Industrial" from 1919 through 1939, dominated for several years by Carl Gaertner. The first two May Shows honored Henry Keller and Frank Wilcox with Special Prizes for Maintained Excellence in their oils, watercolors and etchings.

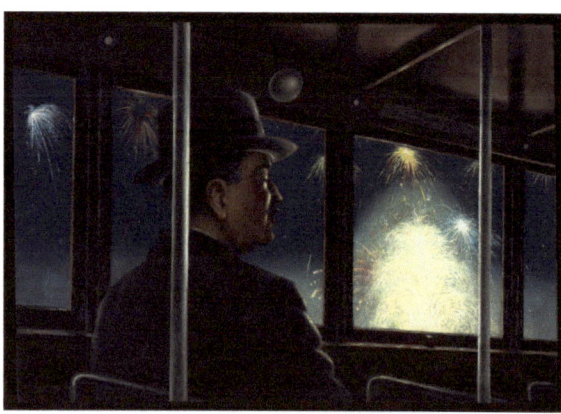

Fig.20 Carter, Clarence "Milliken at the Century of Progress" ©Cleveland Museum of Art

During the 1930s, in order to further promote the best art in the May Show, William Milliken arranged exhibitions to travel to New York, Boston, Philadelphia, Pittsburgh and Chicago. This effort, coupled with the fact that many of Cleveland's finest artists also exhibited in annual competitions in the same cities, helped keep a national spotlight on Cleveland's creativity.

CLEVELAND SCHOOL OF ART – A GOLDEN AGE

The main reason for referring to this group of artists as the "Cleveland School" was the large number of quality artists working in many different mediums for several decades, between the Wars. Some CSA graduates moved away from Cleveland to attain fame elsewhere, like Abel Warshawsky, William Zorach, Clarence Carter, Margaret Bourke-White and Charles Burchfield. But in the 1920s and 1930s, the Cleveland School of Art boasted an incredible faculty in all major categories: Henry Keller, Grace Kelly, May Ames, Frank Wilcox, August Biehle, Mildred Watkins, Louis Rorimer, Clara Deike, Carl Gaertner, Paul Travis, Kenneth Bates, Edris Eckhardt, Otto Ege, Cora Holden, William McVey, Max Kalish, William Eastman, Glenn Shaw, Willard Combes, Kae Dorn Cass, Walter Sinz and Viktor Schreckengost.

Teaching careers at the Cleveland School of Art (later Cleveland Institute of Art) allowed summer breaks from teaching to travel throughout the United States, Canada and Europe providing new, inspirational subject matter. Keller, Wilcox and others made several trips out west and up to the east coast of Canada on the Gaspe Peninsula. George Adomeit and friends preferred Provincetown on Cape Cod. William Grauer spent summers in West Virginia, teaching art classes.

Paul Travis (1891-1975) broke the mold when his 1927-28 sabbatical year took him through Africa, from Cape Town to Cairo. Additional funding for his trip came from the Natural History Museum and the Karamu House's Gilpin Players, so Travis could collect artifacts for them. This incredible experience changed his outlook on artistic creativity and his work became brighter and more expressive than most of his colleagues. Classical compositions morphed into semi-abstract explosions of activity. He painted dreams, fantasies and figural compositions full of humor.

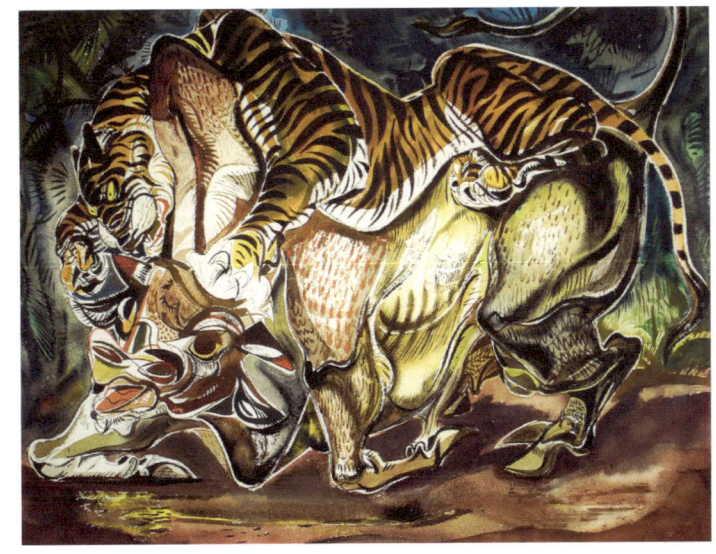

Fig.22 Travis, Paul B. "Tiger and Bullock"

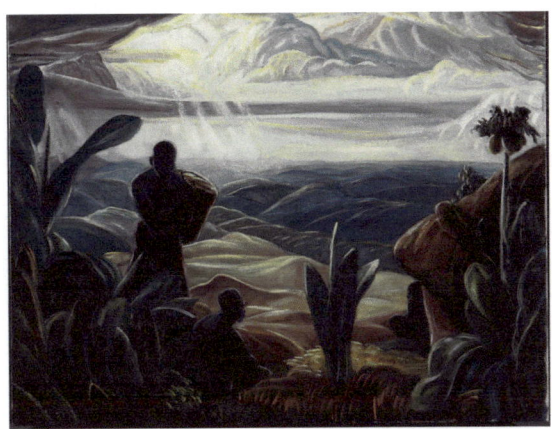

Fig.21 Travis, Paul B. "My First View of the Congo Forest" ©Cleveland Museum of Art

Frank N. Wilcox (1887-1964) was hailed as the "Dean of the Cleveland School" for good reason. After graduation from the school, Wilcox taught numerous subjects for forty years, including drawing, printmaking, design and painting. He taught his students the art of observation, taking them out to look at a retail store window, memorize all aspects and return to class to replicate them through drawing and painting. Wilcox himself had a photographic memory and produced thousands of study drawings and paintings that he used as teaching aids and references for his own finished work. He was also intrigued with history, especially regional and statewide. In 1933, he published an illustrated book called Ohio Indian Trails, which stayed on the New York Times best seller list for months. Others followed, another illustrated book titled Ohio Canals (published posthumously in 1969) and a limited edition, large format book called Weather Wisdom, comprised of 24 color screenprints and accompanying text. Weather Wisdom related stories of how the annual weather cycles affected agrarian life in Ohio. Wilcox constantly included people in his compositions to relate the human story of the image portrayed.

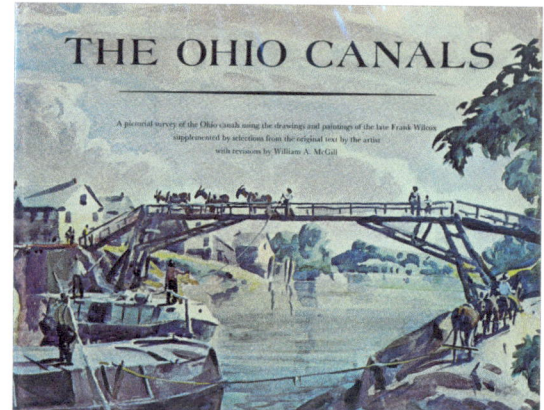

Fig.24 Wilcox, Frank

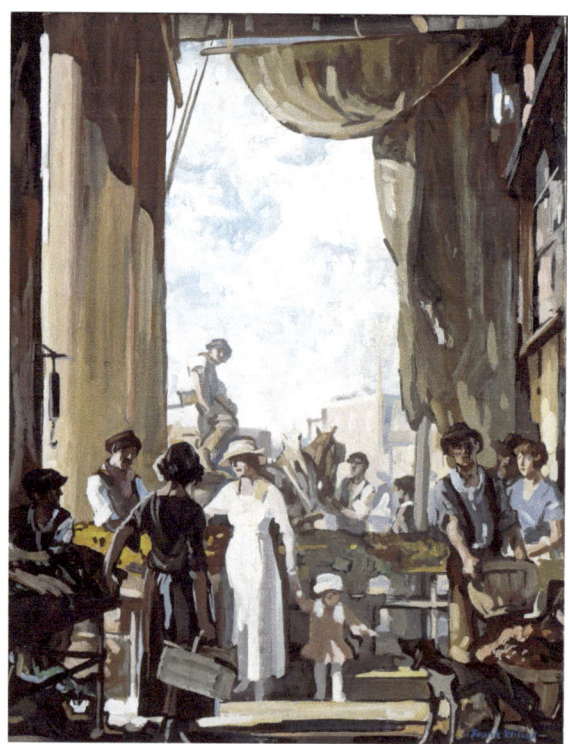

Fig.23 Wilcox, Frank "The Old Market"
©Cleveland Museum of Art

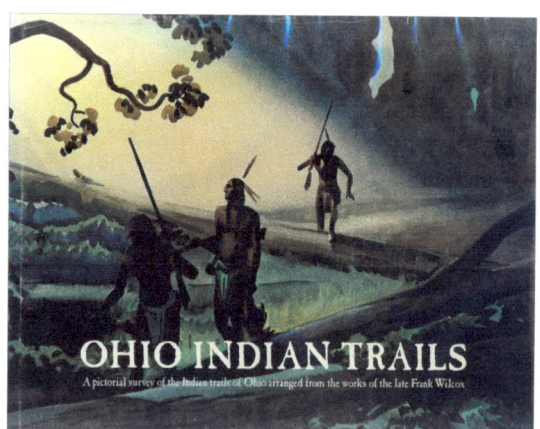

Fig. 25 Wilcox, Frank

OTHER ARTISTIC VENTURES

Between 1912 to 1931, the Cowan Pottery Studio employed many of the prominent ceramic artists of the time, R. Guy Cowan led a group consisting of Edris Eckhardt, Wayland Gregory, Alexander Blazys, Edward & Thelma Winter, Walter Sinz, Russell Barnett Aitken and Viktor Schreckengost. Their beautiful nouveau and deco creations were extremely popular in local homes. The most famous piece is Schreckengost's Jazz Bowl, produced on request from Eleanor Roosevelt. Cocktails and Cigarettes follows a similar theme.

Similarly, other arts businesses evolved, to provide innovative decorative elements for local residences and businesses. Horace Potter and Louis Mellen established an enameling and silversmithing business called Potter & Mellen. The Rorimer-Brooks Studio produced

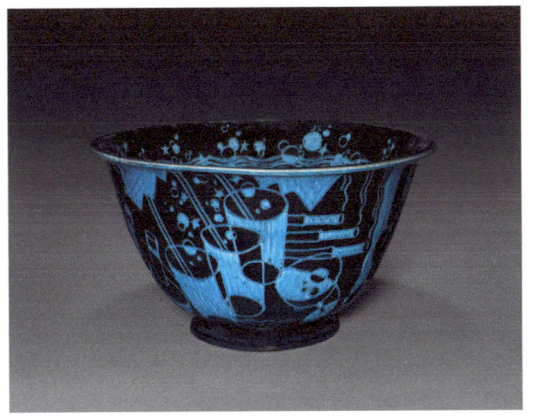

Fig.26 Schreckengost, Viktor "Cocktails and Cigarettes" ©Cleveland Museum of Art

award-winning furniture and Rose Iron Works created elaborate metal décor. Several sculptors taught and developed commission careers that extended beyond the Cleveland region, including Herman Matzen, William Zorach, Max Kalish, William & Leza McVey. Matzen was head of the CSA Sculpture department and produced a number of large, public works depicting Tom Johnson, Richard Wagner, Moses, Cain & Abel, and Pope Gregory IX. William McVey taught at the Cranbrook Academy of Art and the Cleveland Instutute of Art producing commissioned works of personalities George Gund, William Milliken, Albert Michelson, Jesse Owens, Luke Easter and Martin Luther King, Jr.

The Stock Market crash in October, 1929 shocked the nation and precipitated banks failing and the rise of unemployment from 1930 through 1933. In March of 1933, Franklin Roosevelt initiated the New Deal and by December, created the Public Works of Art Program to aid artistic workers and lift the spirit of the country.

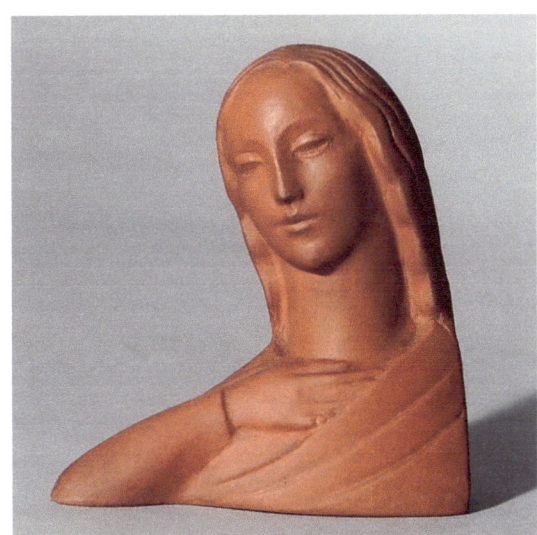

Fig.27 Sinz, Walter "Female Bust"

The Works Progress Administration (WPA 1933-43) provided local artists an opportunity to ply their creativity, from mural painting and sculptural elements, to ceramic objects and prints. Clarence Carter, Edris Eckhardt, Kalman Kubinyi and LeRoy Flint were project leaders and artists, with a strong, supporting group that included Hughie Lee-Smith, Dorothy Rutka, Jolan Gross-Bettelheim, Russell Limbach, William E. Smith, and Stevan Dohanos. Civic pride was prevalent in graphic images of the city and its workers, and characters from popular books like Alice in Wonderland and Uncle Remus were rendered as ceramic pieces. William McVey's 4 ton, limestone sculpture, Old Grizzly still resides in University Circle at the Natural History Museum. But a darker side was also presented graphically, that of poverty, unemployment and racial

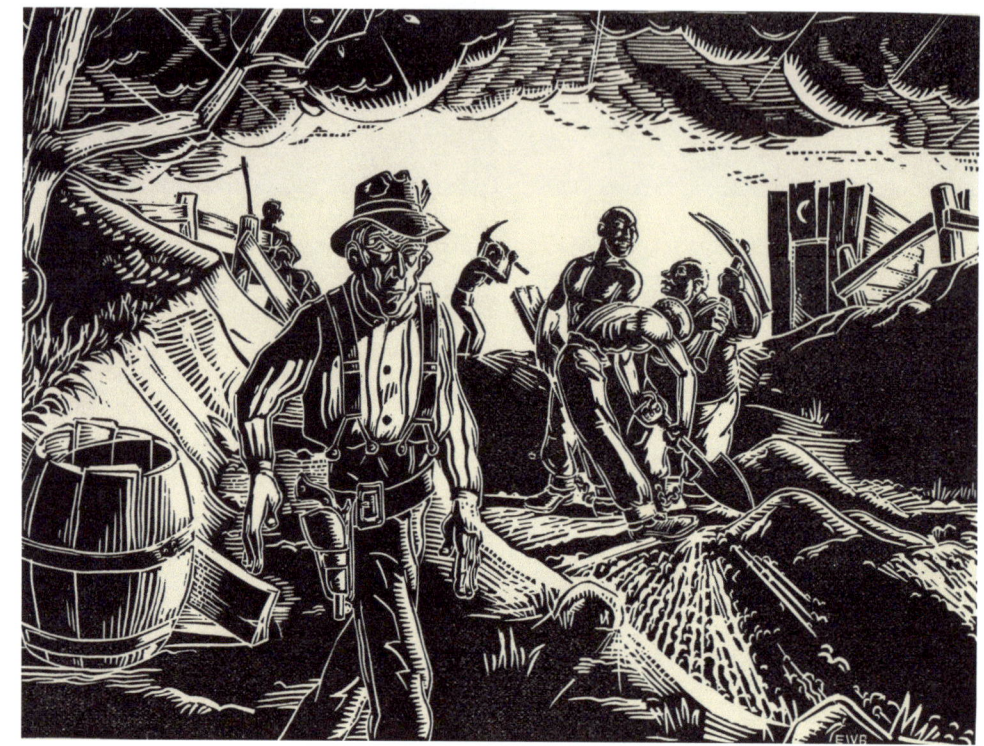

Fig.28 Brown, Elmer "Ol' Peckerwood" ©Cleveland Museum of Art

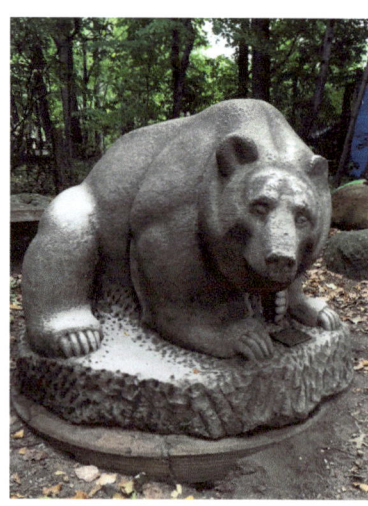

Fig.29 McVey, William "Old Grizzly"

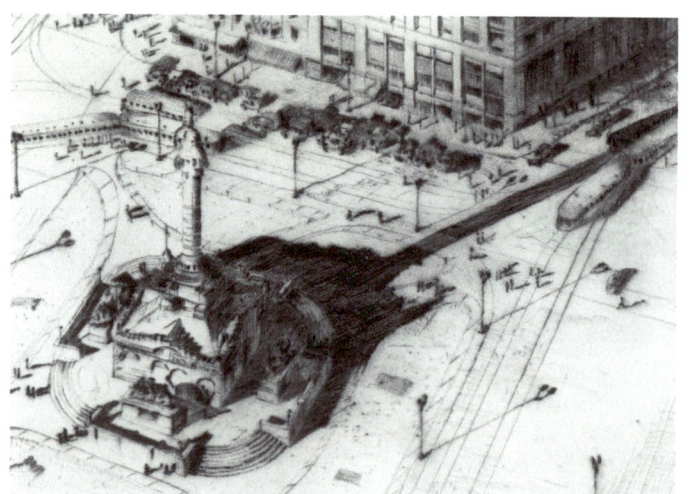

Fig.30 Popkins, Samuel "Soldiers and Sailors Monument"

inequalities and tensions.
The Cleveland Print Makers Club was established in 1930 by Kalman Kubinyi and three dozen members, to practice and promote printmaking. By 1932, they started the Print-a-Month series, literally producing an original print each month that was offered for sale to encourage the public to appreciate and be able to afford original art. The artists were encouraged to be innovative in their printing techniques and develop new techniques in the process. This wonderful project lasted for a total of 48 prints, ending in May, 1936.

World War II brought more strife to the world and the lives of local artists. The "second wave" of Cleveland School artists, which included my father and his contemporaries, had their art school careers interrupted, while they went to war around the world. Cultural events and the art school were both negatively affected as the war effort consumed everyone's attention. The new demand for war materials did boost local industrial production and employment. After the war, a general shift occurred, emphasizing interest in more diverse industrial design and the art school followed by minimizing the fine arts in favor of more applied design courses. By 1948, the Cleveland School of Art became the Cleveland Institute of Art, the older teachers were retired and Viktor Schreckengost led the new wave of design-oriented programs.

My father, William E. Scheele (1920-98) used his artistic talents in ways that went beyond the mere production of art. He served time in the Army Corps of Engineers, in the European Theatre. Due to his artistic ability, he was put in charge of camouflaging General George Patton's tanks, trucks and other equipment. He also found time to paint watercolor sketches of the soldiers and battle environments of which he was a part. Upon his return to the States, he finished art school and went to work in the exhibitions department of the Cleveland Museum of Natural History. In 1949, when the museum had to move from its Victorian house environment to a completely new location in University Circle, Scheele came up with a plan to create the new museum and was appointed Director due to his innovative vision. Opening to the public in 1958, the museum offered more open and colorful displays of specimens and creatures from around the world, in a "walk through time" presentation. Scheele served as the museum's

Director from 1949 to 1972. Following a similar path of his favorite teacher Frank Wilcox, Scheele wrote and illustrated a total of seven books on early animal and human life on Earth. Prehistoric Animals, published in 1954, taught the reader how to pronounce scientific names, showed skeletal structures and realistic images of dinosaurs and other early creatures. The books gained immediate acclaim from schools and librairies, proving that applied art and creativity are important in all aspects of life.

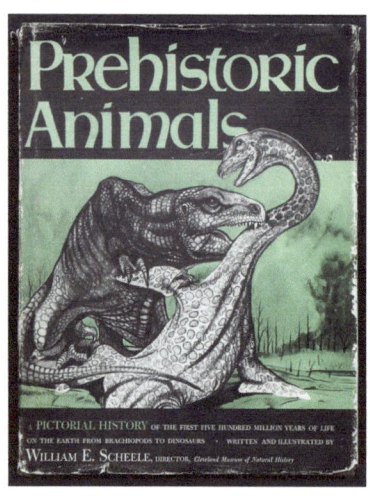

Fig.31 Scheele, William E

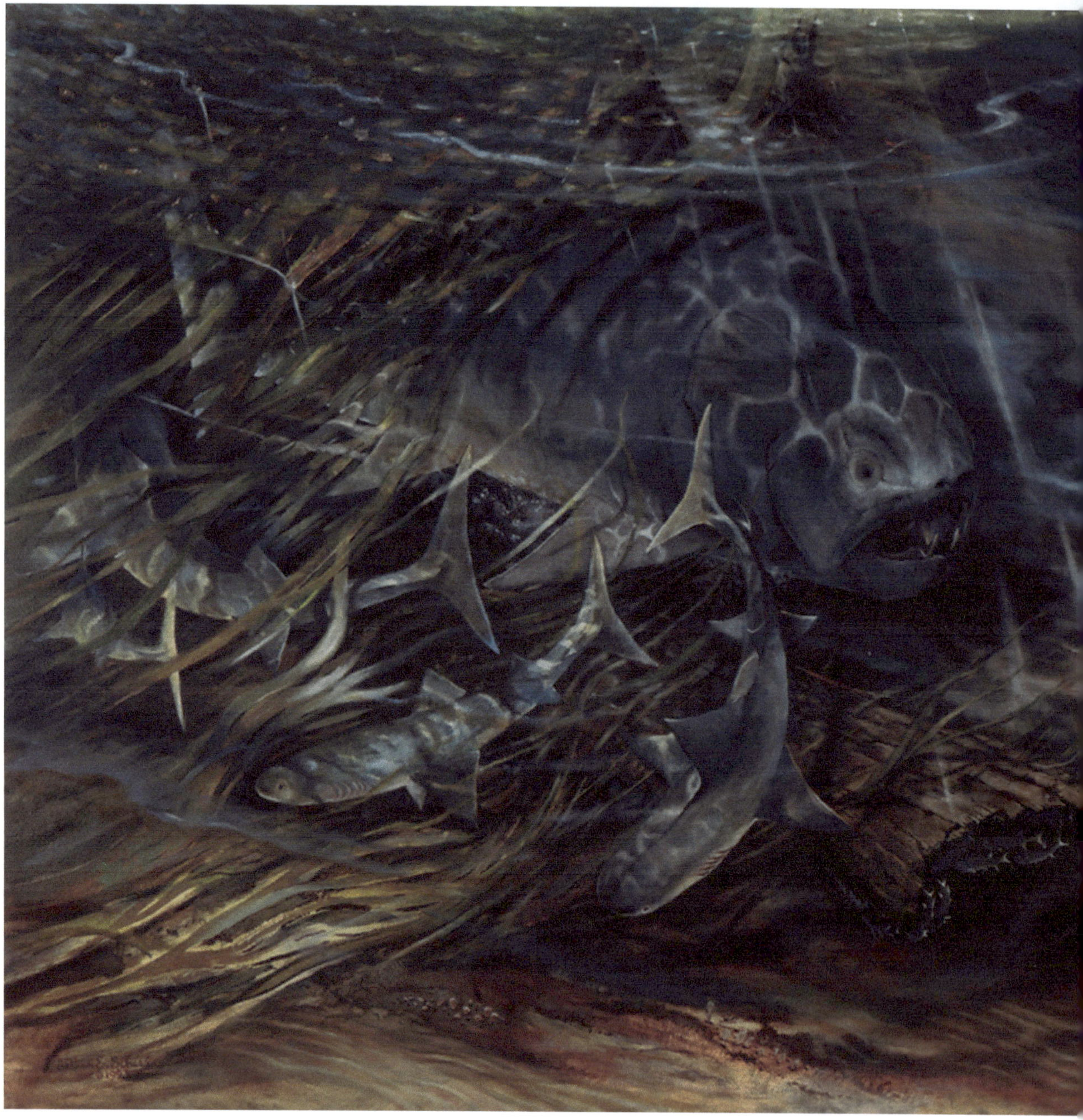

Fig.34 Scheele, William E. "Devonian Incident"

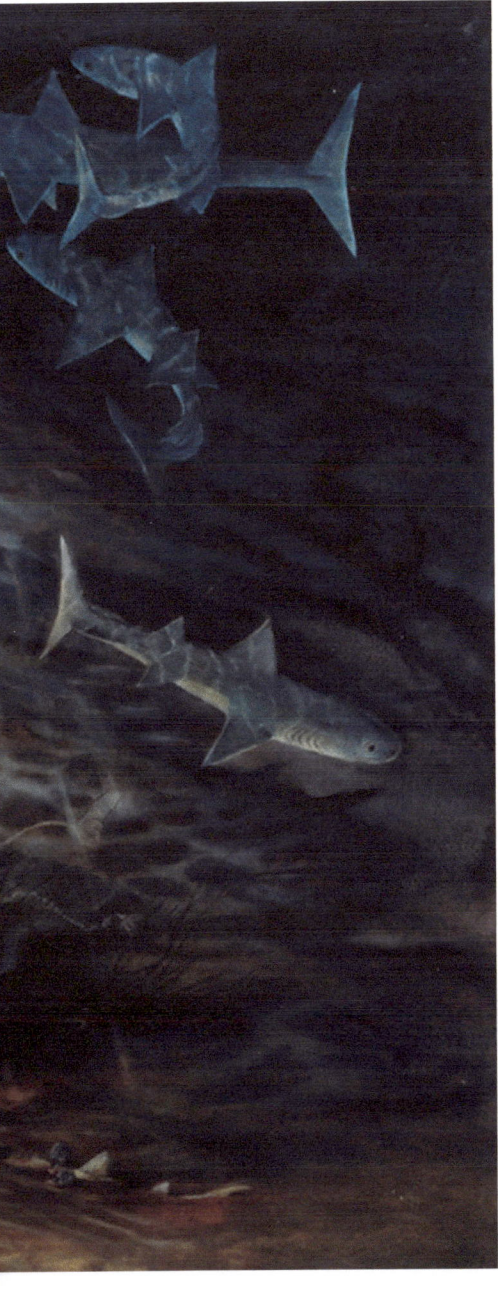

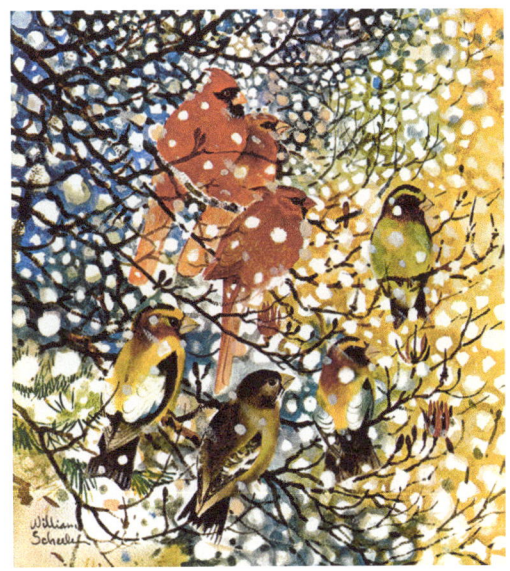

Fig.35 Scheele, William E. "Winter Birds"

CONCLUSION

It can be said with certainty that the Cleveland region has produced a great number of creative visual artists from the early 1900s through the 1950s. Their numbers were large and consisted of men and women with enough talent to compete with others nationally. I feel strongly that this was a "Golden Age" for Cleveland, as it established institutions like the art school and art museum in becoming important locally and nationally. It was a period of time when all of America was growing and changing at a rapid pace and the art produced during this time reflects those changes and becomes a visual history that future generations can look back on with pride.

This essay is not meant to be encyclopedic in its scope and cannot begin to elaborate on the many artists that populated the Cleveland region during this time period. There is a chronological list of artists (birth & death years) and list of reference publications for further research. The collections of the Cleveland Museum of Art, the Cleveland Institute of Art, ARTneo and the Artists Archives of the Western Reserve all have work to be seen and appreciated.

May 2018
William G. Scheele

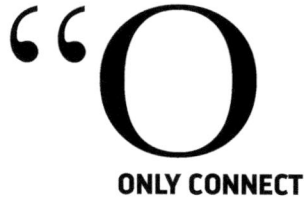

"O

ONLY CONNECT

DOUGLAS MAX UTTER

Let's strike that "rustbelt" word from the record. Corroded though its underbelly may be at times, Cleveland, Ohio can be better understood in other terms. If there were, as the narrator of The Naked City used to intone, "Eight million stories in the naked city," there are well over one million stories in Cuyahoga County -- though admittedly no more than 400,000 within the downsized city of Cleveland proper; let's say half a million stories, in the scantily clothed city. My own tale has been the slogging narrative of a working, writing, exhibiting painter-artist, a citizen in a town with a lot of history, endowed with great museums, concert halls, universities, and natural beauty. The much ballyhooed Rock n' Roll capital is in truth a big-time, serious culture town in ways that go far beyond the pop music scene. It's also a place where a life in the arts is rewarded, if not by great fame or wealth, then by rich and various encounters and by a network of connections that covers the globe. As an artist and a writer about the visual arts, as a lover of both Pop and classical music, and as a (very) long-time resident of Cleveland, I insist that our city is culturally explosive, crisscrossed to an unusual degree with the paths of scientific, literary, and artistic greatness.

For example, as the child of a biochemist, I have reason to know Cleveland was a remarkable biochemistry town (actually it still is), in the 1950's-60's, a town where many key concepts and structures of human metabolism were first researched. As a reader, I know that the Cleveland Public Library has long been considered one of the best in the country. As a lover of classical music, I know there is no ensemble anywhere that outshines the Cleveland Orchestra, and that few music schools compare to the Cleveland Institute of Music. As an enthusiast of Rock and other Pop forms it's been my privilege to hang out everywhere from La Cave (in the early 1960's) and the Agora to the Euclid Tavern in its glory days, the Phantasy Night Club, The Grog Shop, the Beachland Ballroom, Mahall's on Detroit, and a dozen other venues that feature or featured big name performers, at all the points of Cleveland's wildly swinging compass. As a painter who has lived abroad and in New York City, and thus been lucky enough to know a number of the world's great public art collections, I can attest that the Cleveland Museum of Art is a treasure and a gift to the people of our city beyond any reckoning. As an educator and writer about the personalities, trends, and aims of contemporary art, I've come to know and appreciate our region's college and university art departments, which are an important source of talent for the national spotlight. The Cleveland Institute of Art has nurtured or been nurtured by some of America's best artists, from Charles Burchfield, and Viktor Schreckengost to Robert Mangold, Edwin Mieczkowski, Julian Stanczak, and Dana Schutz.

That's just a few among the hundreds of influential painters, sculptors, ceramicists, conceptualists, performers, cartoonists, architects and designers whose art began in Cleveland, or who were shaped by schools in the area, and by unique qualities and resources of the city, in important ways.

There are problems with this argument, no doubt. The limitations imposed by Cleveland's ebbing population have made it impossible for the city's artists and arts institutions to prosper to anything like the same degree as in New York, or Chicago. But let me repeat: the Cleveland Orchestra and the Cleveland Museum of Art are beyond any doubt among the best on the planet – a very neat trick for a town that even at its zenith in the early 1950's was only the nation's sixth largest metropolitan area. The sullied, brutal magic of oil and steel, of Rockefeller and Carnegie, started the ball rolling. But that was a long time ago, and the ball rolls on. I would like to tell some tales of my own Cleveland, stories of a few people I've met over the past half-century, and about the way that great works of art sometimes seem to pop up out of the ground, wherever you are in Northeast Ohio.

When I speak globally, I'm indulging a fantasy of wholeness – I'm kidding myself. If, like Whitman, I contain multitudes, the infinities of the real are nevertheless beyond my imagination. And that goes for the so-called "art world," too. If there's one thing we learn from art history, it's that perspectives of time and scholarship constantly change our view of the art of the past. It follows that if, as they jibe, "the past isn't what it used to be," how true that must be of the present. How much art that will be considered characteristic of our time by future generations, must presently be unknown, or despised? In a way the international Art Fairs, the Biennials and Triennials that have altered the outlines of the global art scene (in actuality the trends within a few widely scattered, well-heeled markets) in recent decades, are a valuable response to the multivalent impact and usages of art in an age of profound transformations – to the complexity of human culture, considered as a whole. Whether these "global" curatorial events broaden the arts' playing field or not, at least they move it around, and endorse (in principle, anyway) a search for aesthetic outliers, for the art of abjection (but once the abject is open for such business, what new categories of abjection must be generated?). Yet the bottom line remains the same: the scene of art is subjective in nature, infinite not geographically or even culturally, but in psychological terms. From that standpoint it matters very little where an artist or work of art is "discovered" or enters into any canon of historical significance. But I do believe art completes the circuit of some truth ("Only connect," wrote British author E.M. Forster) when it crosses the short (vast) distance to one other mind, one other world.

Not all connections are created equal. Cleveland, Ohio, is about to join the age of global connectedness with the first iteration of the FRONT Triennial exhibition, opening its many doors at several city-wide venues this July. Cleveland hasn't been a particularly populous city in recent decades, but it does have plenty of big city problems, and a few big city advantages, many of which will find voice at FRONT. If you count all the people who contribute to the mix in Cuyahoga County and somewhat beyond, you find there's actually a couple of million to contend with – enough to be politically significant, and perhaps sufficient to make some kind of aesthetic critical mass feasible. There are all those institutions I mentioned before, and the sports teams and steel manufacture. And then there's the odd, in-between, on-the-verge feel of the place. Cleveland sprawls along a surprisingly beautiful, volatile lake that looks quite a bit like an ocean. It boasts a few buildings that have often served as a sampling of downtown America in the movies, at least (though the Terminal Tower was the second tallest building in the nation until 1964). There are still more plays being staged in Cleveland than anywhere in the country outside of New York, plus all kinds of concerts all the time. And there are a ton of artists.

I'm one of them, a visual artist working in often unconventional paint media. I began to exhibit my works in the mid 1980's, and I found that, despite all the hullaballoo in local publications, there wasn't a reliable audience for contemporary art in Cleveland, and very few reputable hometown-based art galleries. These related circumstances have changed and improved, yet even now an absence of long-term commercial venues tends to drive artists away, dispersing them to Chicago and LA and New York. Despite all that, good-sized art communities do take root in the so-called Forest City. Their numbers are fed by several of the region's university art departments (Kent State, Akron, Cleveland State, Case-Western Reserve), and the historic Cleveland Institute of Art. Nowadays the lives and flickering careers of locally-based visual and conceptual artists are enriched if not sustained by local institutions such as CMA and MOCA Cleveland, SPACES and Zygote Press, the Morgan Paper Conservancy, and CMA's new West Side affiliate the Transformer Station. In the late '80's only the first three of those existed, and galleries such as the William Busta which were to gain momentum through the next decade hadn't yet emerged.

For a time I was able to show my work in New York. Circumstances eventually led me away from the big city, however, and after forays to various other cities and countries, I mainly pursued a hard-scrabble career back in Cleveland. Like many other emerging artists my work was reviewed in local and regional newspapers and magazines, though sales weren't much impacted and remained far from brisk. As youngish parents with two children, my partner and I needed whatever income streams could be improvised, so I joined the group of art writers who contributed to that era's flurry of arts coverage. My first articles were printed in Dialogue, a Columbus, Ohio magazine devoted to state-wide arts coverage. Soon I was also writing for the Chicago publication New Art Examiner (distributed internationally), and the long-time Cleveland-based cultural magazine Northern Ohio Live. From 1996 I contributed weekly reviews to the Cleveland Free Times, and later on an occasional piece to the Plain Dealer. After the millennial year, however, the print world began to head slowly south. Of the publications mentioned above, only the Plain Dealer remains in business.

A few of the artists whose work is reproduced in this book were part of that pre-2000 scene. Most were not, either because they weren't around back then, or because the art they produced didn't fit in with common gallery and museum interests and concerns; curators and boards have their own agendas, and media attention tends to follow along. Since then Cleveland's "art world" has grown quite a lot. Replacements have emerged for some of the lost publications, and I've contributed my share of art and essays, especially to CAN Journal, which covers the arts in a quarterly print publication and ongoing blog post (CAN represents and supports a membership of more than eighty member organizations, including CIA and the Cleveland Museum of Art). But the point that I want to reiterate is the idea that the very best art produced here and now or in any other place and time may well be invisible to the galleries and magazines and museums that aspire to "curate" it. If post-modern thinkers like Jacques Lacan and Gilles Deleuze, Judith Butler and Julia Kristeva can be believed (or understood), art in the post-colonial era is a very slippery and dangerous activity. Its job (they think) is to pierce, rend and reconfigure the membranes of language and reason that sequester the conventional self from the "other." Art transgresses, salvages, interrogates, consumes, threatens. Art is the truth, and in our postmodern situation is very often the truth as abjection (at least for Kristeva), a savage and misshapen thing that we have driven from our side, which can strike us dead with a glance. Such difficult beauty oscillates between the far edge of radical foreignness, and the unsearchable archive of selfhood. "The self is only a threshold, a door," wrote Deleuze, But who has really stood at that door, and opened it? Very seldom does art, either in Chelsea or the gallery districts of Chicago, Los Angeles or anywhere else, reach a memorable level of intensity or profound psychological relevance. That it could be containable anywhere with tall columns, clean floors, and a hefty pricetag, like a pack of hyenas roaming Saks in gilded tennies, seems improbable.

BUT WHERE, THEN?

Cleveland comes to mind, though please understand that geography and civic pride are not at issue here. But as a partial account of my own artistic subjectivity and its formation I would like to tell a few stories from my life, here in this book that samples Cleveland's current art production. Read them for what they're worth – as anecdotal evidence, perhaps to support a theory of strange provenance – but at least to illustrate that there's artistic life of many kinds, alive and well on the north coast. And while the stories I recount here are about artists who did achieve wide recognition quite early in their lives, I've been fortunate to meet (and write about, elsewhere) many brilliant artists who live or have died in obscurity.

Until I was about 15 years old my parents and I lived on a street in Cleveland Heights at the brink of the eastern line of bluffs that rise above the city. Sometime around 1958 a young African American architect named Robert Madison built two houses, one of which was for his own use, up at the end of the street nearest to where we lived. It was a location that had been lightly wooded up till then, across from a deep ravine running down toward University Circle. Much later Madison would be widely celebrated as a pioneering figure, but in the 1950's he was more anonymously brave, staking out territory in what was still a uniformly white community. His houses are still there, and the community is still a desirable place to own property, except that now and for most of the past fifty years it has been racially integrated. This happened with a minimum of racial tension, at least by Cleveland standards, but I can't forget that there was only one African American child (and one Asian) among my 300 or so classmates during the six years I attended the neighborhood elementary school. Perhaps Madison chose that corner lot because it was beautiful, located at the end of our long, curving, hilly street. I'm very glad he did, whatever the reason. I was beginning to take drawing seriously at that time, and I still have one or two pencil sketches on thick manila paper. They show the earthmoving equipment that was used to dig the foundations of Madison's modestly modern, comfortable houses. For me my first outdoor drawings and the awkward machines they depict seem to push against the paper, reminding me of the strength of new beginnings.

During those years a German couple lived in a peaked, dark brown house right next door to us. We didn't know them well, but we did have enough of an acquaintance to occasionally be invited into their living room for one neighborly reason or another. Since my parents and I toured the Cleveland Museum of Art often, I was familiar with the work of the nationally known painter Charles Burchfield. CMA displayed his work prominently and owned at least one very striking, experimental work titled "Churchbells Ringing, Rainy Winter Night." At that age I was not in a position to appreciate how extraordinary it was to see a private house crowded with paintings and drawings by such a modern master, but they made quite an impact on me. I was used to the large-scale prints of impressionism "lite" paintings that my mother bought at Higbee's – street scenes by Maurice Utrillo, Degas-like dancers by Moses Soyer, and a few more challenging works, Picasso, Diego Rivera (Mom taught herself how to make frames for these – we went together to a lumber yard to buy boards, and hardware stores for tools and stain). But we were seeing a whole different level of home exhibition on our visits next door. Burchfields ranged around the living room and up the stairs, along with wonderful drawings and watercolors and oils by other artists associated with the Cleveland School, in particular William Sommer, and Burchfield's teacher at the Cleveland Institute of Art in the early years of the 20th century, Henry Keller. But it was Burchfield they knew and loved the best. Our neighbor (let's call her Mrs. B.) told us that she and her husband often drove cross country in that pre-Interstate era, to the artist's studio in upstate New York. They came home with a new painting, or two or three, every time. So it happened that mixed into the developing sinews of my childish character was this quite un-American idea -- that people could buy original art, they could live with it. And not just any art in this case, but paintings advanced for their time, dealing with visual impressions and psychological nuances in a multi-sensory way. For better or worse the depiction of sonic resonance in Burchfield's "Church Bells" painting and his semi-hallucinatory images reverberating with the artist's trademark watercolor flourishes, made a lasting impression on my young mind.

Later we lived in a slightly more upscale Cleveland Heights neighborhood, not far from where prohibition era lawman Elliot Ness's mansion still stood when I was in high school. But of more benign cultural significance was the home of George Crile, Jr., son of the founder of the Cleveland Clinic, and his wife Helga Sandburg Crile, author and daughter of the Chicago poet Carl Sandburg (we owned copies of Sandburg's books of poetry and his very famous biography of Abraham Lincoln). This was just across the street from our corner house, a block or so from Euclid Heights Blvd. One of the Crile's neighbors was Sherman Lee, the much admired Director of CMA during those years, noted sinologist and all-round expert on Asian culture. During WWII he had been one of the Army's better known "Monument Men," assisting in the liberation and restoration of cultural artifacts. And his next door neighbor happened to be Dan Moore, another highly-placed figure in wartime cultural affairs, an influential figure in Cleveland politics and father of a young painter I would get to know and write about in later years, Harriet Moore Ballard.

It was an interesting place to grow up, really more than I was able to fully appreciate at the time. Cleveland didn't seem like the boondocks; if our city was marginal, it certainly redefined that concept. Cleveland for me and many others has been a place where it is oddly possible to grow up believing one might actually become an artist through the development of a relationship to the whole world, and not only to an academic framework of concerns. That one might – in fact must – be an artist before one is an educator, or a citizen, just as one must be a person in true earnest, examining one's own heart and core, in order to be moral or authentic. That one's naiveté must be bone-deep.

There are other places and conditions in my own story. My parents and I lived for a year in Australia, and sometime later spent a year in England. I was able to visit museums in Europe as a teenager, and was tutored in oil painting very briefly by a member of the Royal Academy. I learned further sketching techniques on British TV, which aired a weekly "Sketch Club" show. Soon after that (it was 1961) we were back in Ohio, where I attended classes at the Cleveland Institute of Art. In the 1970's I lived in NYC for several years. I was also a student at Case Western Reserve University for a while, where I concentrated on classical languages and literature. Eventually I married a sculptor and together we had two children. I worked as an independent contractor for a time, refinishing interior woodwork. And I began to paint in earnest. In the mid 1980's the heroic (if ironical) themes and dimensions of Neoexpressionism made an impact on my work, and on my ambitions for it.

As a tyro arts writer at the end of that decade and on into the 1990's I soon discovered that Cleveland was home to thousands of women and men who considered themselves artists, divided among widely different communities and venues. The editorial question at places like the Free Times was first of all, who do we cover and why? How does a regional alternative newspaper find a focus among all these groups and individuals? Are they all as important as they think they are? My first article for that publication was a review of a show at Cleveland Independent Art, a relatively short-lived gallery on Perkins Avenue around East 40th Street. The gallery's owner-director was Julie Fedevich, who had ties to the art community though her alma mater Kent State University, and also via the William Busta Gallery where she worked and was influential for several years. Another source of cutting edge, downtown -flavored art for her new gallery were her many contacts at the crossroads of rock n roll and so-called high art, centering around venues like the Euclid Tavern (Julie had introduced her friend the seminal Cleveland rock n roll illustrator and artist Derek Hess into William Busta Gallery's roster), The Agora, and the Grog Shop. Later that list would include (and be survived by) the Beachland Ballroom, under the leadership of Cindy Barber. But at this earlier period Barber herself was actually running the Free Times. Maybe because it is a small city, great art and great music often connect in Cleveland. It's a pairing that echoes across socio-economic groups, beginning in University Circle with its matching treasures, CMA and Severance Hall, built at opposite ends of Wade Park Lagoon. I don't think the Cavs, the Browns, or the Indians enjoy a similar tie-in with the arts, but the new century is young yet.

Cleveland has no central art district, though in the 1960's there were a few galleries downtown, most of them not far from Playhouse Square. One, at least, was run by prominent Collinwood-born artist Shirley Aley Campbell, known for her large-scale paintings of unconventional and controversial subjects (she did a series of heroically huge Hell's Angels portraits that toured far and wide, making it as far as Moscow). Always daring, she opened a gallery of her own in the 1960's, in the same general area where Bonfoey's Gallery remains even now the city's longest lasting and most successful showplace for the region's contemporary art. Campbell's place didn't last long; very few galleries do, even in places with thriving markets for contemporary art. Cleveland has never quite been one of those. A lot of newspaper column inches were (and are) devoted to announcing the opening and closing of places that try to sell art. The more determined among those do often make a comeback, some more than once. Such a place was William Busta Gallery, which beginning in 1989 opened three times in three different locations, shutting its doors most recently in 2015. There's no consensus about the value or importance of any regional art ventures, but many aficionados thought Busta was the city's all-time best gallery. It regularly introduced major Ohio-based talents, and provided solo and group shows that kept track of a few artists' progress over the years. These are functions that any serious art gallery needs to perform, obviously (you might think), but rarely do. Plus, audiences must be reached, a collector-base strengthened and informed. Documentation of shows and works and artists is also sorely needed, as are market-related standards like consistency in pricing, replacing the vagaries of artist's whims and the craziness of auction houses, where fine art often sells for next to nothing, sabotaging careers and galleries alike.

It's hard to make a living here, so most serious artists in Cleveland have tended to seek gallery representation in other cities, accessing larger and more established markets. Others just leave as soon as they can – an observation that brings to mind another tale of Cleveland connections. When I was about sixteen years old a friend from school was over at our house. He was looking at my latest paintings at one point (I rarely showed them to anyone, and took no art classes in high school), and mentioned that I might like to meet his brother-in-law, who was a cartoonist working at American Greetings. I was something of a snob about pop culture and I had my doubts. Nevertheless, one evening the following week we took a bus down the hill to the corner of 105th and clambered up a fire escape to the back door of his sister's apartment, at the rear of a small brick building (long since demolished). Brother-in-law Robert was tall and thin with a prominent nose and heavily-framed eyeglasses. He and Russell's sister Dana welcomed us with the sort of attention that teenagers don't always get. They were very kind to us. After a while, as we sat on a sofa in the living room, Robert, who created his narrative cartoons under the name of R. Crumb (he was not yet well-known outside of American Greetings) began to show us a few hand-inked books he was planning to publish soon. Child-snob or not, I was blown away. I'd never seen anything like Crumb's radically in-your-face humor and commentary. I was familiar with Mad magazine, as was every adolescent of that period, but Crumb's take on black humor left Mad in the dust. The books were a little smaller than standard composition notebooks, crammed full of wonderfully drawn, expressive figures doing rotten things against a backdrop of squalid urban scenes. Slowly we went through all of Fritz the Cat's adventures with his long-suffering, lowlife animal friends. No holds were barred as Crumb satirized racist political paranoia (the Chinese, depicted as evil crows, were tunneling through the earth toward Cleveland), and made fun of drunk sex, psychedelic camaraderie, and all the swirling twilight pleasures and confusions that turn into mud when you've reached your limit of bad trips. It was 1967, so Crumb was about twenty-four, old enough to seem guru-like to my teenage self. Not that I became an acolyte – within a few months he was gone and I never saw him again. He migrated to the Mecca of the hippie era, San Francisco's Haight-Ashbury District, where he quickly became a celebrity. Indeed he was one of the best known chroniclers of that disaffected, independent-minded era, celebrating and ridiculing the Summer of Love and its long, sour aftermath. His cover for Big Brother and the Holding Company's Cheap Thrills album came out less than a year after our weirdly cool encounter, in 1968. The daemonic, doomed Janis Joplin was of course lead singer with the band, and Janis herself had commissioned the artwork from Crumb, whose work she adored. Cheap Thrills was purchased by everybody in any way attuned to the zeitgeist, myself included. My own small amount of hipness I owed in large part to Crumb himself and his hospitality. He loathed our fair city, it's been reported, and I can't blame him. But it happens that Crumb made some of his best-known work in the obscurity of certain northcoastal places, and, by the way, often in the company of people like Gary Dumm, who with his partner Laura has contributed to this volume of Cleveland art, published so much farther down the road. Encounters, connections echo in unexpected ways and places.

Another artist I met and wrote about when I was in my early fifties, just as she was about to become became very famous, is Dana Schutz. This tale may make a point about Cleveland as fertile artistic territory and cultural crossroads even better than the one about Crumb. Dana and I actually met in 2003, but the story begins about 3 years earlier, when my friend and former student K and I got together to look at K's recent canvases. We were at the Cleveland Institute of Art one evening soon after that year's spate of BFA exhibitions. Upstairs at the so-called Factory annex (now the main building at CIA) on Euclid Avenue, graduating painting majors occupied long rows of cubicles as mini-studios. Usually these too-small rooms were crammed with papers, paintable objects, working studies and works in progress, but now they were mostly empty. I was curious to see what K (who would graduate the following year) had been up to. But I'm not sure we ever made it to her space, because I was distracted by a number of colorful oil paintings, small and medium-sized, leaning everywhere in the big white room against the sheetrock partition walls. I stopped and scratched my head, maybe, or just stood there looking gobsmacked. It seemed to me that these weren't normal paintings, even in the quite wild and crazy, sophisticated context of CIA. I was fifty by then, I'd seen quite a lot of life, and paint – don't get me started. But these paintings were in a class by themselves. They were, well, f*****-up. And they were funny.

For instance, there was a blue, red, and yellow one that seemed to depict a girl with long blonde hair. Her nose was exploding, as far as I could tell. Another, narrower image on panel showed the back of a woman's head. The truly peculiar focal point in that one was a big ball of paint chips, which looked like long hair bound up in a knot or bun, extending three or four inches out from the surface. Several others featured a woebegone, bearded young man. These works appeared to have an "implied narrative," but they were being ironic about their irony, and as a result were surprisingly fresh, emotionally speaking. Bad things were happening to this guy, and somebody didn't care at all. It was that casually amused character that I sensed, lingering outside the picture frame, who made these paintings read as fresh. Meanwhile, the poor young man appeared to be stranded on a desert island, achingly sunburned; his hair was a mess. He was sitting as if posing in one particular painting, facing the viewer, clueless, resigned. His white shirt was in pitiful tatters; he sat on a pile of straw; the sea was wide and blue behind him in the distance. In others he looked like a missing link, or one of the poor half-human animals in a horrific Robert Louis Stevenson tale. This was around the time that the reality show Survivor was big, so it seemed to me the painter was having some highly original fun with bogus meta-narratives and Pop culture, and probably his or her own love-life. 'Who did these?" I asked K. She explained they were the work of a girl named Dana. "She's wonderful. She sings like a bird."

Dana Schutz soon went on to grad school at Columbia University, earning unusual accolades and early recognition in shows around the country. She'd just finished up her MFA a few months before when I drove to New York to interview her for the inaugural issue of an arts and letters publication named Angle. A series of major winter storms buffeted my old Volvo wagon, coming and going, but the day I dropped in on Dana was clear. Her studio was on 12th Avenue on the upper west side not far from the school, all but under the West Side Highway. I was glad the painter Amy Casey was with me on that trip. Her own academic career at CIA had overlapped with Dana's, so they knew each other. But as K had indicated years before, Dana is one of the easiest people in the world to talk to. The only ice that needed breaking was the ice in the discarded coffee cups sitting around Dana's freezing cold, cheerfully disordered space. I met with her again just a few weeks ago to talk about her show at Transformer Station called "Eating Atom Bombs." She's changed very little in the long interim – in many ways she still seems like an art student. Yet these days she's the mother of two, and an established force in contemporary painting. Then, as now, she wears her hair (probably a little shorter these days) in a mass of reddish brown curls, and of course jeans, tennis shoes, sweatshirt, pea coat – and a big, funny fake smile she plasters on for photographs, which is also a real smile; it makes her look like one of her paintings. Following a year of controversy surrounding her depiction of Emmett Till she's understandably a bit wary of the world and its ways, I think, and a little tired (like any mother of young children who also works very hard), but as friendly and genuinely modest and forthcoming about her work as anyone I've ever met. We talked during that first meeting long ago about the paintings I'd seen in Cleveland, many of which had been shown by that time at PS1 in Long Island City, and in Los Angeles at Roberts and Tilton Gallery. We stood (it was too cold to sit, and I don't remember any chairs) and stared at the large paintings in progress all around us, which would soon be displayed in an upcoming show at the LFL Gallery (later Zack Feuer Gallery) in Chelsea. The biggest one was more than half-done that day. Called "The Chicken or the Egg," its deep blue and violet and black colors composed a very simple landscape, a nocturne showing a lake and low hills. In the foreground the artist (I think it was Dana herself) in shadow, adjusted a crazy, fancy machine. Around and behind her stretched a starry, starry night, dominated by a yellowish full moon (very much like a fried egg) shown also reflected in the lake. So it was a mash-up of a night scene in nature, with a planetarium lightshow running at full throttle. Reality, projection, depiction, the mysterious role of the observer, the ninja-like stealth of the artist…a whole lot of questions and associations, laid out in broad strokes with the unassuming omniscience of a storybook illustration. But that's Dana. I was blown away, as I was when I first saw her paintings and have been many so times since. Amy Casey and I got back to Cleveland an arduous day or two later, after navigating a howling blizzard on the Interstate. One of Dana's pictures (a detail of a painting titled "Hello Helen") eventually ended up on the cover of the first print issue of Angle, a magazine which I co-founded that year with my fellow art writers Amy Sparks and Dan Tranberg, following the demise of the Free Times (which left us all under-employed). Angle survived for several years as a 501c3, producing a few dozen issues of a beautifully designed and printed magazine (available by subscription or for free at designated pick-up spots) before failing for lack of funds in 2007. What could have gone wrong! That's right – money. Looking back, the fact that a publication like Angle lasted even that long was a tribute to the Cleveland community's commitment to responsible, experienced arts coverage.

These days most of my writing-for-hire appears in CAN Journal, which after five years in operation in the Cleveland-Akron area is still going strong. CAN is the brainchild of poet, artist, editor and all-around advocate for a better world Mike Gill, who was also at one point the arts editor at the Free Times. Gill conceived the magazine as the voice of a consortium of arts organizations and individuals, produced on a quarterly schedule. As I mentioned earlier, CAN now has brought together a large number of member organizations that includes most major players in the area, including museums, galleries, and performing arts organizations. Remarkably, perhaps uniquely, there's room for critical writing in this mix of public and private sector support. And both the page count and writer compensation have more than doubled over these last few quarters. CAN has become an indispensably important part of Cleveland's current arts scene as it heads toward the century's third decade. As the force animating an unusual regional coalition, CAN is mounting its own FRONT Triennial juried exhibition this year. The idea is to complement the international exhibitions around town, and of course to attract the attention of out of town audiences.

The subtitle for FRONT Triennial is "An American City." The presence of this new international arts event in Cleveland can only work to the city's advantage, and is to be enthusiastically welcomed. Hopefully it's the first of many future triennials. I'm especially pleased to note that FRONT has restored an historic building designed specifically for African American physicians' offices during the racially fraught 1960's in Cleveland's Glenville neighborhood adjacent to University Circle. This unique office building was the work of none other than the architect Robert Madison, and serves as the headquarters for a number of long-term artists residencies that are part of this complex event. But I'm also glad to notice that among the aesthetic investigations FRONT will elicit from participating artists there will be some that look at (or react to) experiences of the self that aren't necessarily determined by curatorial ambitions, however up-to-date. After all, artworks are not quite part of the "real" world, which includes Art Triennials. Does the rather self-conscious phrase "An American City" mean anything important to art? We'll see. And is Cleveland itself best understood in those terms? It's so much more.

"ONLY CONNECT!…AND LIVE IN FRAGMENTS NO LONGER!" (HOWARD'S END)

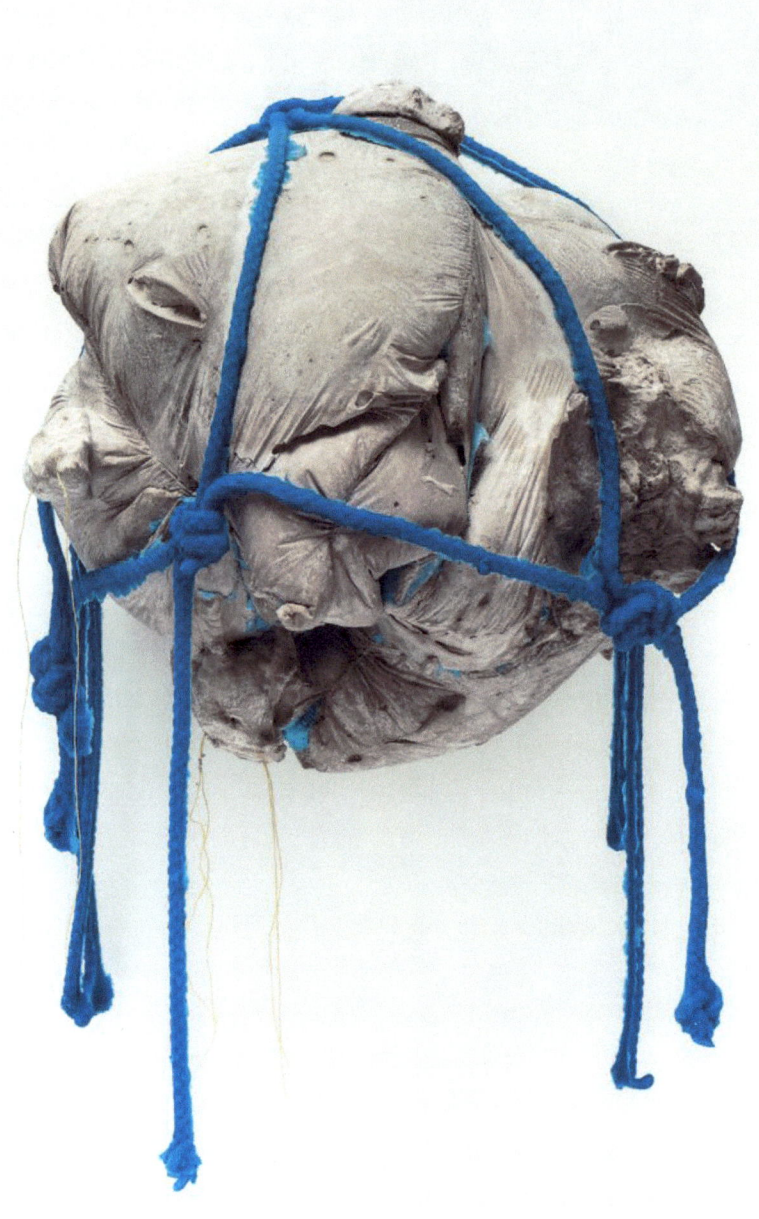

"M

My sculptures are influenced by Cleveland's industrial life, particularly the mysterious businesses that I find while exploring the city by bike. They can appear closed down from the outside, but on summer days, when large overhead doors are open, I see a full, vibrant life inside."

Fig. 36 "Escape to Sky"

"C
Cleveland, win lose or draw it's home. It's a collective experience that we as Clevelanders live and die by. We will always rise above, no matter what the odds are, Cleveland is a city of winners and no one can tell us otherwise...yes it rocks."

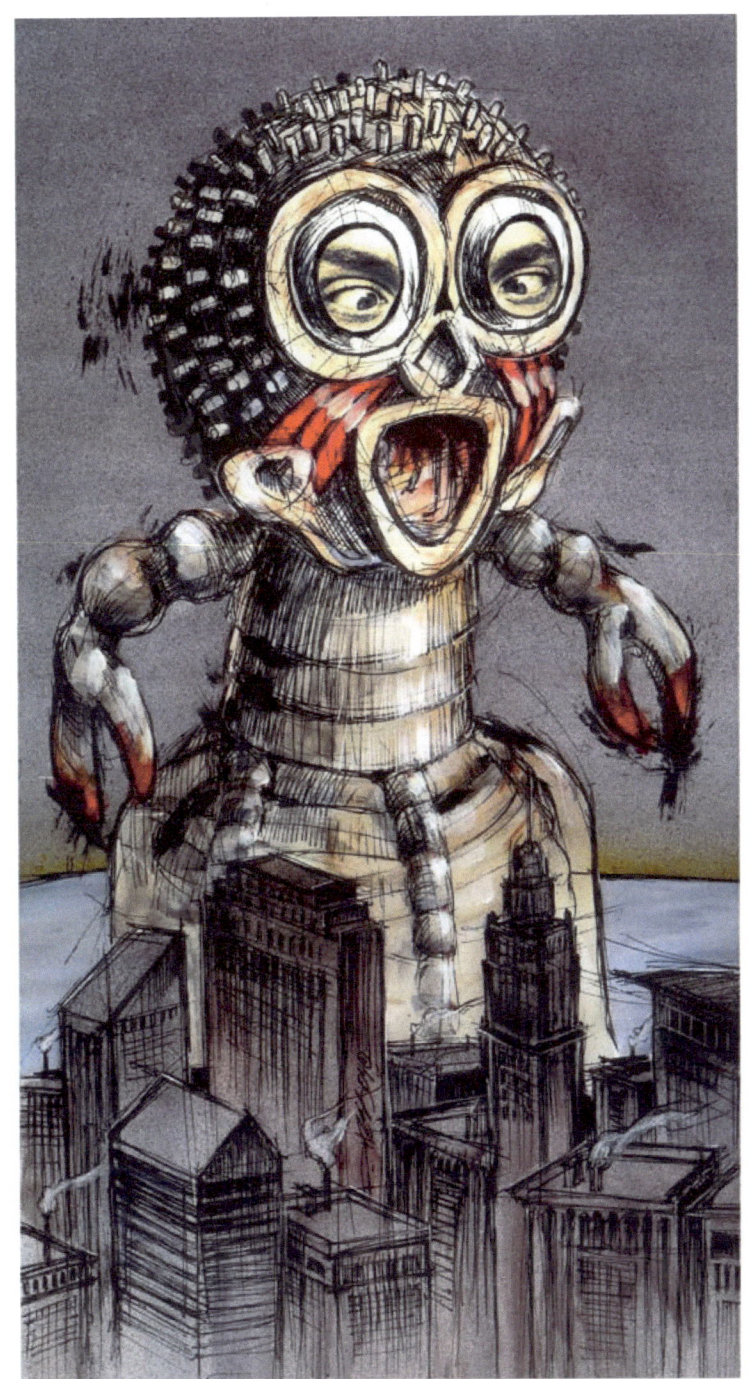

Fig. 37 "Horrible that ate Cleveland"

"H

Harvey was and Laura and I are life long Clevelanders who agree with the character on the back cover of American Splendor #1 who says 'We're stayin' in Cleveland and fighting'!"

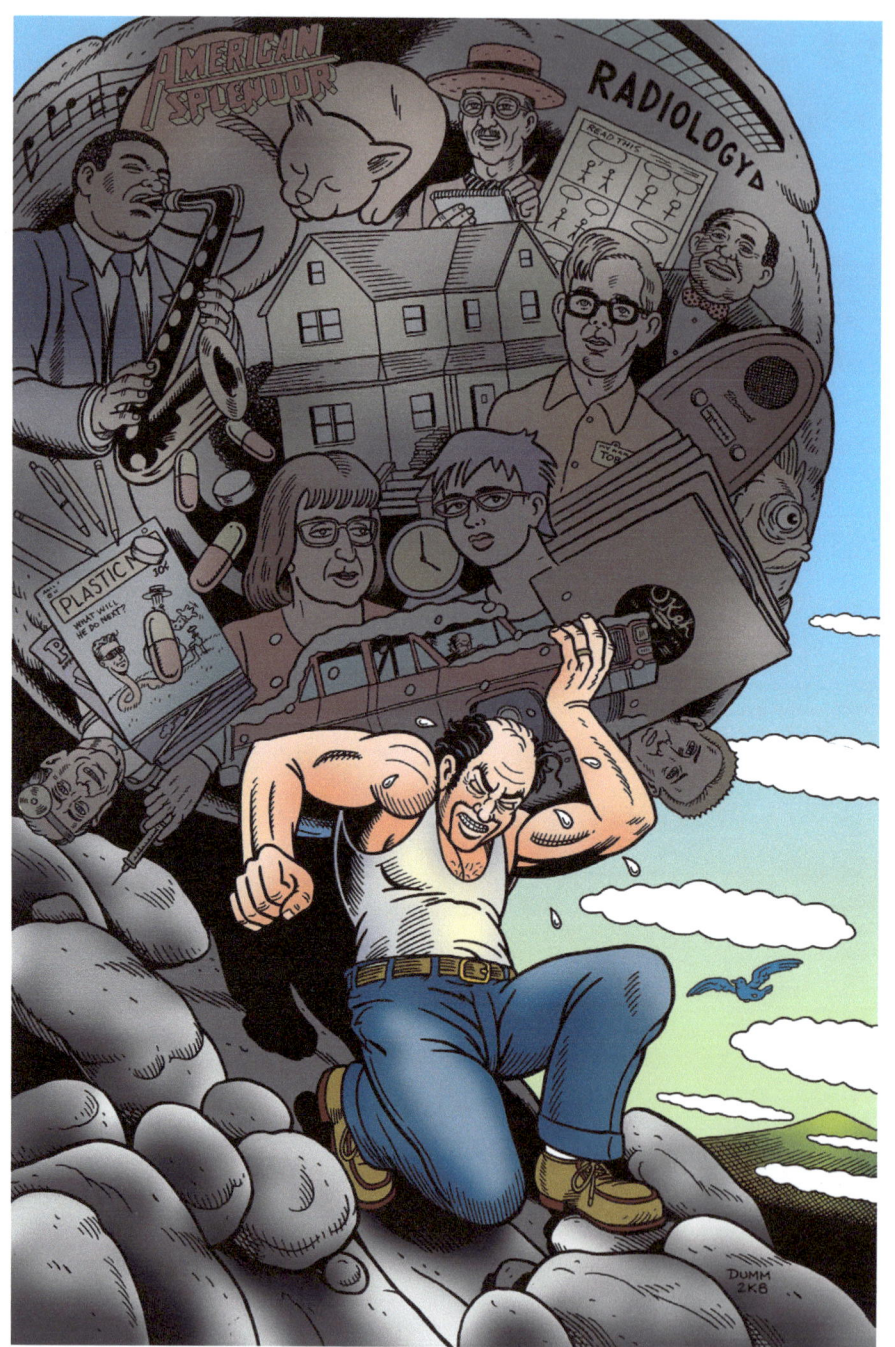

Fig.38 "Harvey P. As Sisyphus"

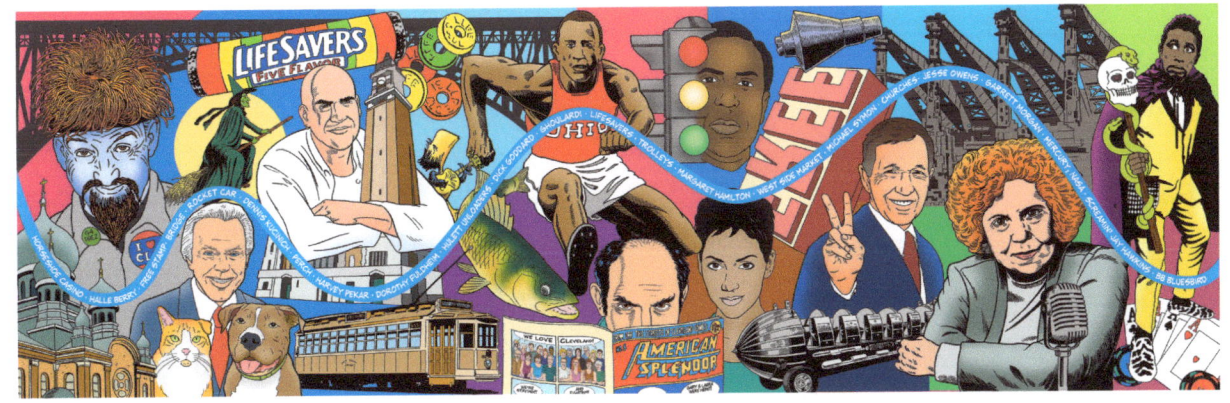

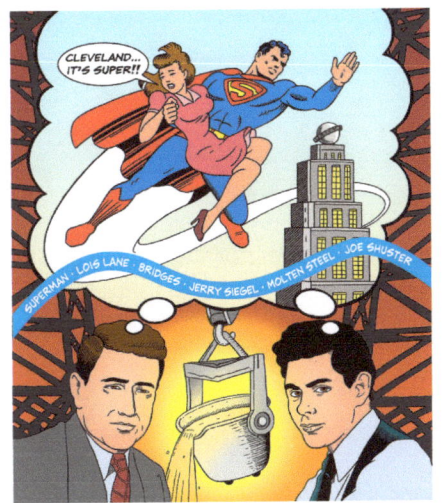

Our Love Letter to Cleveland
by Gary and Laura Dumm
September 10, 2013

These murals were created to pay homage to the creative people, wonderful places and thoughtful inventions that have made Cleveland a greater place to live and work.

"Our Love Letter To Cleveland" mural was made possible by a 2013 Cuyahoga Arts & Culture and Community Partnership for Arts and Culture Creative Workforce Fellowship awarded to Gary Dumm.

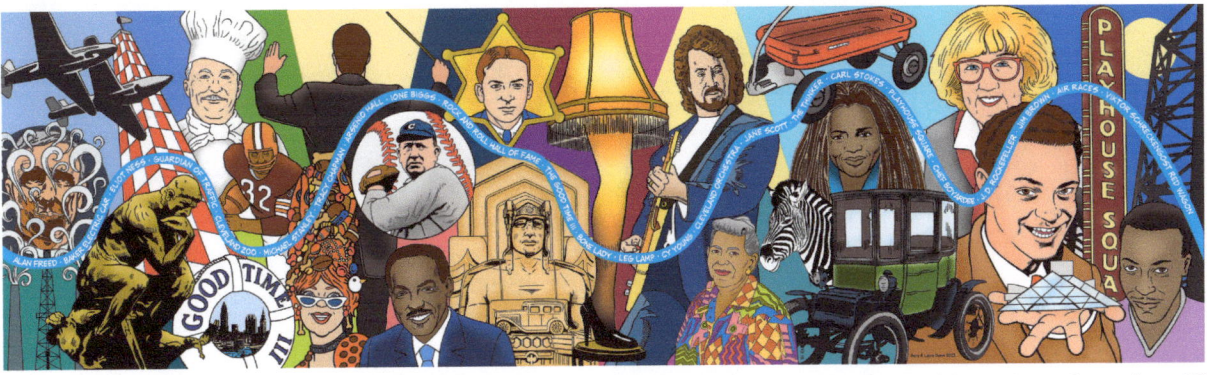

Fig. 39 "Our Love Letter to Cleveland"

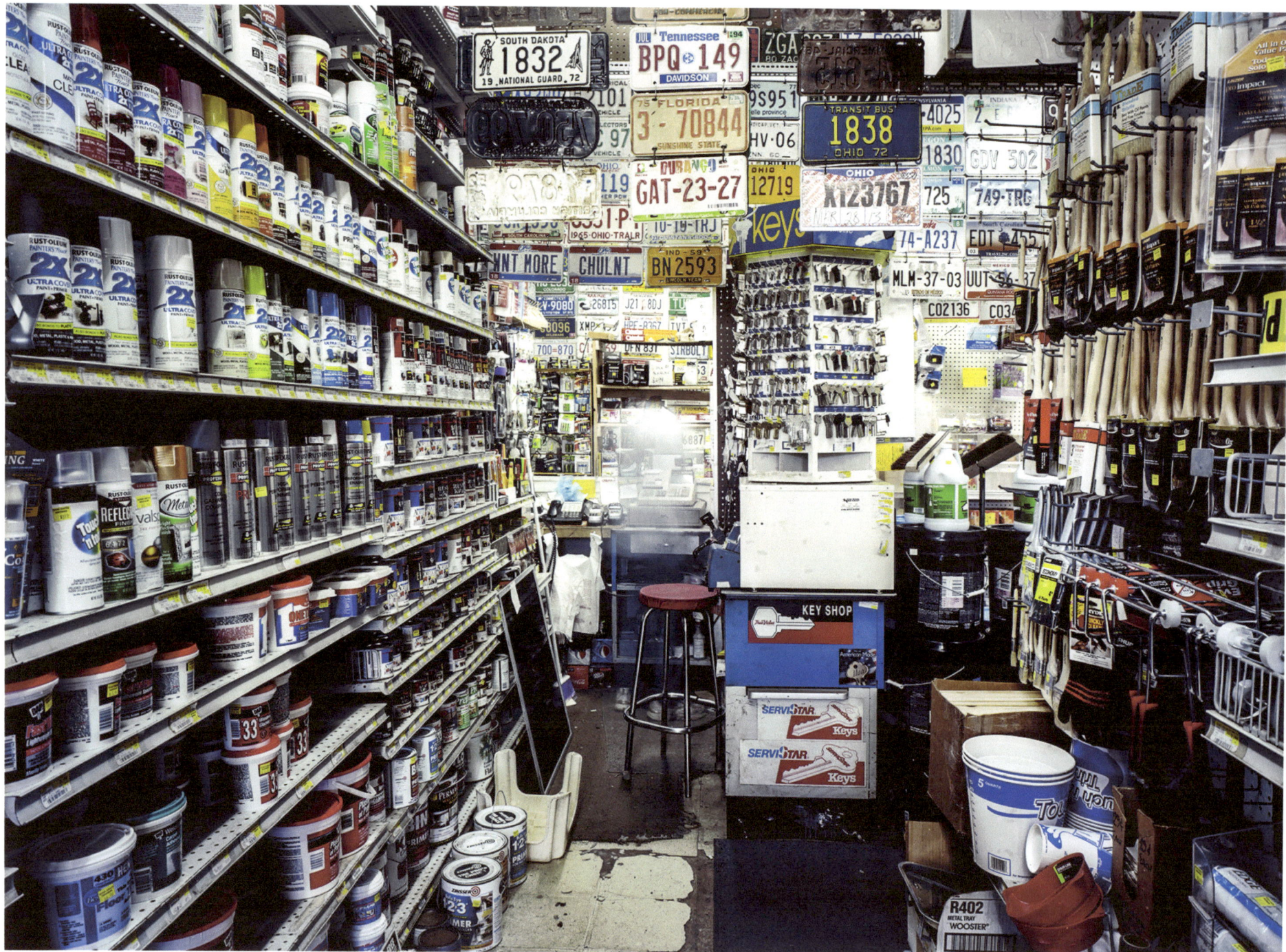

Fig.40 "Cedar Center Hardware"

"C

Cleveland is a city built by people who made things. Certainly cars and steel but also the entire fabric of industrial America. This project is a tribute to those people and to the people now that appreciate the satisfaction of making. This is part of series on traditional hardware stores. They are survivors. They are a contrast to big box emphasizing making and fixing things rather than consuming."

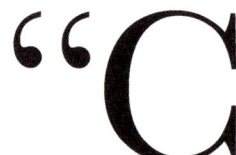

"Cleveland relates to us all. It has its shining moments, dim sorrows, deep losses, magical victories, and a sense of community like no other city I have lived in. Whether it was back in the rusty 70s where as a child I would approach "Gate D" hoping for an innocent Indians victory or now when Terminal Tower is shining bright welcoming all in celebration of what we have accomplished! We are a city with grit, dedication, glory, color, soul, and most of all the strong belief that our Cleveland will stand above the rest. Watch us shine."

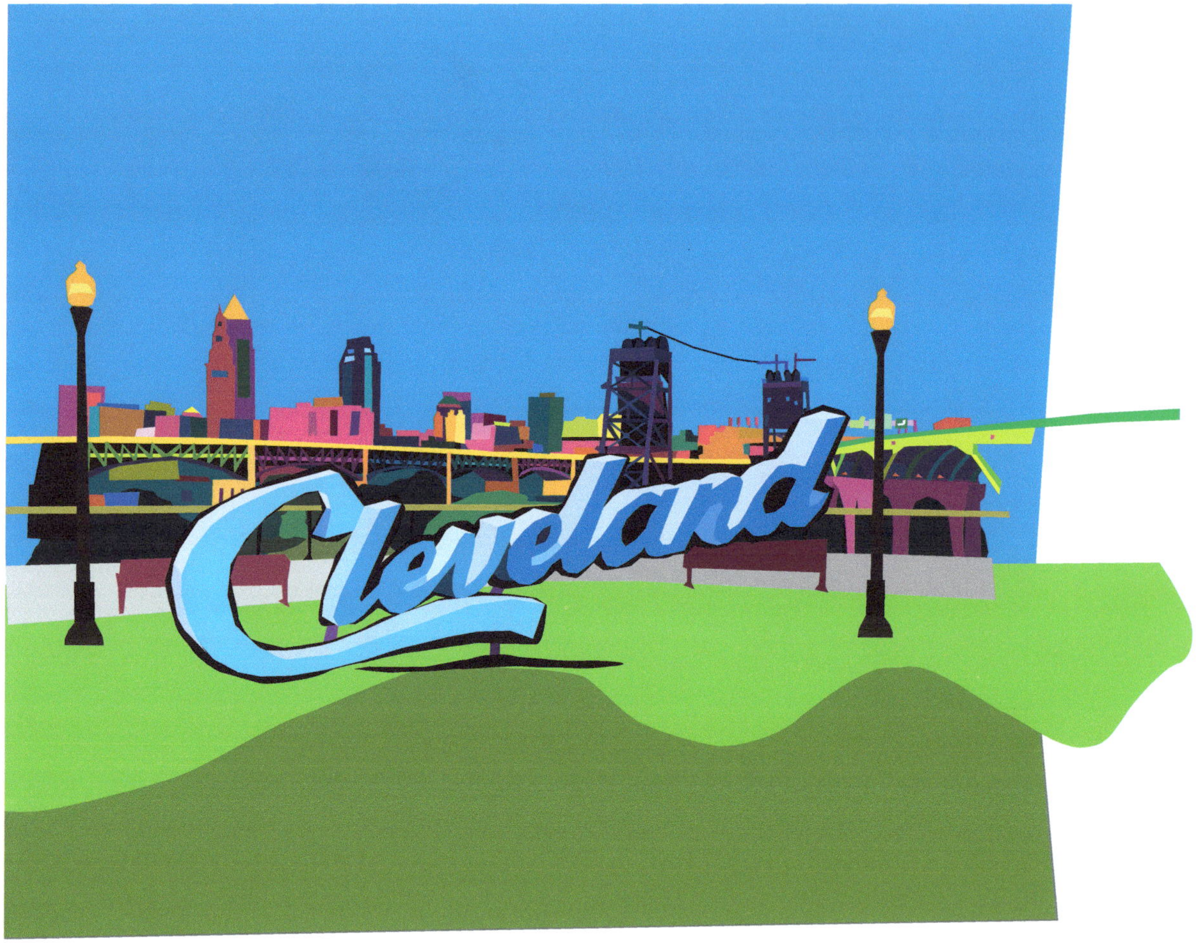

Fig.41 "CLE"

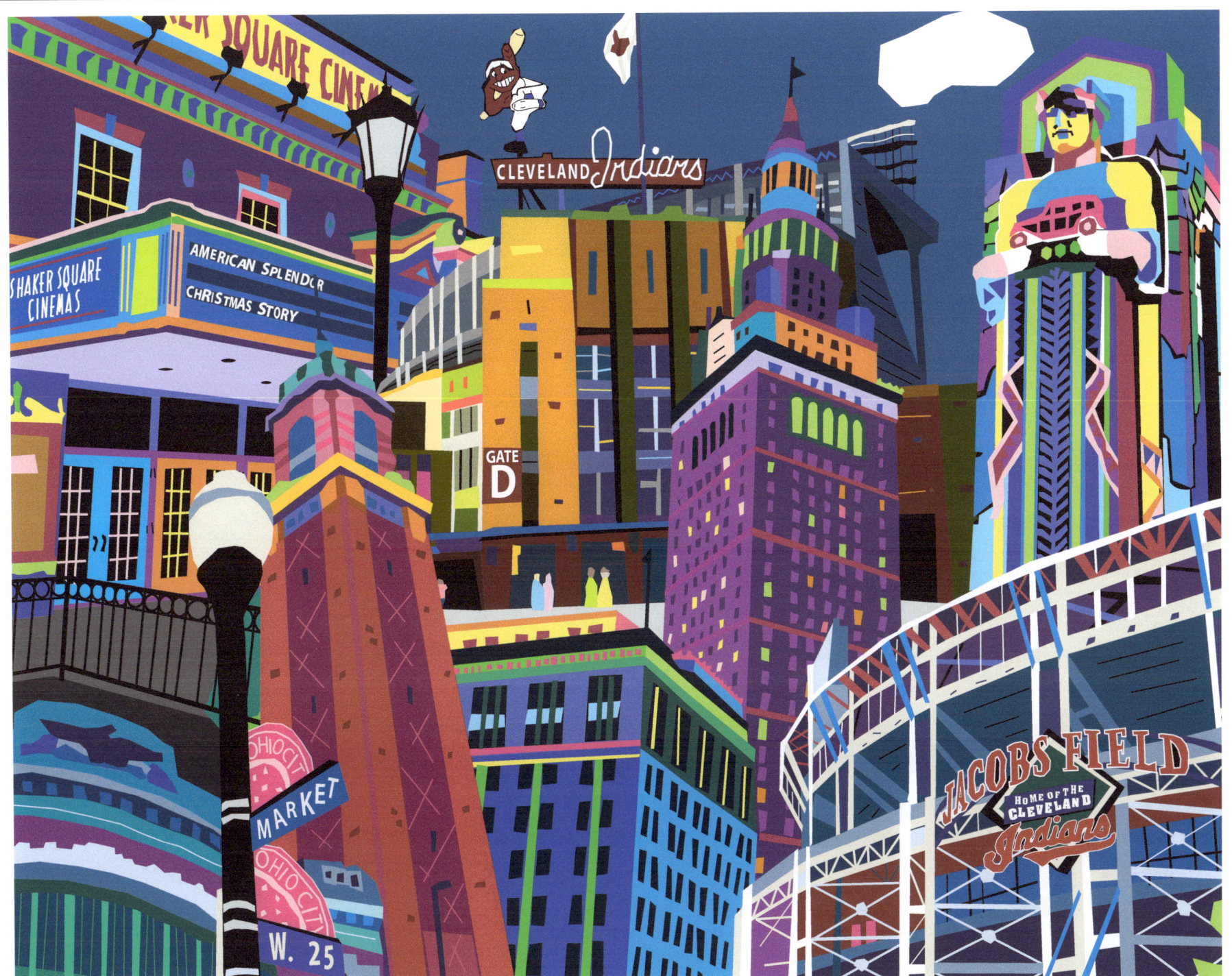

Fig. 42 "Cleveland"

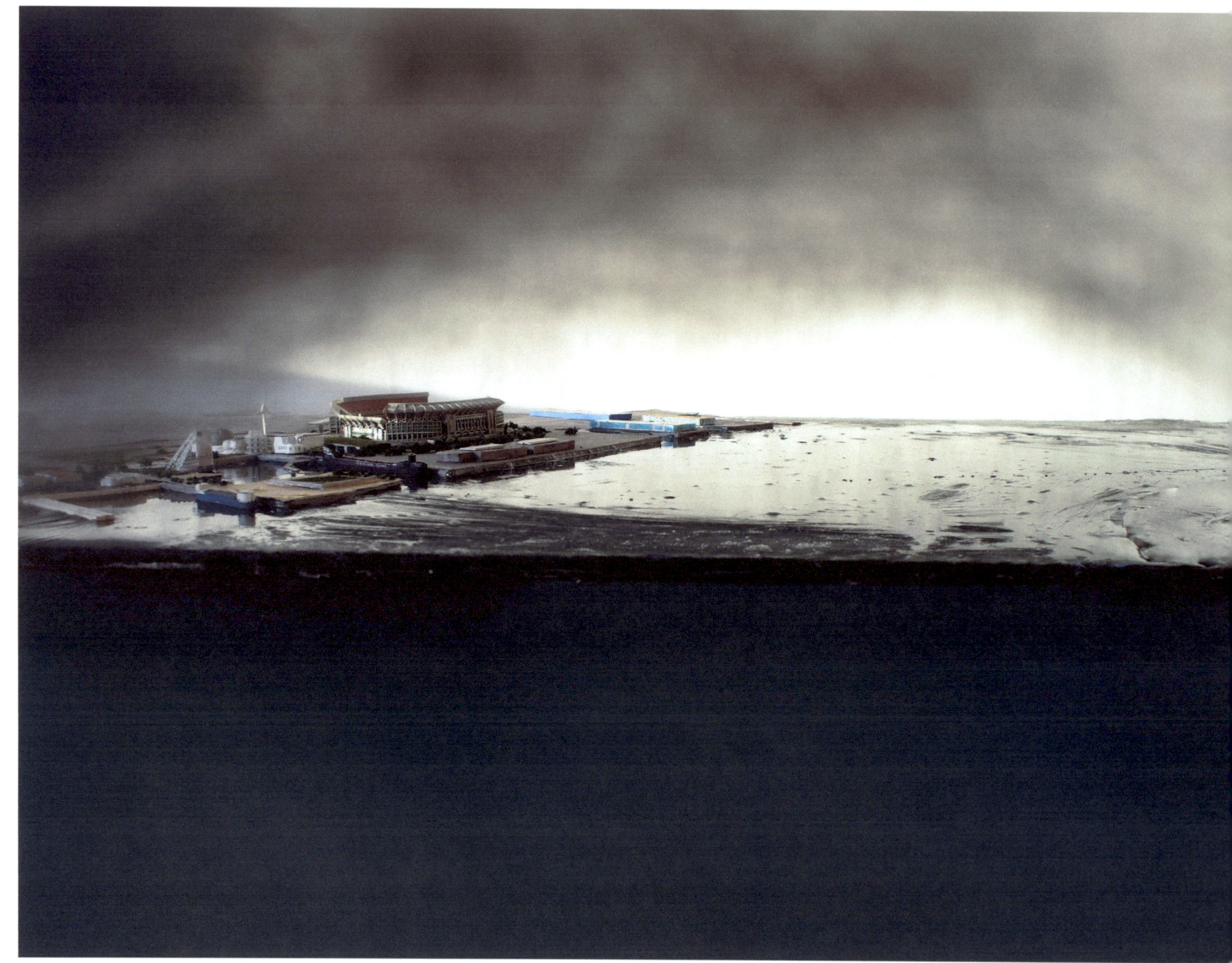

Fig. 43 "Under the Stadium"

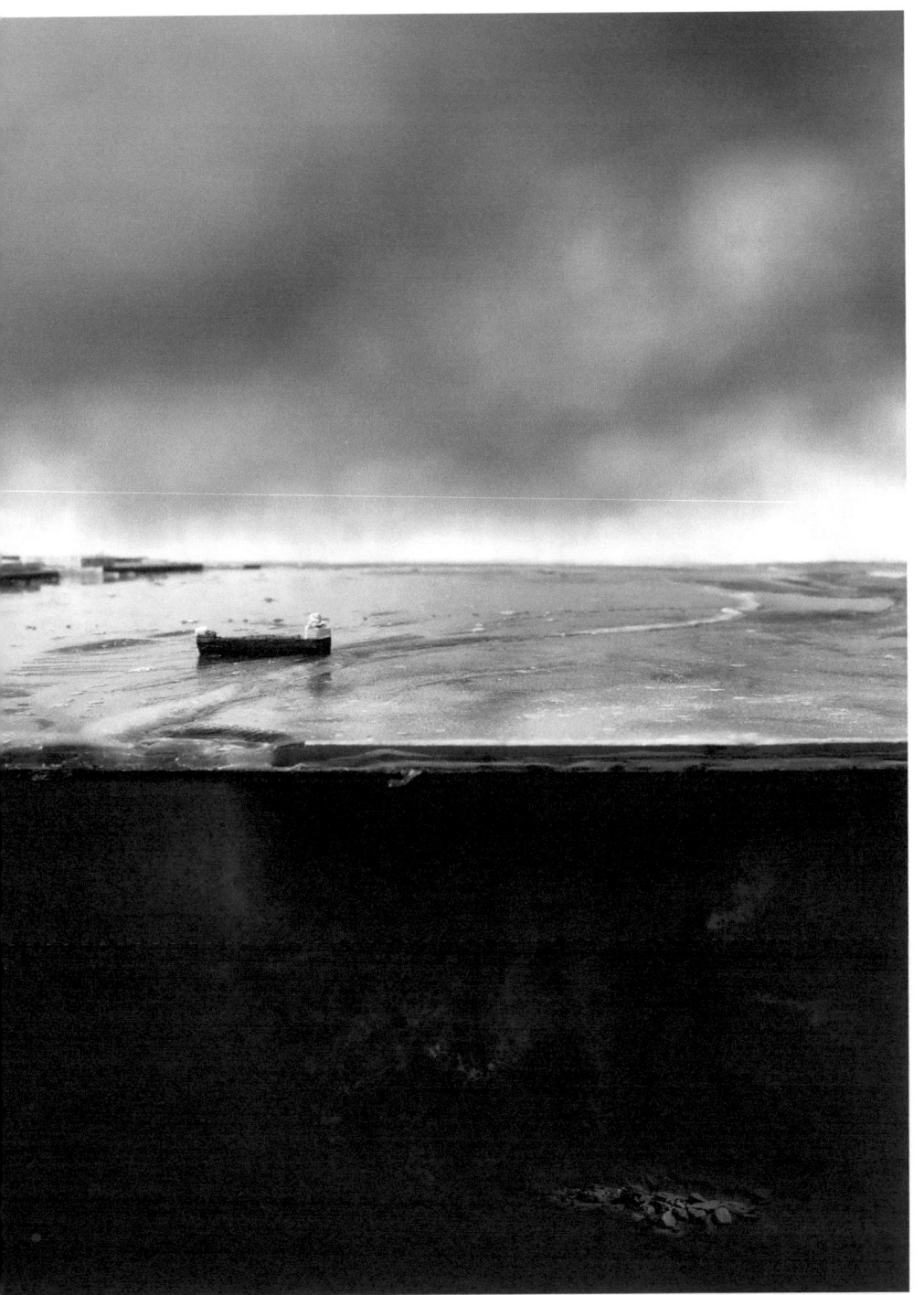

Fig. 44 "Looking for Artificial Reef"

"**H**Having grown up around the Great Lakes, I find the landscape along Lake Erie offers both solace and inspiration, and its presence inevitably spills over into my artwork."

In 1997 the Cleveland Municipal Stadium was demolished to complete the construction of a new Cleveland Browns Stadium. Portions of the old stadium were dumped into Lake Erie at three strategic points to create artificial reefs that would serve as habitat for fish and wildlife. Under the Stadium is a tableau photograph that peers at the new sports arena from the vantage point of the lake. This constructed photograph allows the viewer to see a cross section of the city skyline as well as the mysterious depths of Lake Erie. The second panel, Looking for the Artificial Reefs, shows the remnants of the old stadium as it currently sits in the off shore waters of the lake. This diptych shows both the old and the new, and in doing so alludes to the city's progress as well as offers a new perspective on the nature of sports in our urban centers. For the quiet endeavors under the lake have restored over 1,000 feet of fish habitat, but such efforts are often uncelebrated compared to the attention granted to our professional sports arenas.

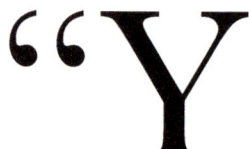

"Yes, the dictionary spells it "tingling", but that doesn't rhyme quite right. In Cleveland we spell it "tingeling": as in "Mr. Jingeling, how you tingeling". Anyways, Clevelanders don't care about spelling and they don't care about Santa. Who wants the man in red when you can have the man in green? Halle's 7th floor might be gone but it's still closer than the North Pole. In the land of CLE, Mr. Jingeling (or as I call him, Christmas Ghoulardi) rules the holiday landscape. Whether it was Halle's, Higby's, or Tower City, The Jing loomed large. I read that the very first man in the suit was a cop, and that the keys on a large hoop (for Santa's shop, or something) were in fact for the city's jail cells. Reigning from '65 to '95, the appropriately named Earl Keyes (pictured) was the Jing of my youth. Some other guys have played him since and I think that's great. Cleveland is too tough to die and so is Mr. Jingeling. May his keys jingle and jangle forever.

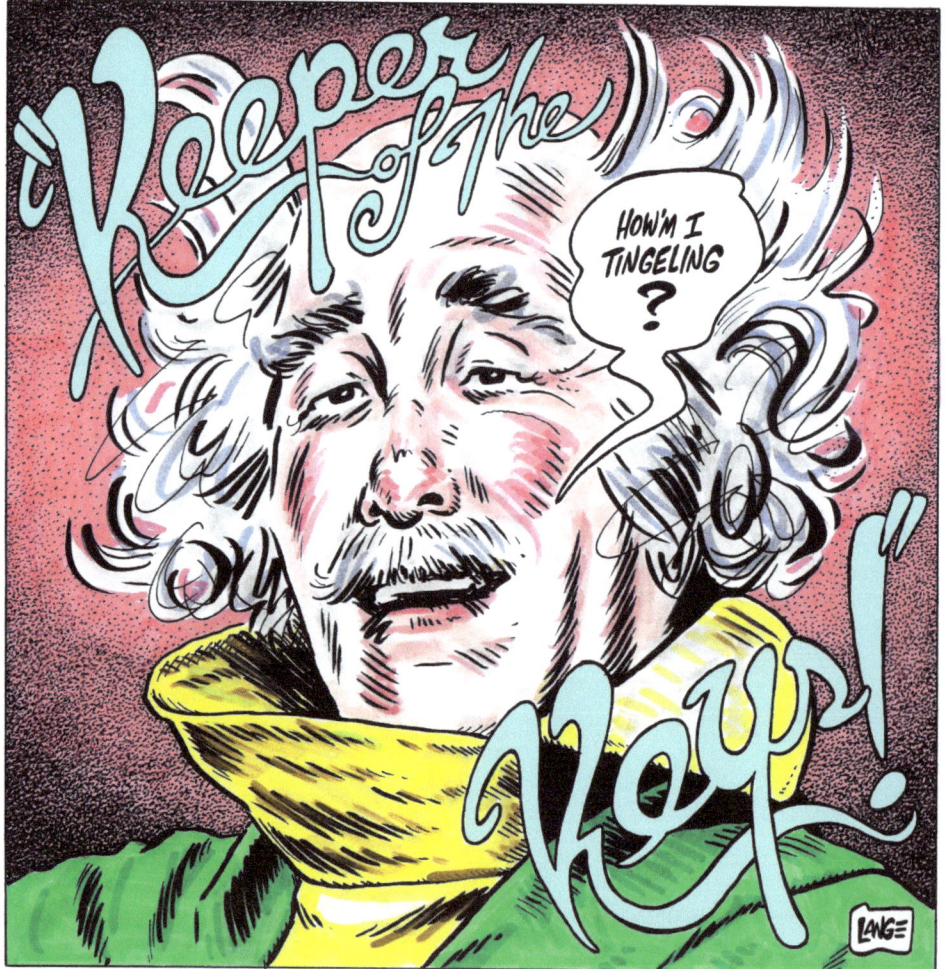

Fig.45 "Mr. Jingeling"

"P

Peter Laughner, Peter Laughner, Peter Laughner. Say it three times and it feels like he just might appear. The patron saint of local fuck-ups, there's something special about Laughner- a Dickensian specter, wrapped in chains like Jacob Marley visiting Ebenezer in the night. But who was he? I'm not sure anybody knows. He died so young and left so little behind, and anyways, the legend has long outgrown the man (he's been dead longer than he lived, papa ooh mow mow). What we do know: He was a poet, a folkie, a leather jacket fuck-up, a trendsetter and man about town, a drunk, a drug shooter, insecure, ambitious, an embodiment of both creation and destruction, a dark prince amongst peasants; He was a Punk. Laughner is mostly

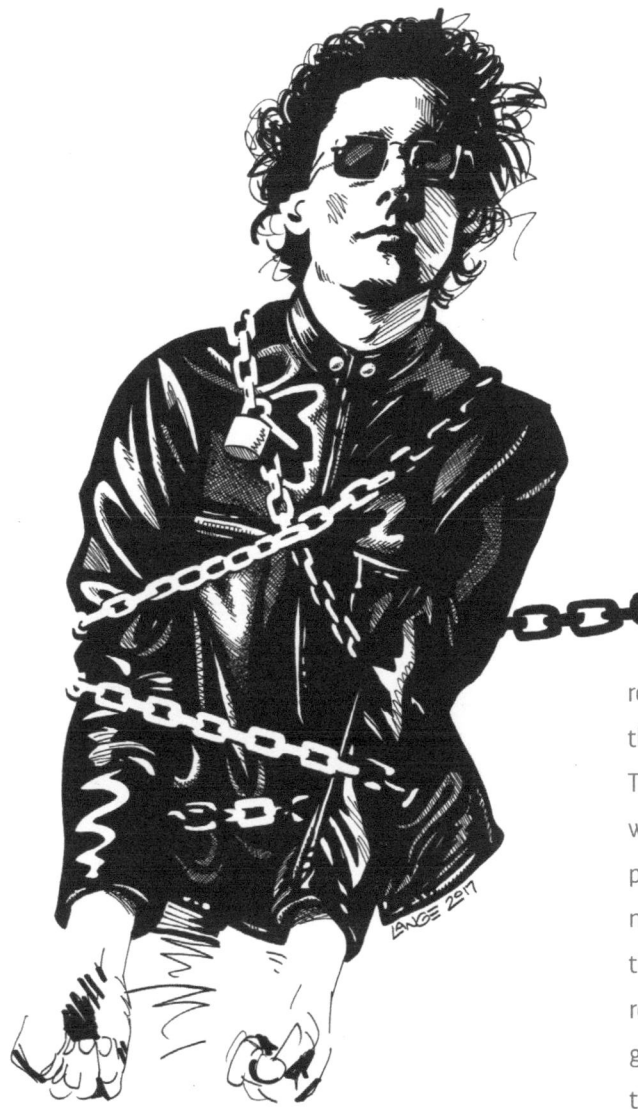

Fig. 46 "Peter Laughner"

remembered for his work with the bands Rocket from the Tombs and early Pere Ubu. There were other groups too. Some played out only once. Others never even recorded. And yet... there are bootlegs, demos, radio recordings, writings, ephemera, gold. For those willing to look, the well is surprisingly deep. Laughner's candle-twice-as-bright life mirrors Cleveland's own industrial heyday- something beautiful, violent, sublime. And far far too short.

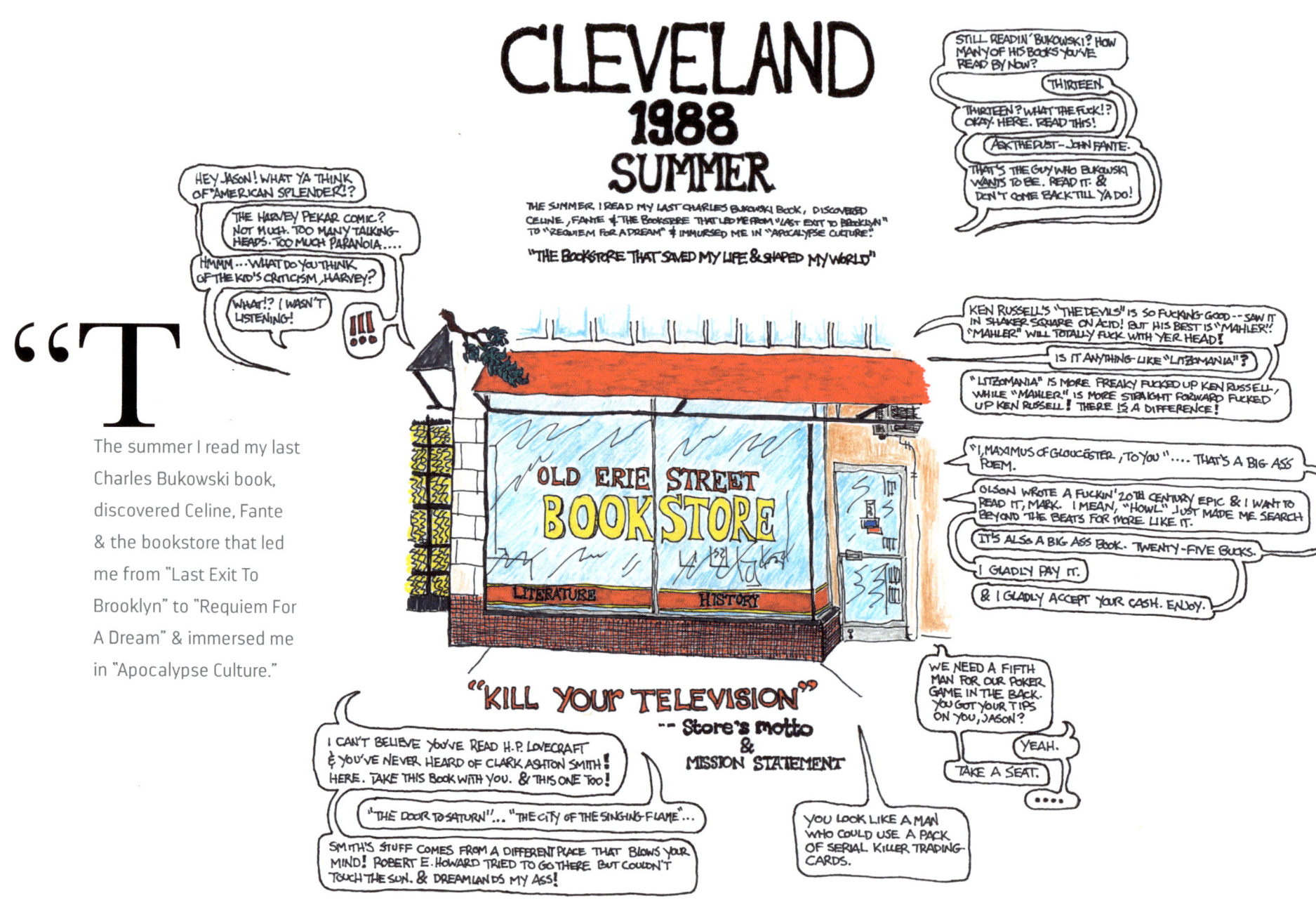

"T

The summer I read my last
Charles Bukowski book,
discovered Celine, Fante
& the bookstore that led
me from "Last Exit To
Brooklyn" to "Requiem For
A Dream" & immersed me
in "Apocalypse Culture."

Fig. 47 "Cleveland 1988"

"Cleveland Fish Platter with Matzoh Ball Soup and a Salad. The gefilte fish, pickled smelt, trout lax, and trout caviar are all made with lakefood from Lake Erie and it tributaries. We wanted to show our guests how far we've come since the Cuyahoga River burned. Cleveland's waterways are a success story that should be celebrated and enjoyed. What sense does it make to import seafood from hundreds of miles away when we have well managed stocks of delicious lakefood in our backyard. There's no greater reflection of who we are as a community than the foods we enjoy. Clevelanders are resilient, strong, and hopeful for a better tomorrow. Eating foods from our now clean lakes and rivers is a testament to our drive to sustainably carry on."

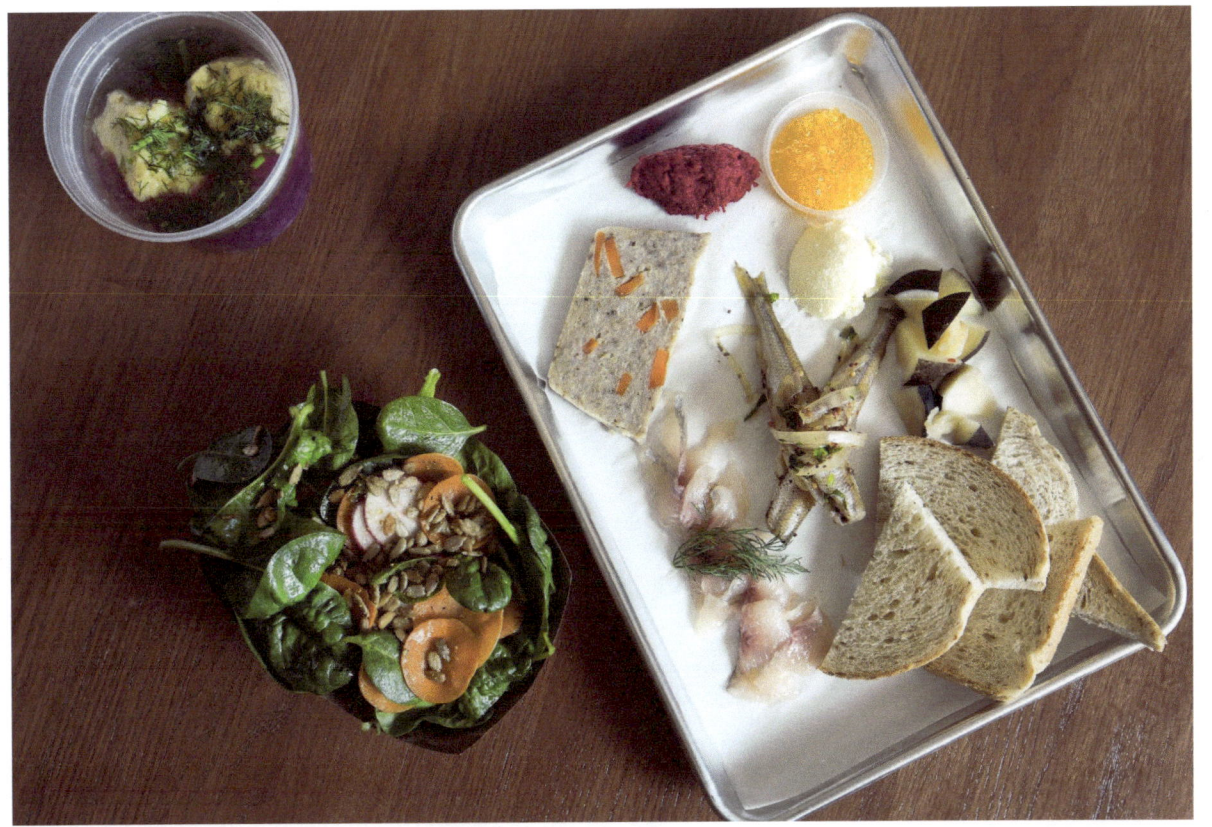

Fig. 48

"Cleveland artists can make something out of anything. This piece was made right after the Great Recession and I found the pillow on a tree lawn. I started to develop these found objects where objects that were abandoned and left for useless became an entry point for a new conversation about displacement, the sub prime mortgage crisis, and other things that were happening to people. Integrating text and using neon amplified the voice of the character that sat on this cushion and allowed to animate these characters to come to life and ultimately be heard."

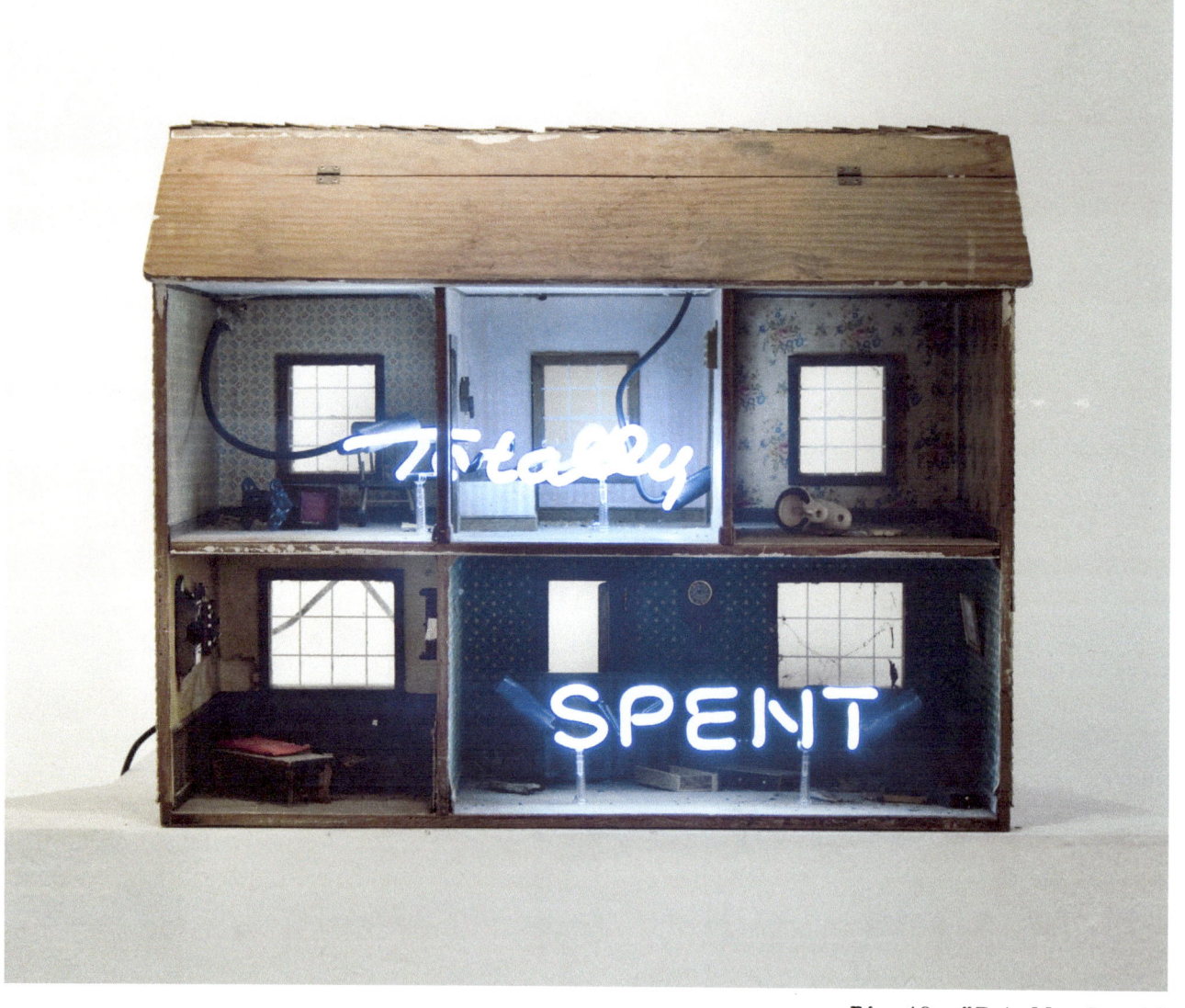

Fig.49 "Totally Spent"

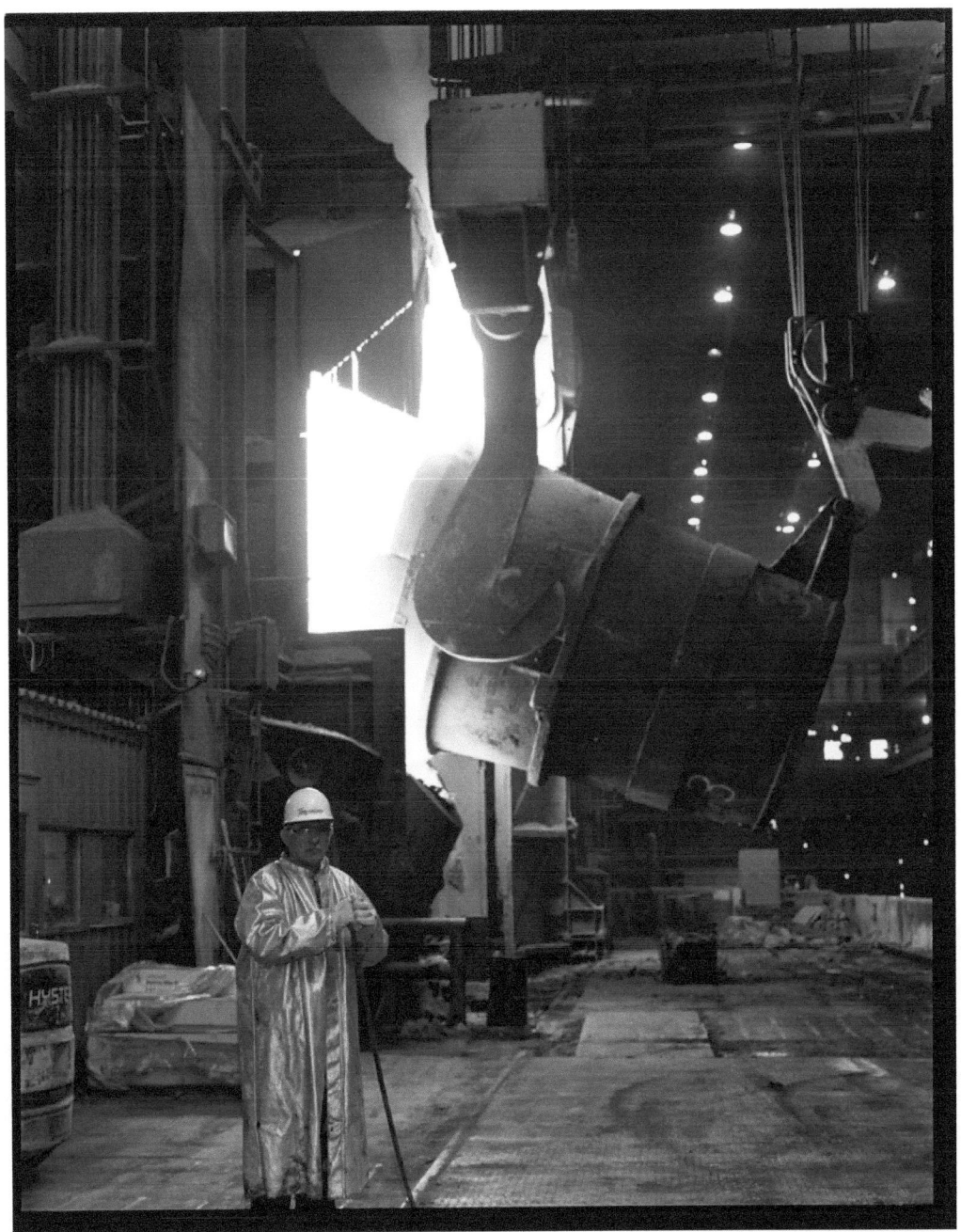

Fig. 50 "ISG/Mittal Steel's head safety officer Tom Krizman"

"I

I am a Clevelander.

My great-grand parents settled in Cleveland in 1911. My son and grandsons are proudly the fifth and sixth generation of our family to enjoy Cleveland's intellectual, cultural and commercial treasures.

As a portrait photographer I have photographed in every corner of the City. Since opening my studio in 1975 I have documented the incredible diversity of our places and faces.

I have travelled wide and far. I have explored most of the United States and visited countries on five continents. In all of my travels, there ain't no place like home."

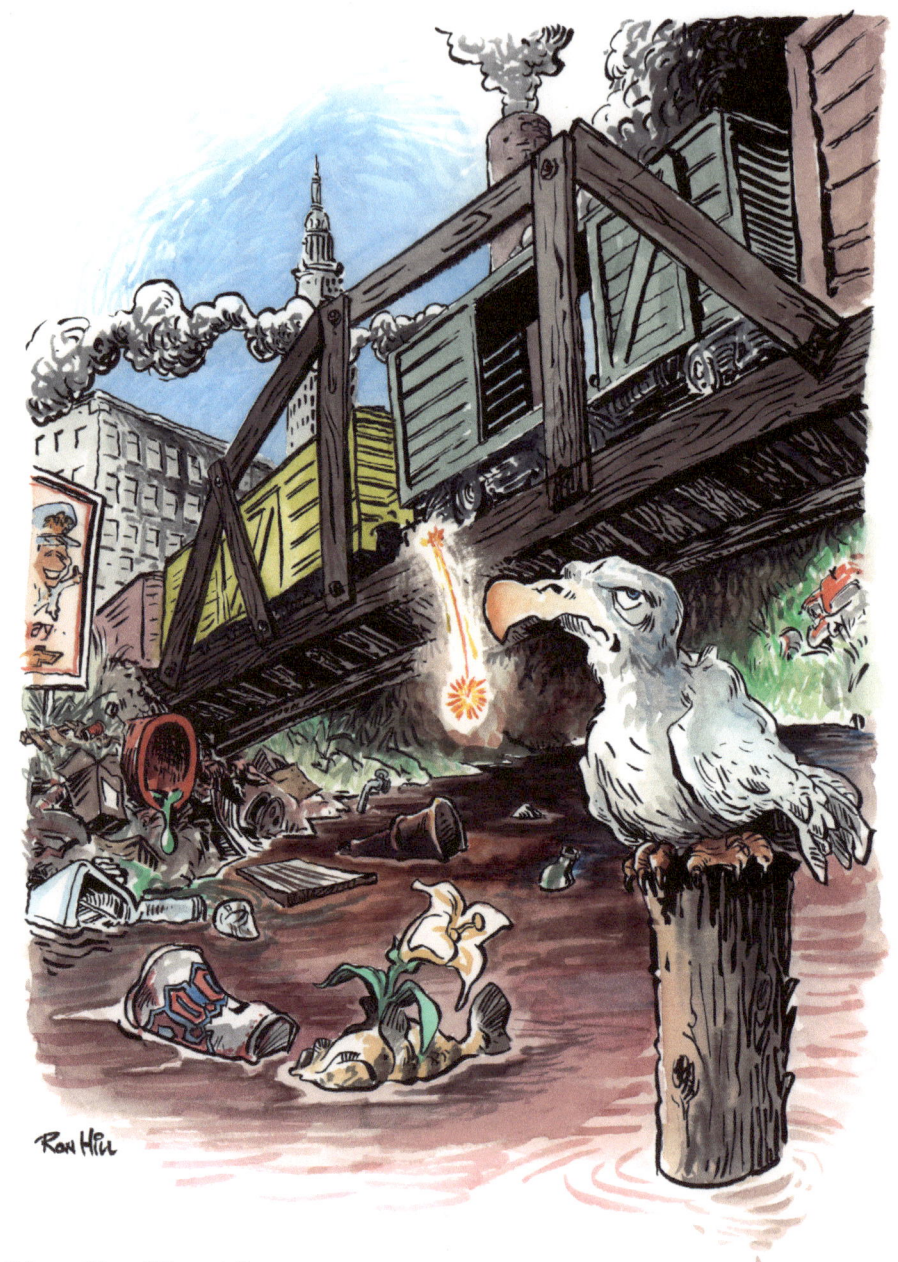

Fig. 51 "Spark"

"F

For 19 years I have been publishing editorial cartoons for six Cleveland-area, weekly newspapers, but I also work as an illustrator and occasionally enter regional art shows. These four watercolor paintings were created for two different Northern Ohio Illustrators Society shows. The cartoon of the Cuyahoga River was created for a show theme titled The River Burned, and depicts the spark from the railroad trestle that ignited the waters. The three caricatures of Cleveland fright-show hosts were for an exhibit titled All Things Cleveland. Pictured are "Big Chuck" Schodowski (late Friday nights on channel 8), Martin "Super Host" Sullivan (Saturday afternoons on channel 43), and Ron "The Ghoul" Sweed (late Saturday nights on channel 61). These were all shows I loved as a kid in the 1970s."

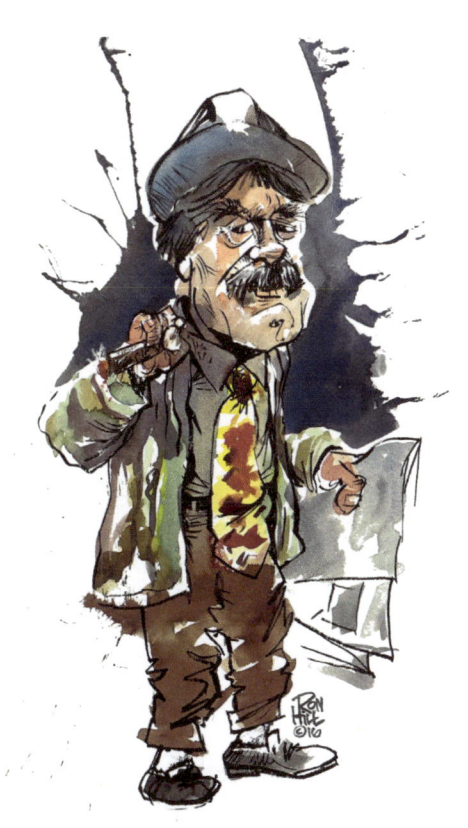

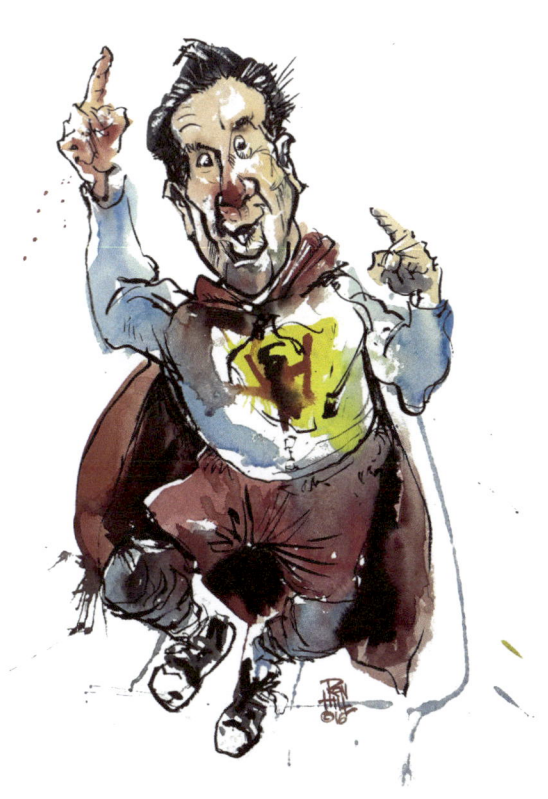

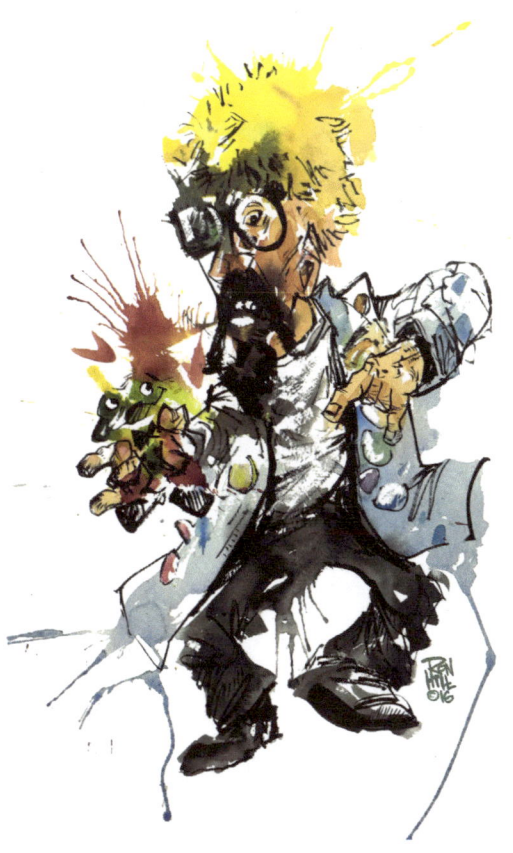

Fig. 52 "Stash Kowalski"   Fig. 53 "Super - Host"   Fig. 54 "The Ghoul"

"P

Pushing boundaries by dissecting the status quo is a process I think of as seeing between the lines. For example, The Chief – Still Fighting is a parody of a caricature. No matter which side of the PC issue you come down on, you'll have to agree that the Cleveland Indians' beleaguered Chief Wahoo has taken a political beating. I've re-imagined him wearing boxing gloves, a winning grin and a black eye. Naturally, he's poised "on the ball" which is exactly where sports fans want to see the team: ready to fight another round for the pennant."

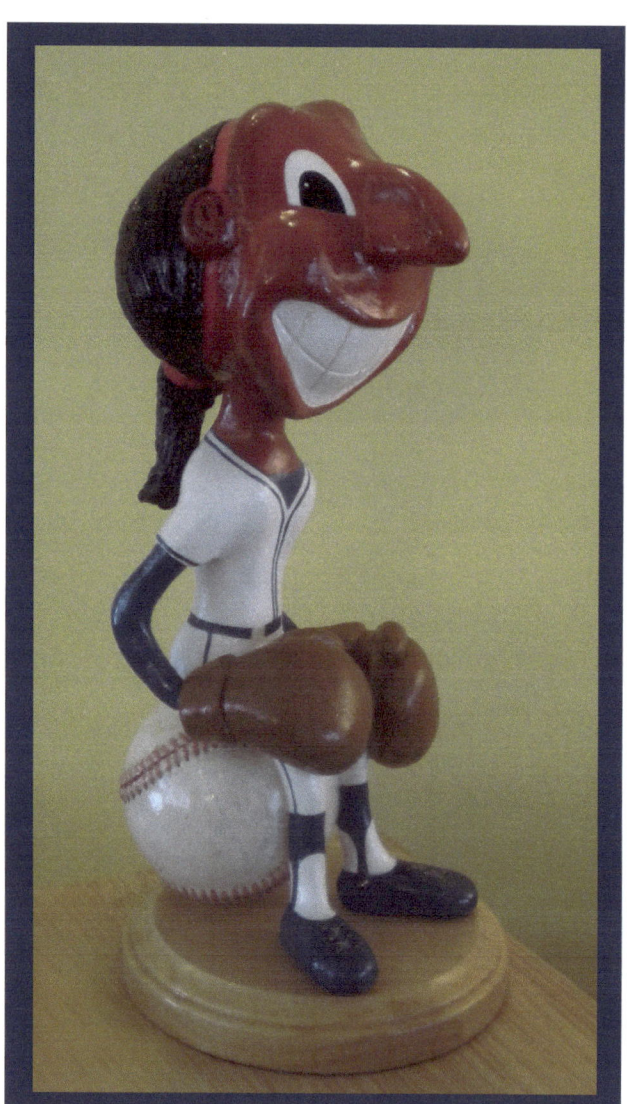
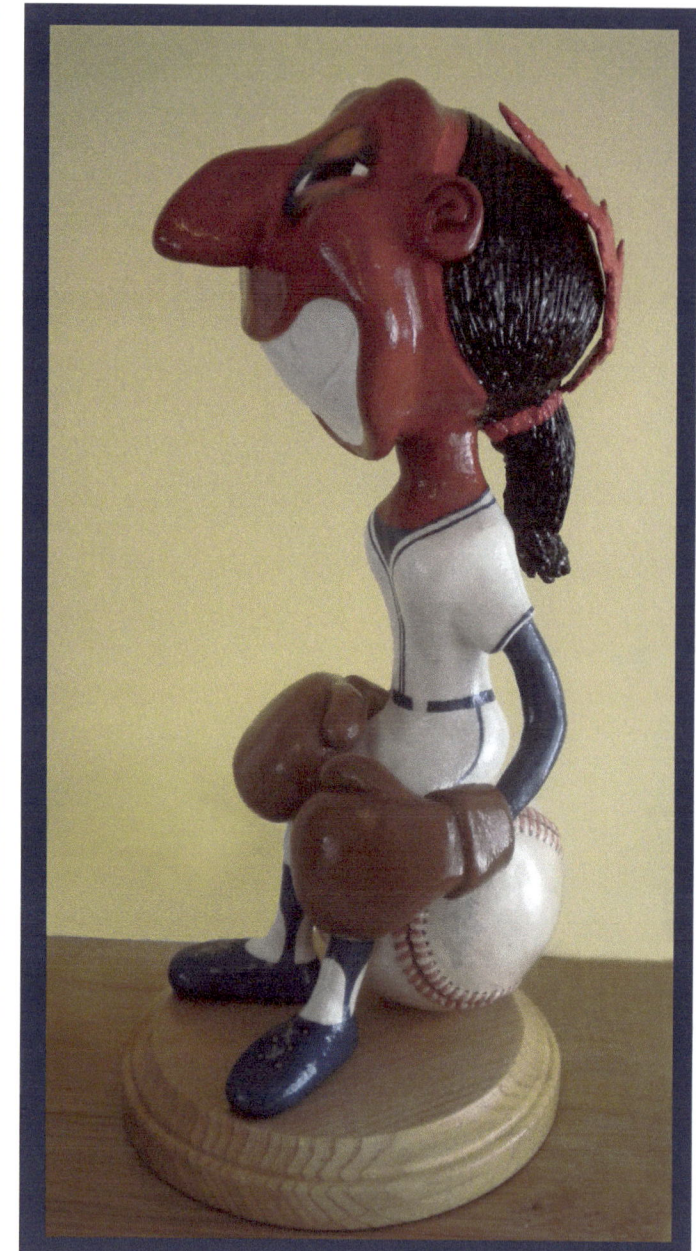

Fig. 55a and 55b "The Chief"

"T

The Cleveland Book Lovers' Map arose out of my interest in literature (I was the book-review editor for The Plain Dealer for five years) and illustrated maps. Northeast Ohio has a rich tradition of birthing successful writers. This map is by no means a comprehensive guide to them all. Instead, I wanted it to delineate people and places that anchor that tradition. And the little line-art girl at the top of the page is someone I drew in a bookstore — which I do with some regularity. All of the art here started out as pen drawings in my sketchbook, which I brought into Adobe Illustrator.

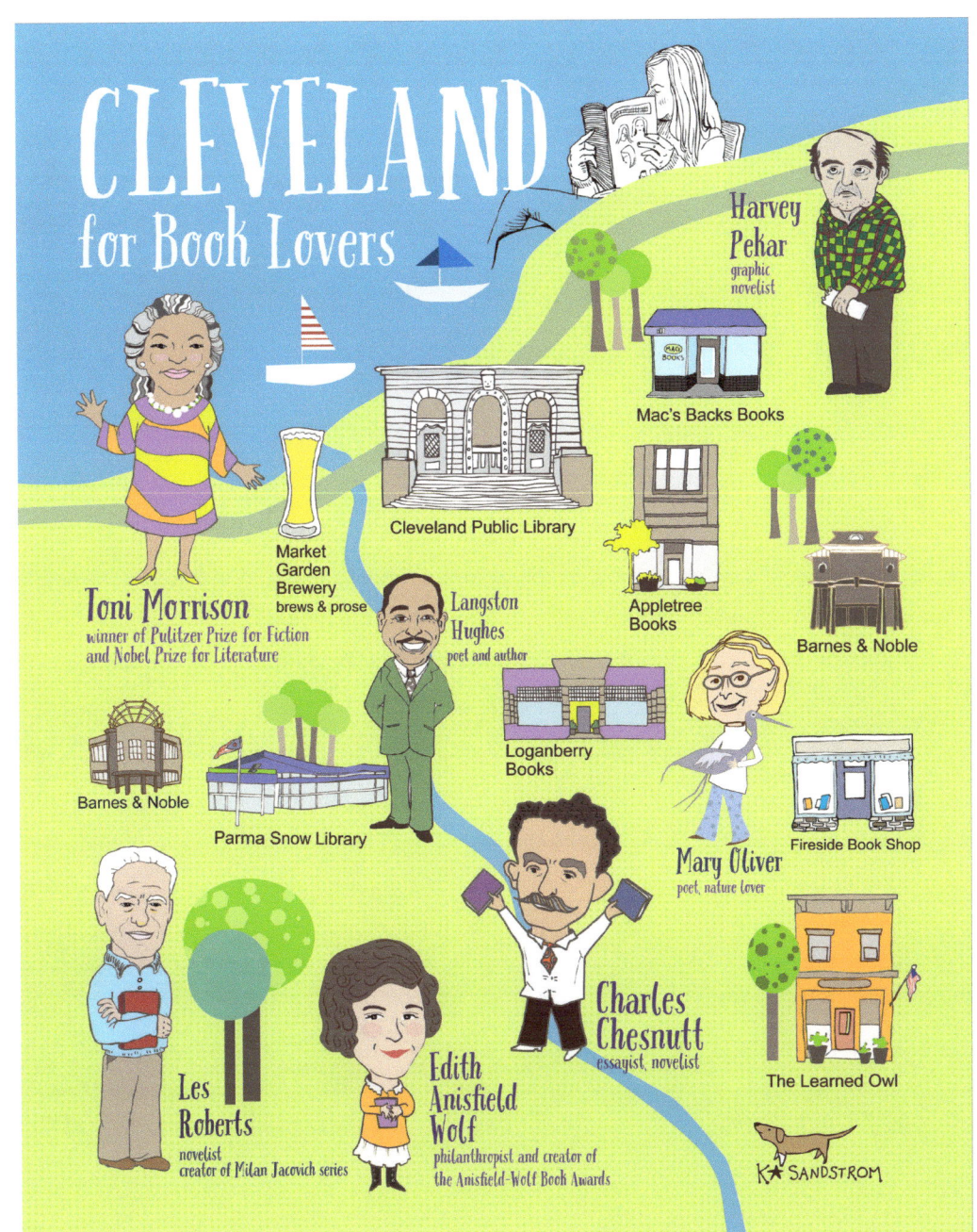

Fig. 56 "Book Lovers Map"

"F

For the last few summers the Rock and Roll Hall of Fame has had bands play at the plaza in front of the Rock Hall. I started attending these events, they were free and they had some great bands performing. I started taking my sketchpad or IPAD with me, and was inspired to do this painting. The people are made up as well as the singer, but I hoped I captured a true Cleveland treasure."

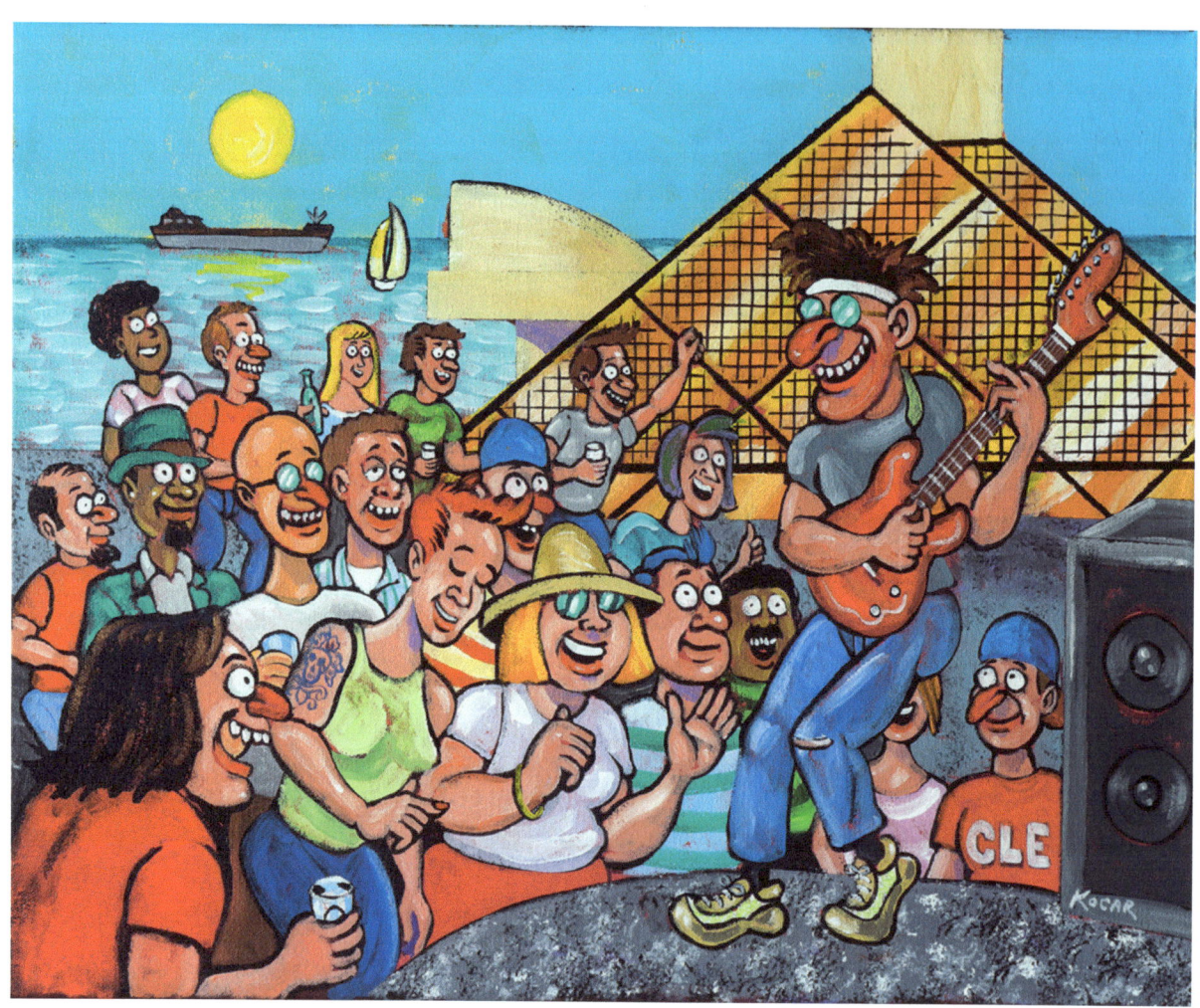

Fig.57 "Summer at the Rock Hall"

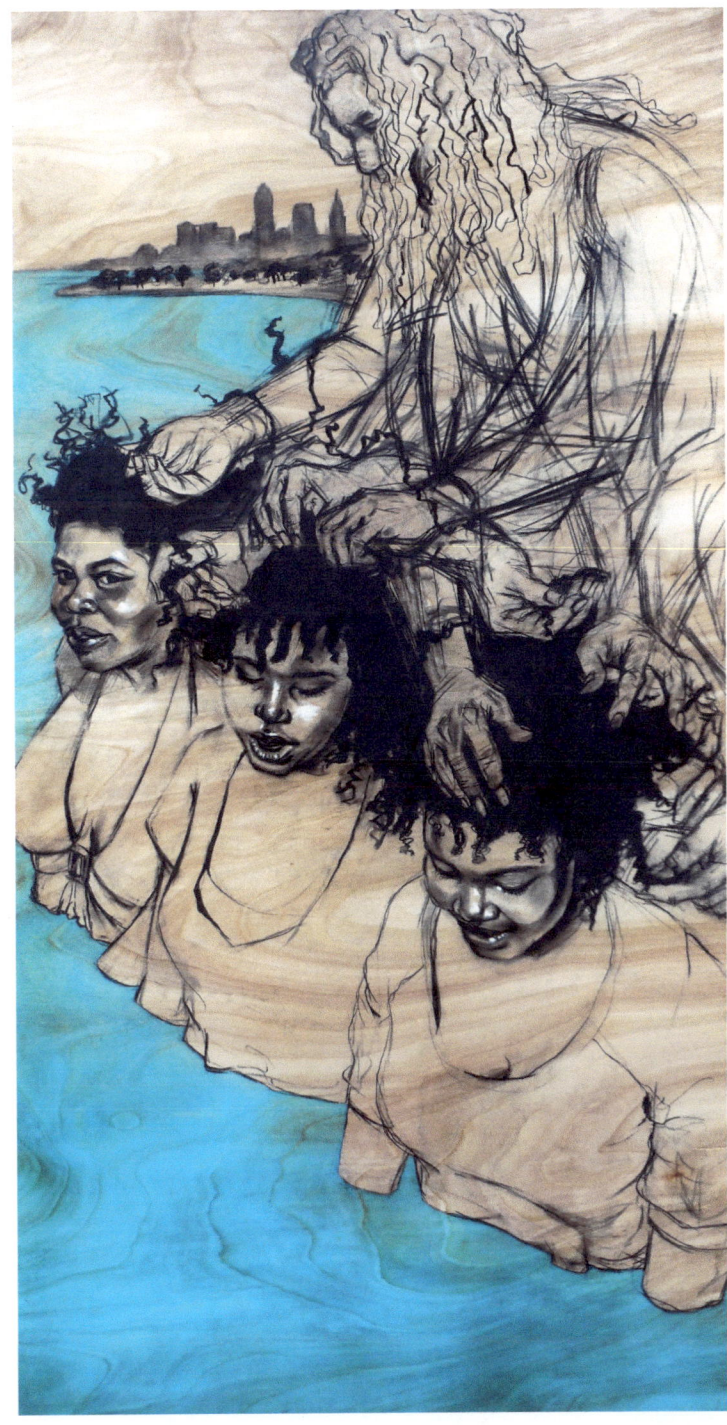

Fig. 58 "Blue Water Still (The Sirens Series)"

"T

The reference photos for this series were taken at Edgewater Beach. The subjects are my next-door neighbors who have become my dear friends and now an extended family. Despite the fact that the daughters are all avid swimmers this was their first visit to Edgewater. A few years back the girls convinced their mother to take swim lessons for her safety. As I spent the day with this incredible family, I realized this fiercely protective nature included me as well."

"I

I always liked the moniker for my hometown: forest city- In my work, the cemetery, another kind of forest city, has loomed large, an interest that has spanned my decades. The idea of conjoining them in these drawings of pooled research came naturally.

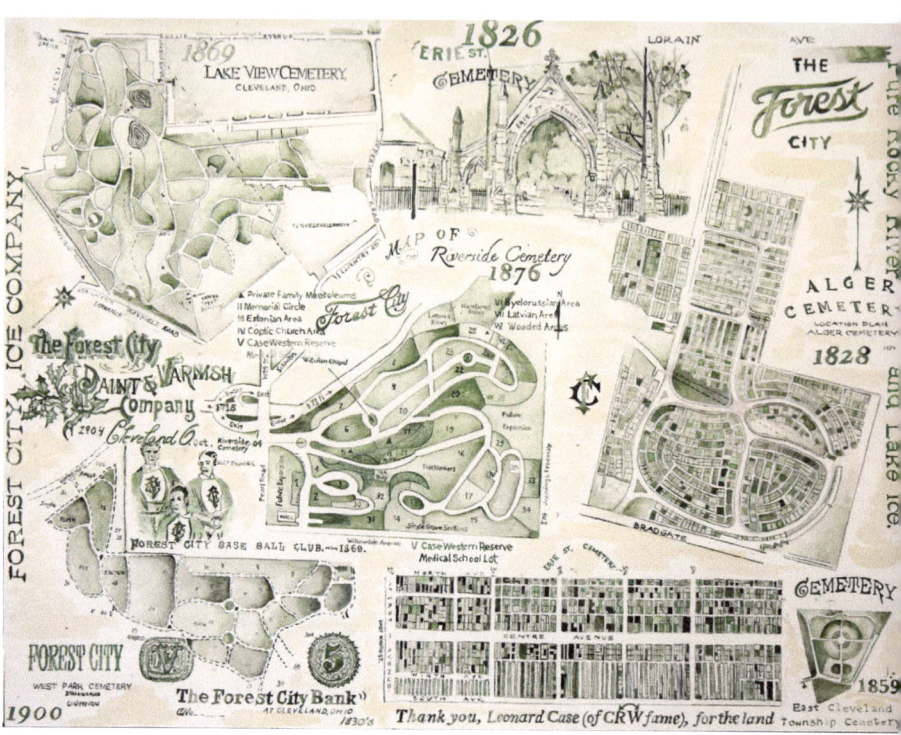

Fig. 59 and 60 "Forest City 1, & Forest City 2"

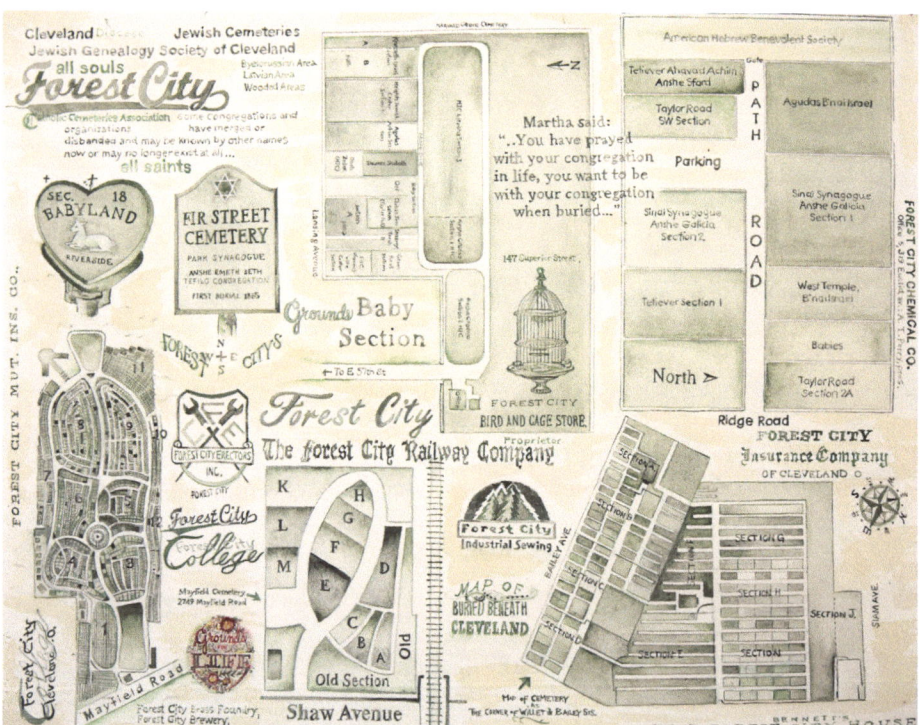

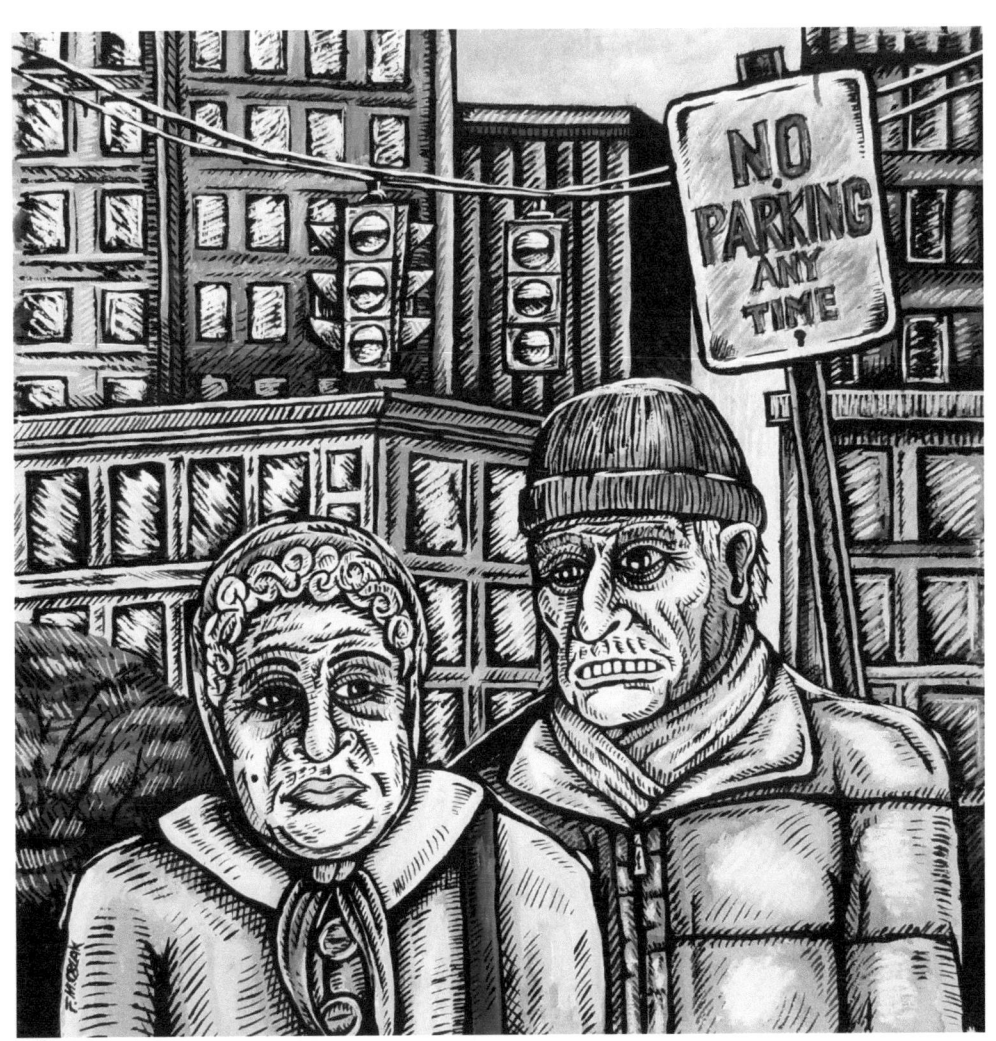

Fig. 61 "Arctic Blast"

"C Cleveland is a city where winter is a major part of city life. In January and February cold fronts and snow move in off Lake Erie from the north, and the city is transformed. I rode the bus to work everyday for about five years, and the Cleveland Public Library was my stop. I noticed that there was something unifying about the freezing cold weather between my fellow bus riders. Of course nobody mentions the weather, but people are more likely to open up about their day as they wait for the bus. Clevelanders are friendly and tough people. With this painting I was trying to convey the shared feelings when the icy wind blows downtown between the buildings, the temperature is sub-zero, and you share a half smile with the person next you, because you know they are feeling it too."

"T

This image is taken from an old project of mine, "Industrial Landscapes." Once, our view of the economic health of Cleveland was centered on industry in areas like the Flats, rather than the "Euclid corridor." We believed social wealth depended on the muscle and brains, the coordinated labor, the ingenuity and dedication of men and women who built our economy, who understood they were workers, and so built strong unions through which they won security, decent wages and dignified working conditions.

When I arrived in 1970, things had already begun to change; Cleveland and Ohio had entered the decline toward the disastrous economic conditions that we have suffered since the flight of industry to non-union areas of the US South and overseas in the 80s and 90s.

Although objectively the glory years of Cleveland's industrial base were already behind us when I arrived, there was still a great deal of manufacturing, transportation and other productive activity. In the 70s

and 80s I spent time in the Flats and other areas documenting the disappearing industrial landscape of our region and the paradoxical beauty it offered. I found this an attractive photographic subject for its display of brain and muscle, teamwork and human effort.

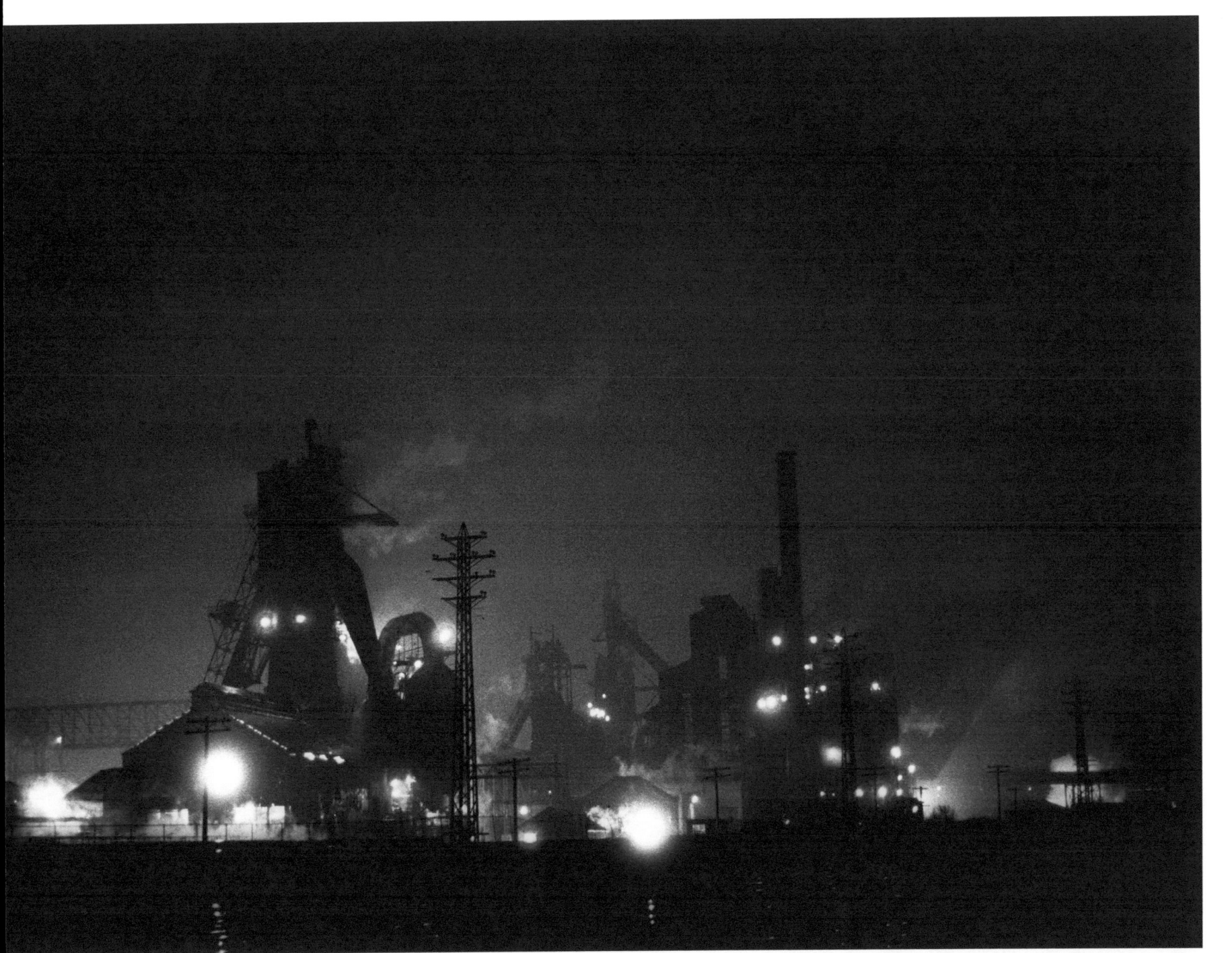

Fig. 62 "Steel Mills, Quigley Road."

"S Some of my earliest memories as a kid in Cleveland were spent around University Circle; going to the Cleveland Museum of Art for art classes, where Van Gogh's "The Large Plane Trees (Road Menders at Saint-Rémy)" forever left a powerful impression on me; and climbing Steggie outside the Natural History Museum, where I was awed by all the wonders inside. On a side note: my brother, Jeff, ratted me out once for stealing a MUSCLE figure from Zayre's, thereby cancelling a trip to the Natural History Museum, which at the time was the worst punishment imaginable. Thanks bro.

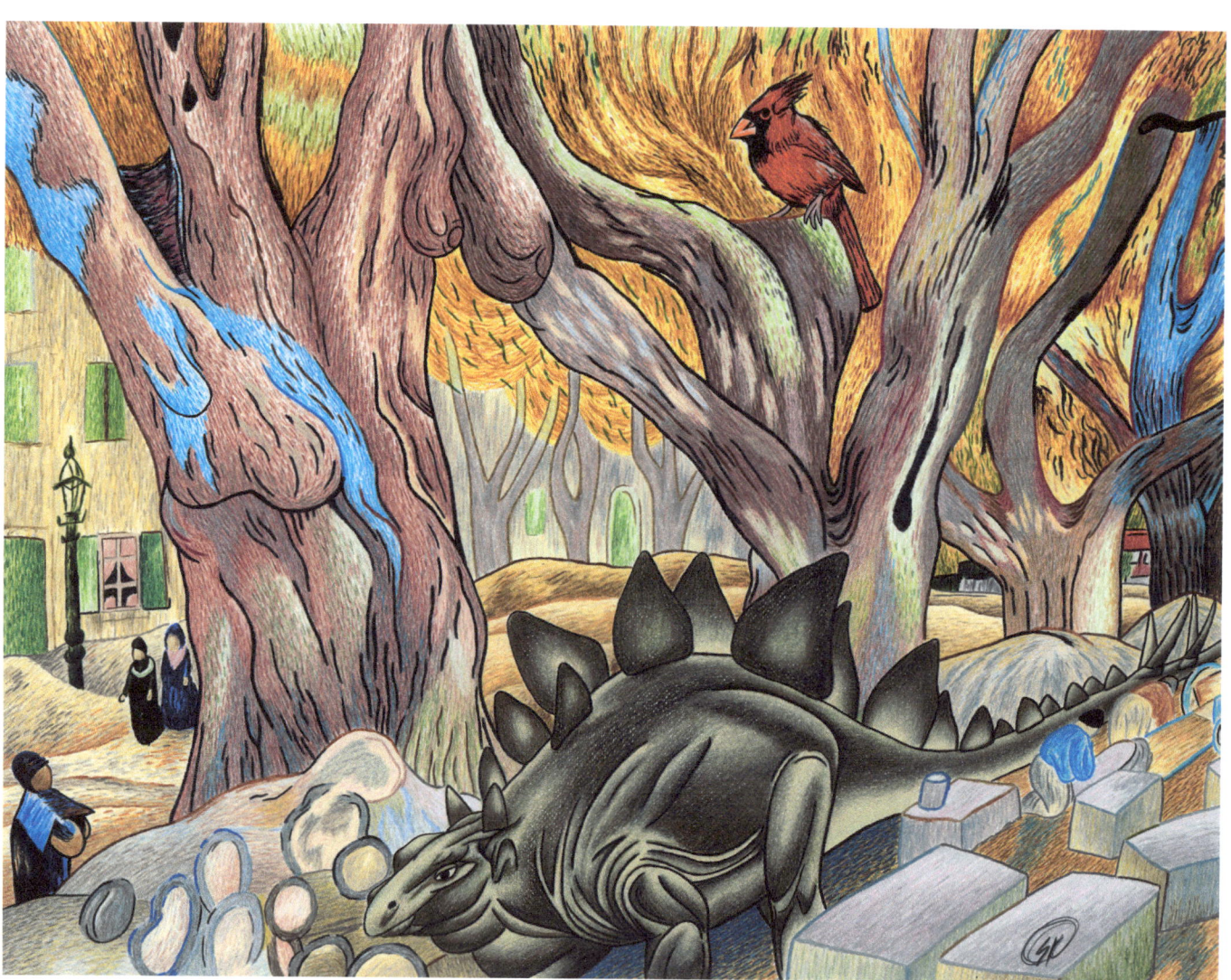

Fig. 63 "Steggie the Road Mender"

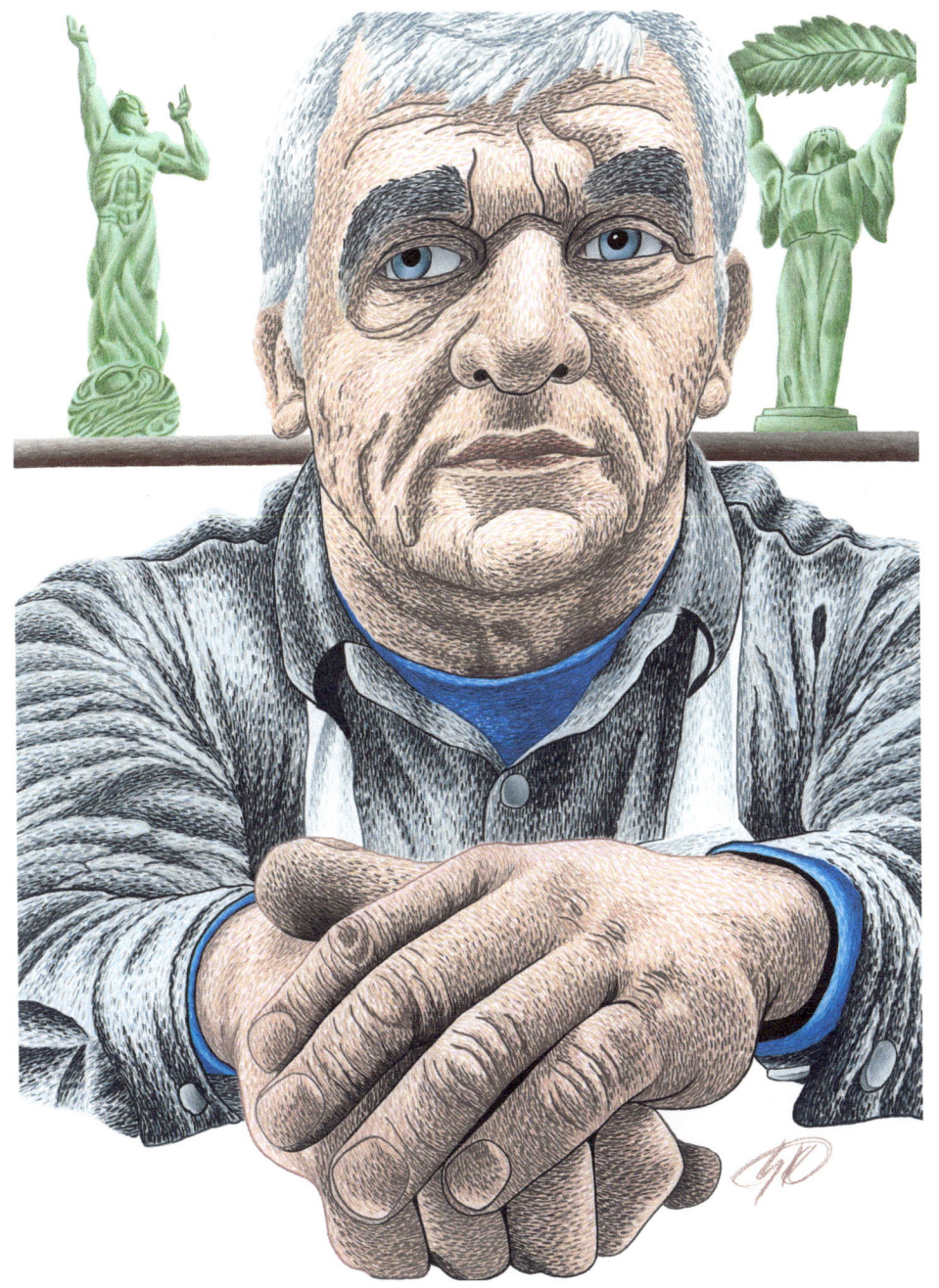

Fig. 64 "Mykos"

"I

It wasn't until living outside of Cleveland when I truly appreciated the great cultural diversity Cleveland has, especially of eastern European decent. It seems like you have to reach a certain age where this truly means something to you. The older you get, the more you understand that "coming home" means "coming to a place that gave poor, scared immigrants looking for a new start a place to call home". I've lived all over the country and nowhere have I found this bond as strong and alive as in Cleveland. This piece is of Miklos Szvcs, a butcher at the West Side Market who came to Cleveland from Hungary in 1986. To me, being of German, Slovak and Russian ancestry, he is the physical embodiment (or maybe a perfect example) of this journey.

#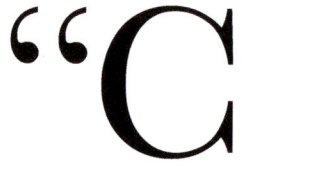

CLEVELAND ON THE ROX

I was born there of course and will always think of it as home, but Cleveland to me now is a haunted place. A place full of ghosts. I walk the streets or go into an old favorite bar and I think of Carol Ann Metoff, Jim Jones, Jill Marotta, Stiv Bators, Larry Lewis, Bryan Gregory, Tim Shaw, Peter Laughner, Duke Snyder... My brother Brian and my own son Richie.

The overwhelming sense of loss is palpable and that in large part is why I don't, can't, live there anymore.

The people I knew there, in the 70s and early 80s, all those years ago, remain the most serious people I've ever met in my life. They lived — and in many cases died — for their love of rock and roll.

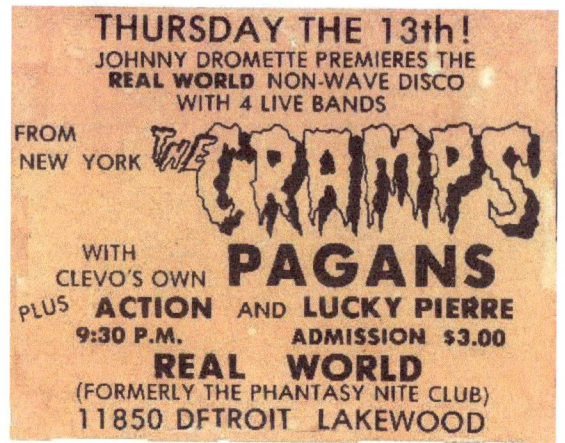

"What's a stripper do with her asshole in the morning?" they'd ask. "Give him twenty dollars and drive him to band practice," you'd say.

You'd run into Nicky Knox at Record Rendevous or Otto Mosher's and his greeting would always be the same.

"Get a job," he'd say. It was kind of like magic. And the truly magical thing was that those people, those serious, doomed people, turned out to be right in the end.

You can go to the Rock and Roll Hall of Fame on East Ninth Street and see their gear. Or listen to the music on the headphones. The Dead Boys, Cramps, Electric Eels, Pagans,

Rocket From the Tombs, Styrenes... Just dial it up.

When Destroy All Monsters came down from Ann Arbor, we always opened. Ron Ashton from the Stooges and Mike Davis from the MC5. True Midwestern rock and roll royalty. A young and scantily dressed singer fronted the outfit, Ashton's girlfriend at the time — Niagara Detroit — and she would writhe on the stage and wail some great rock and roll. Heady stuff for us, a bunch of 20-year-olds who had worshipped at the altar of "Fun House" and "Kick Out the Jams."

So what else was there to do? You could go watch the Indians lose of course, and a big part of our summer days were devoted to that. In the winter, you could slide around on the freeway trying to get to and back from the 2300 Club or whatever other dive you chose to drink at that night, and we did that a lot too. And then there was always LSD, cocaine and heroin, which is why a lot of people aren't here anymore.

You'd sit up on the cliffs overlooking the shimmering waters of the great Lake Erie and watch the big ore ships going back and forth in the distance while little sail or sport fishing boats bobbed up and down inshore.

But it was only rock and roll that saved you from being some kind of factory rat or petty criminal.

And you lived in a town with a tradition of it. From Alan Freed, the disc jockey who first publicly uttered the term, through the Diamonds and the Poni Tails, the Choir, James Gang, Outsiders and Raspberries, you could become a part of a tradition that went back to before you were even born. And we did. With a vengegence.

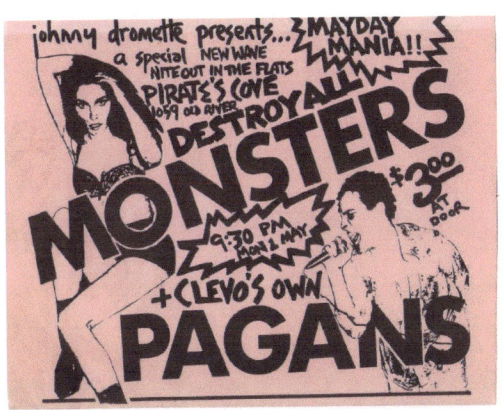

"Fuck art, let's rock," Stiv used to say.

I remember when he died, I remember when all of them died. Carol Ann's death, in February 2017, was particularly devastating. Back in Cleveland in the old days, she had certainly been the Queen of the Underground. A great photographer, preteranturally beautiful, the younger sister of Pagans guitarist Mick Metoff — my best friend — and cousin of Cramps drummer Nick Knox, I knew her since she was fifteen.

When my first wife and I separated in 1983, one thing led to another and Carol Ann, then 21, and I began a relationship. She was a beautiful thing.

We lived at my dope dealer's house. It was winter, and I still remember her tiny pointed footprints in the snow. It lasted a couple of months. I attempted a reconciliation with my wife, who was the mother of my son.

That didn't really work out either but of course Carol Ann was crushed. A couple years later, Mick and I went

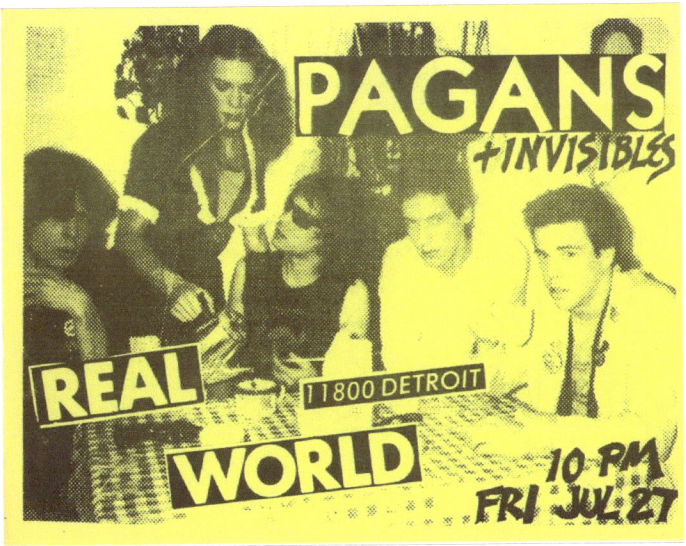

to see Johnny Rivers together at that rib burnoff thing they have downtown. Carol Ann saw her brother and rushed over to greet him. She hadn't seen me though, and when she did she burst into tears and ran away crying.

Decades passed. I left her alone. She raised kids, became a Christian and lived a good life. In August 2016, she joined Facebook. Mick had told her I was on it and she wanted to contact me. I gave her my number. The first time we spoke on the phone I told her how sorry I was that I had hurt her and asked her to forgive me.

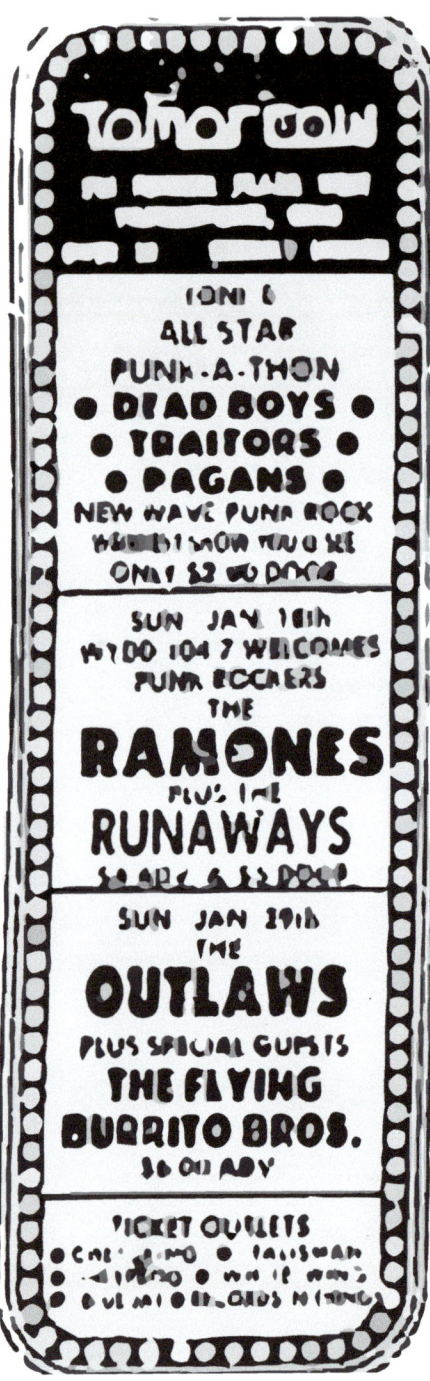

"There's nothing to forgive," she said. "I've always loved you."

After that, we talked almost every day on the telephone. She was back in Cleveland and I'm out in L.A. now. Often we would talk for hours, until our phone batteries died. She was a brave girl. She had a rare form of lung cancer, but never once let on to me how bad it actually was.

After both of our birthdays in February, I tried to call her but there was no answer. I tried to call her the next day but there was no answer again. I asked on her voicemail whether she was pissed off at me about something. Finally I got an email from a mutual friend. Carol Ann had passed. It's hard to figure about this world. You want to love it, but then beautiful and talented people wind up on a slab at the morgue in Los Angeles or Cleveland or London or Paris while the many pieces of shit you've had to endure get to keep walking around and sucking up air.

God bless Carol Ann Metoff, Jim Jones, Jill Marotta, Stiv Bators, Larry Lewis, Bryan Gregory, Tim Shaw, Peter Laughner, Duke Snyder... My brother Brian, my own son Richie and all the rest.

Mike Hudson,
Los Angeles, 2017

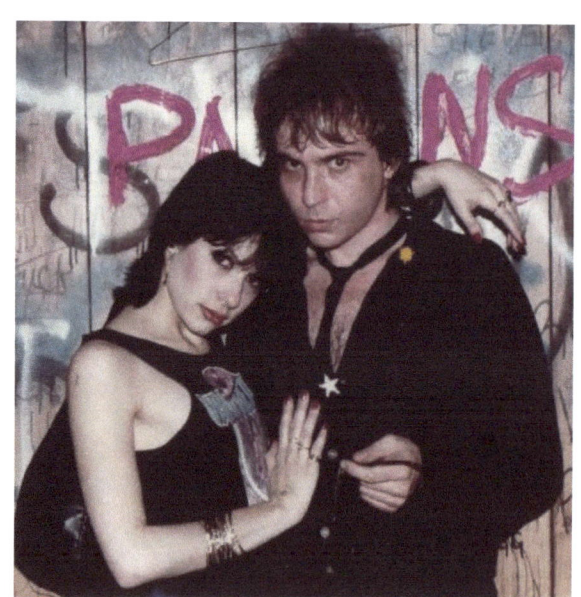

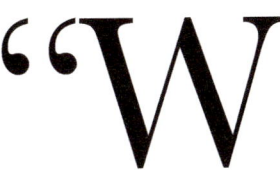

"W When I was 10 growing up in Lakewood, Ohio I hit that age where "cool" started to matter. My role model in my quest was Maynard G. Krebs. Maynard was a sitcom character portrayed by a pre-Gilligan Bob Denver in the weekly The Many Loves of Dobie Gillis. (CBS 1959-1963) Maynard was hip and cool, he peppered his speech with like . . . 'like,' 'man' and 'Daddy-o.' He had a goatee, drank espresso and listened to jazz - not the kind of jazz my parents had which was a singular Jazz at Oberlin by The Dave Brubeck Quartet, Maynard listened to Bird and Diz . . . I wanted to be a beatnik just like him. At my behest, my mother bought me a gray sweatshirt, then 'beatnik-ed it' like Maynard's. She cut off the sleeves and put holes in it. This was not for Halloween, it was for everyday wear. I took being a beatnik seriously. In the show Maynard kept trying to goad Dobie into going with him to see "The Monster That Devoured Cleveland" at the Central City Bijou. By age 10 I was aware

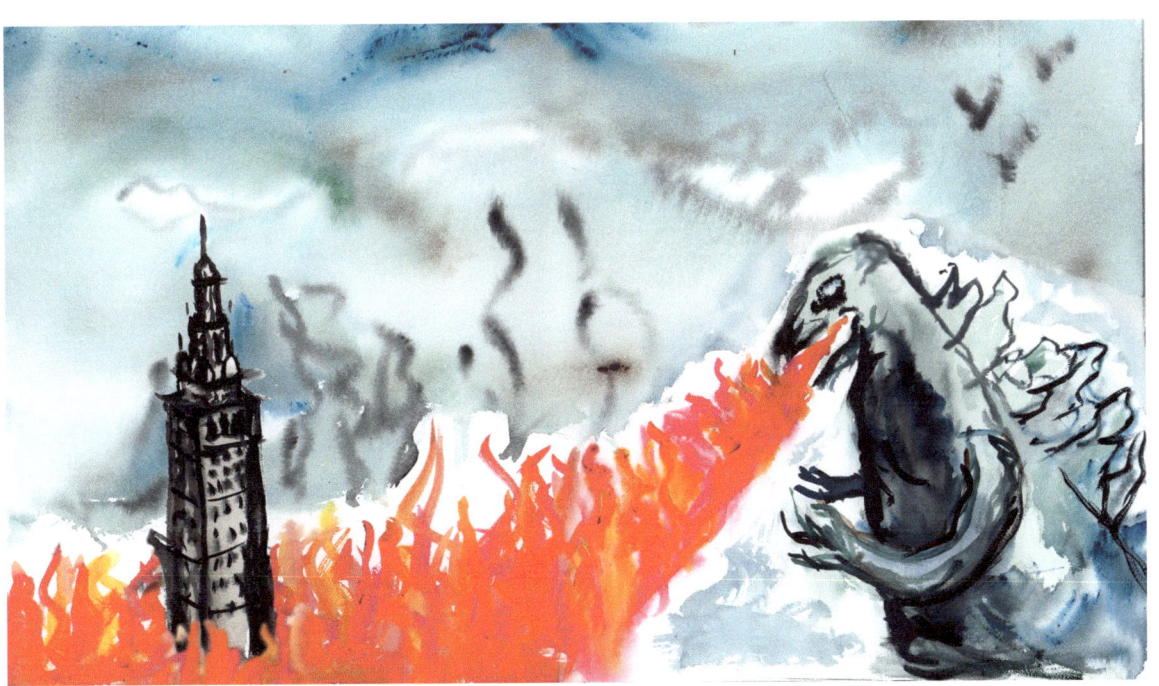

Fig. 65   "The Monster That Ate Cleveland"

that Dobie and Maynard weren't real people, but actors. But the movie? Why should it not be real? Under the aegis of another TV hipster, Chanel 8's Shock Theater host Ghoulardi, I had started weekly Saturday afternoon devotionals at Lakewood's Detroit Theatre. Ishirō Honda's The Mysterians was my first, so I fully expected to see The Monster That Devoured Cleveland advertised in The Lakewood Post some Friday, perhaps along with its sequel Son of the Monster that Devoured Cleveland. Add 50 years to this along with the Kaijū-evoking events of the Cuyahoga

River fire and 9/11, which I watched from Red Hook Brooklyn across the harbor. Then when my band, X____X (resurrected from Cleveland 1978) played The Painted Lady in Detroit in 2016, a fanboy lauded that the band was now 'a monster!' (in fanboy, 'monster' = 'Like way-cool, Daddy-o!') So the title and imagery of our next release came crystal clear in an atomic satori: The Monster That Ate Cleveland. And, Gentle Reader, if you are concerned about the transmogrification of the title from Devoured to Ate? Just don't think about it .

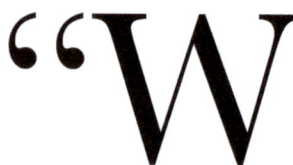

"When I was a child in the 50's I lived with my family on West 4th Street in what is now the Tremont neighborhood. My grandparents lived on the east side. Going to visit them was quite an adventure. A car ride first through the flats, over and under bridges, past loud smoky factories and railroads, then onto the east shoreway. There we'd drive through clouds of smog from the lakefront dump fires, and then we'd see…the Hulett Ore Unloaders! Always working, up and down, unloading ore ships on the lake. We called them "grasshopper legs". I loved them.

They are gone now. Two have been dismantled and saved to be reconstructed on another site. I hope I get to see them again."

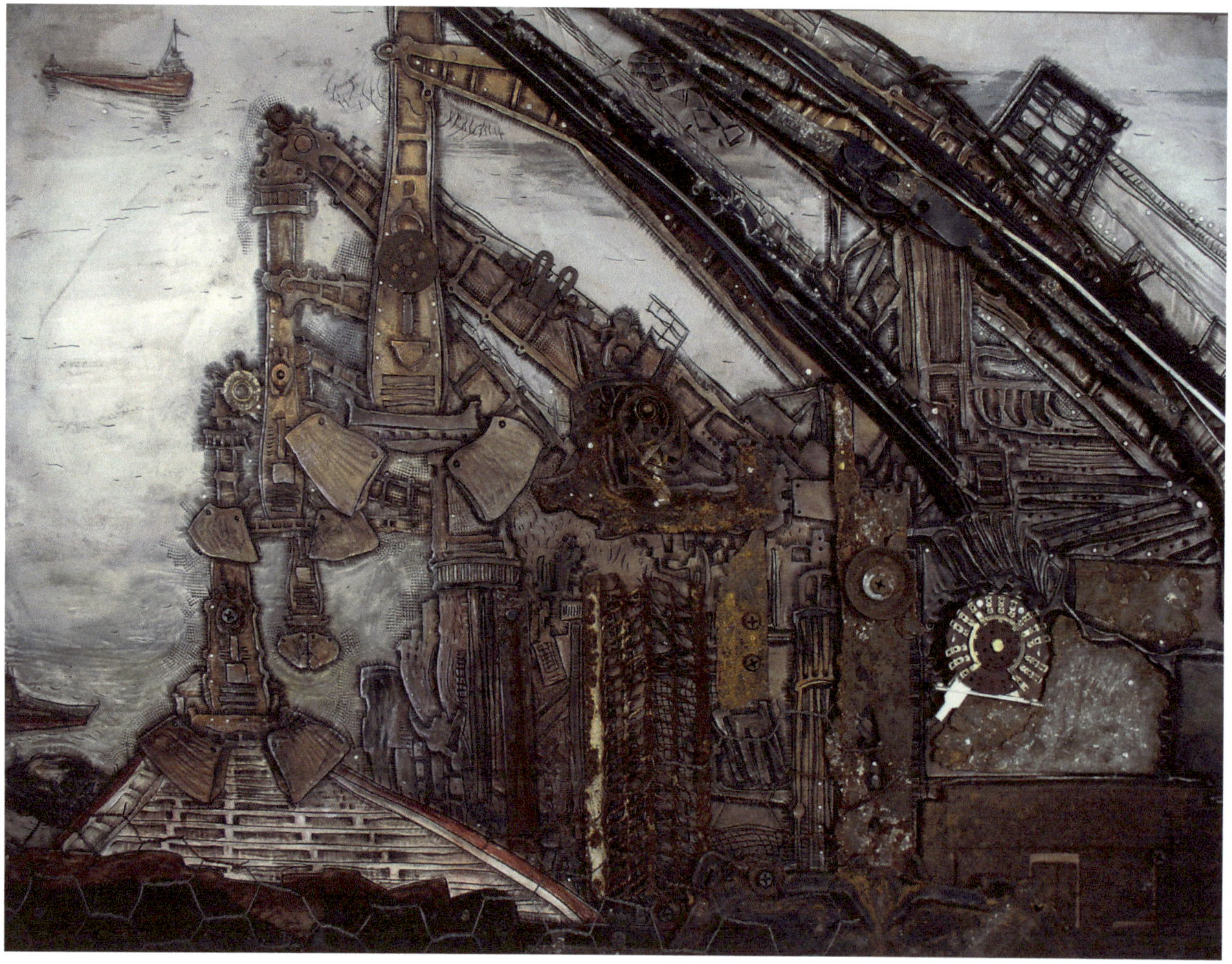

Fig. 66 "Hulett Ore Unloaders"

"O Often when I tell people I live in Cleveland, they immediately think of industry. Even people who live here refer to our town as "The Rust Belt". So there's a stereotype that Cleveland is nothing but factories, smoke stacks, rust, and dust. Our botanical gardens and parks don't get nearly the recognition they deserve. In Spring and Summer, Cleveland is green with life and energy. No matter where you live in this town, you are not far from the park system that surrounds the city. This softer side of the Rust Belt is the inspiration for my floral paintings.

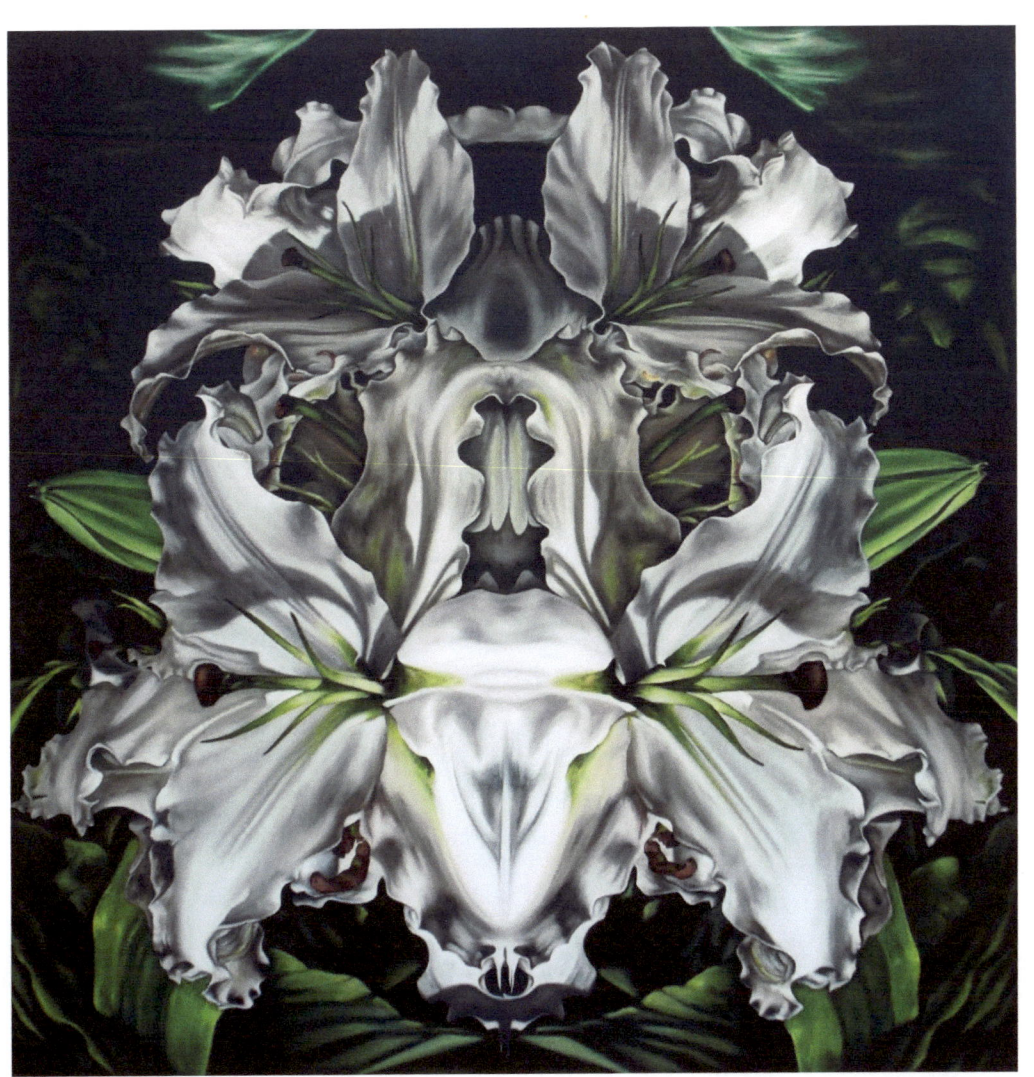

Fig. 67 "Moonlit"

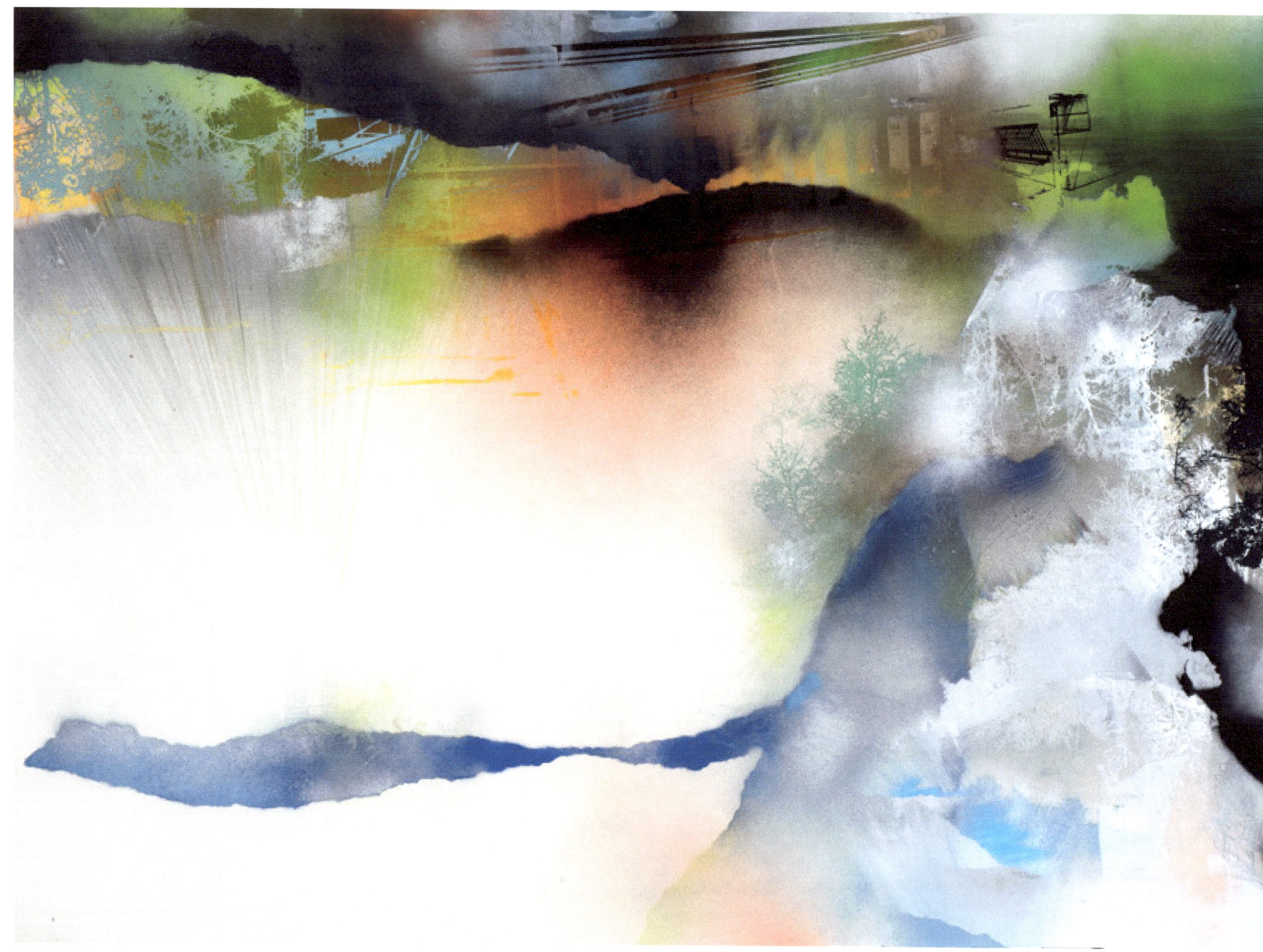

Fig. 68 "Doan brook slowly got buried over 200 years but it pops out here and there, around Superior, up to Coventry (it smells in the Summer)."

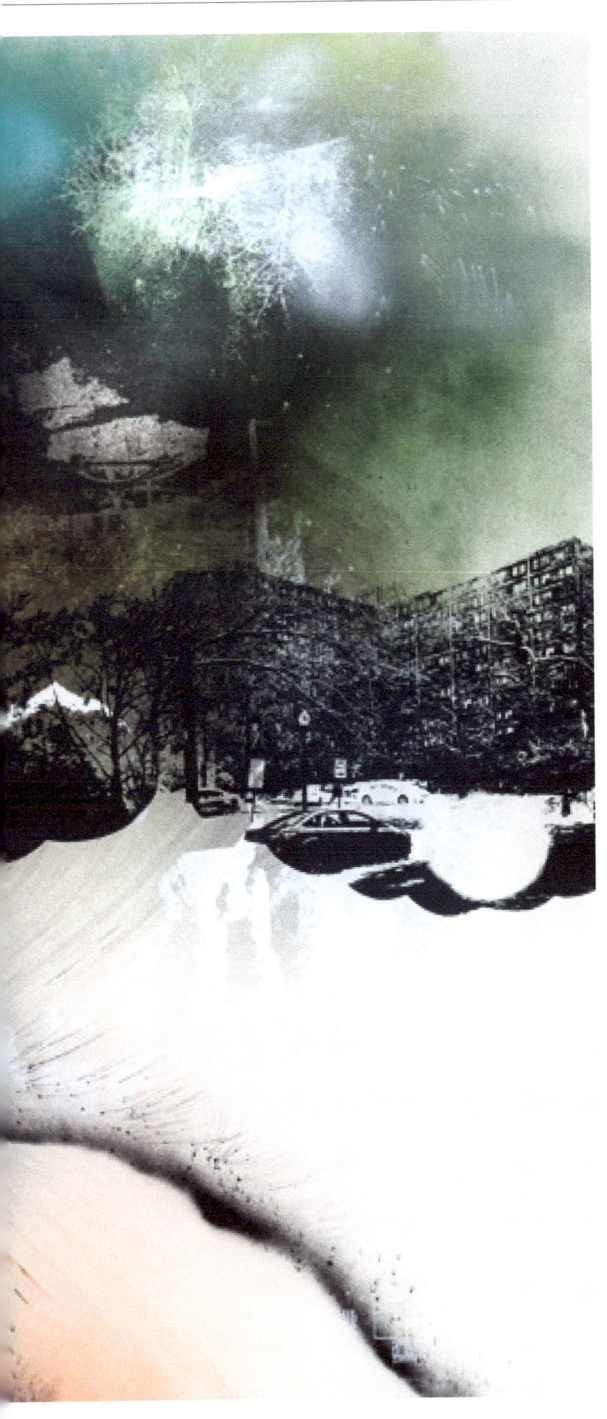

"I It is the most personal relationship I have with the City... the Natural and Urban aspects of Cleveland.

"**I** live on a farm in Freedom Township near Cleveland. This enamel and the others in the series are all interpretations of my respect and love of the land that surround my house. My memories of walks through the landscape, the different seasons and the changes that come with time all influence the final outcome of the piece."

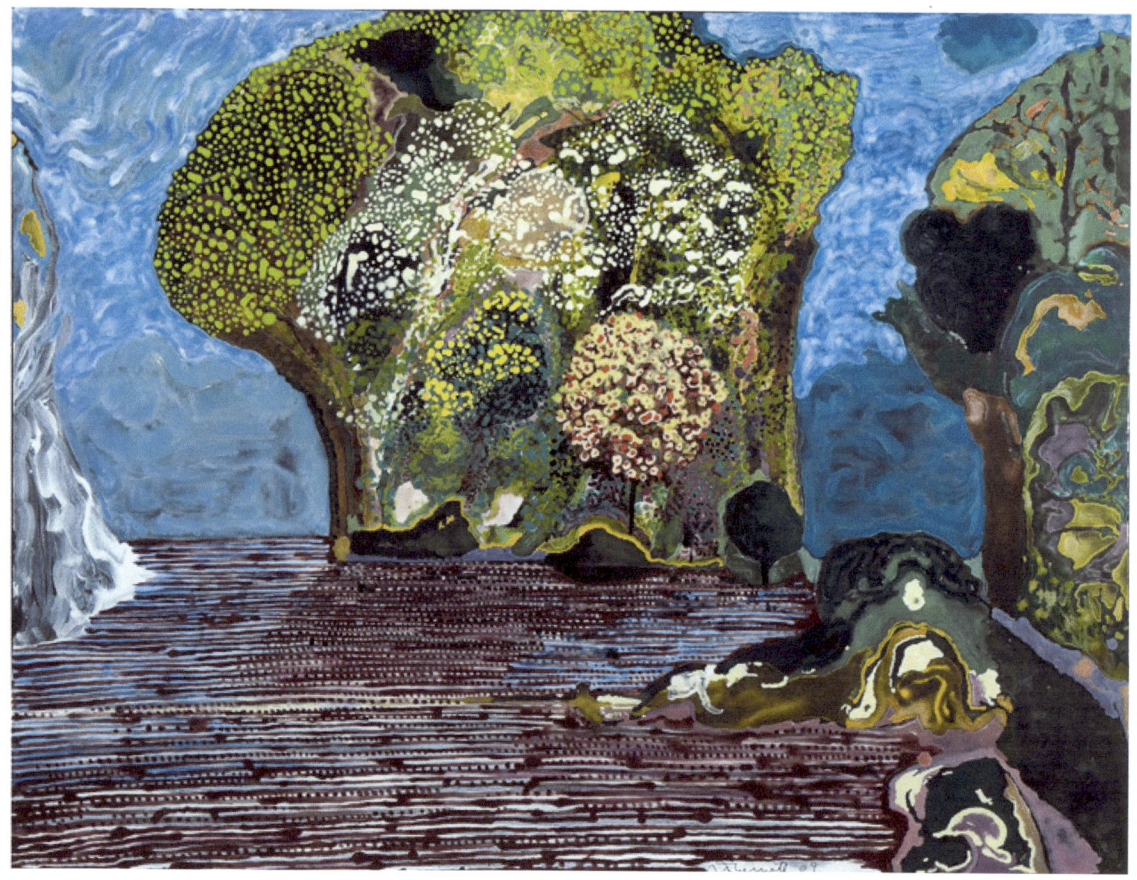

Fig. 69 "A Wet Spring"

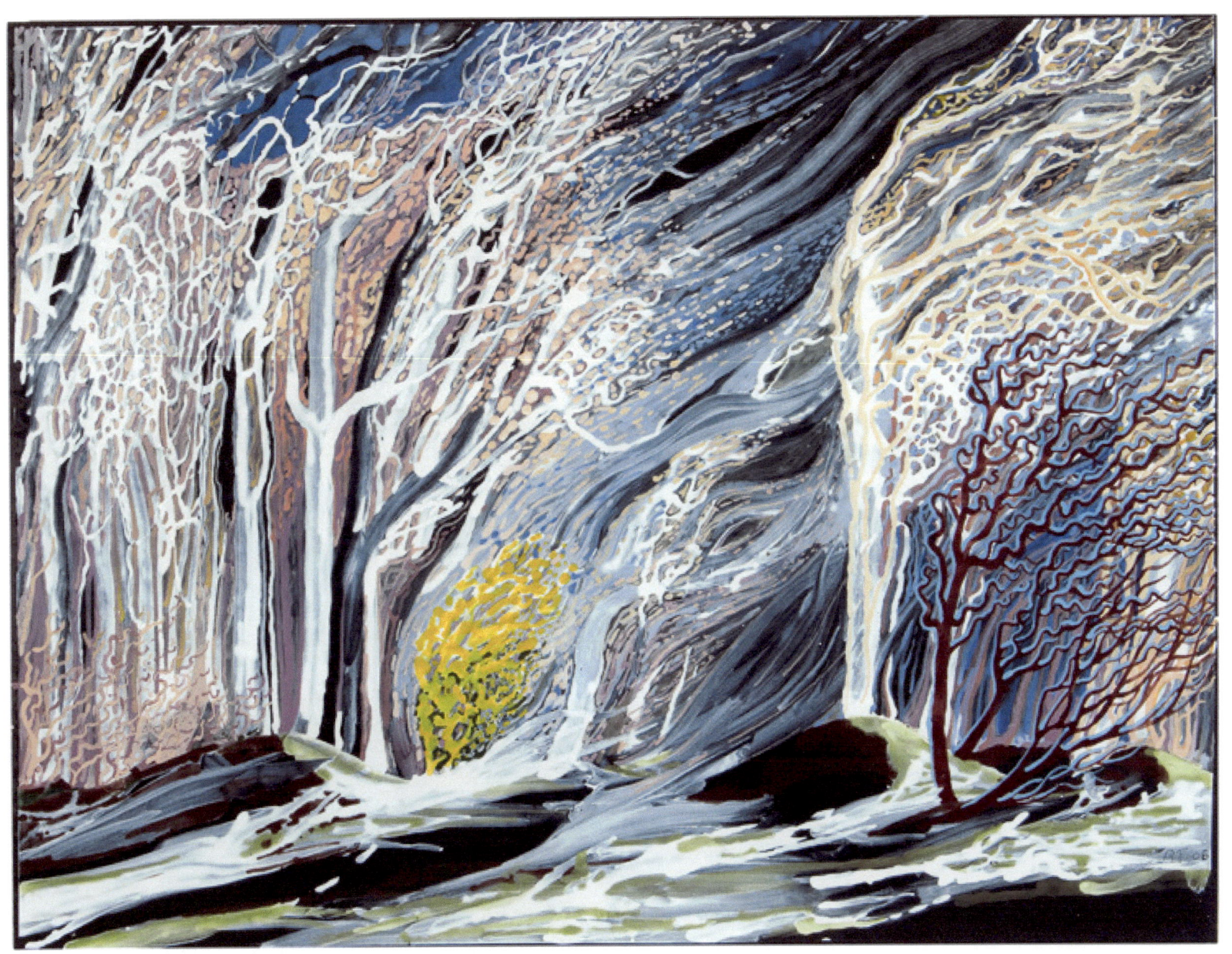

Fig. 70 "Wind in Winter"

"N

Naji's World is my portrait of Cleveland's own celebrity artist and activist, Loren Naji. His exhaustive efforts to fan the flames of the art revolution happening in Cleveland, Ohio have been met with profuse praise and bureaucratic resistance. The globe is a nod to the giant wooden ball structures he sculpts and places in Cleveland Hot Spots. If you look very closely at the globe in my painting, I have placed a heart on Cleveland, Ohio, the town we love and call home."

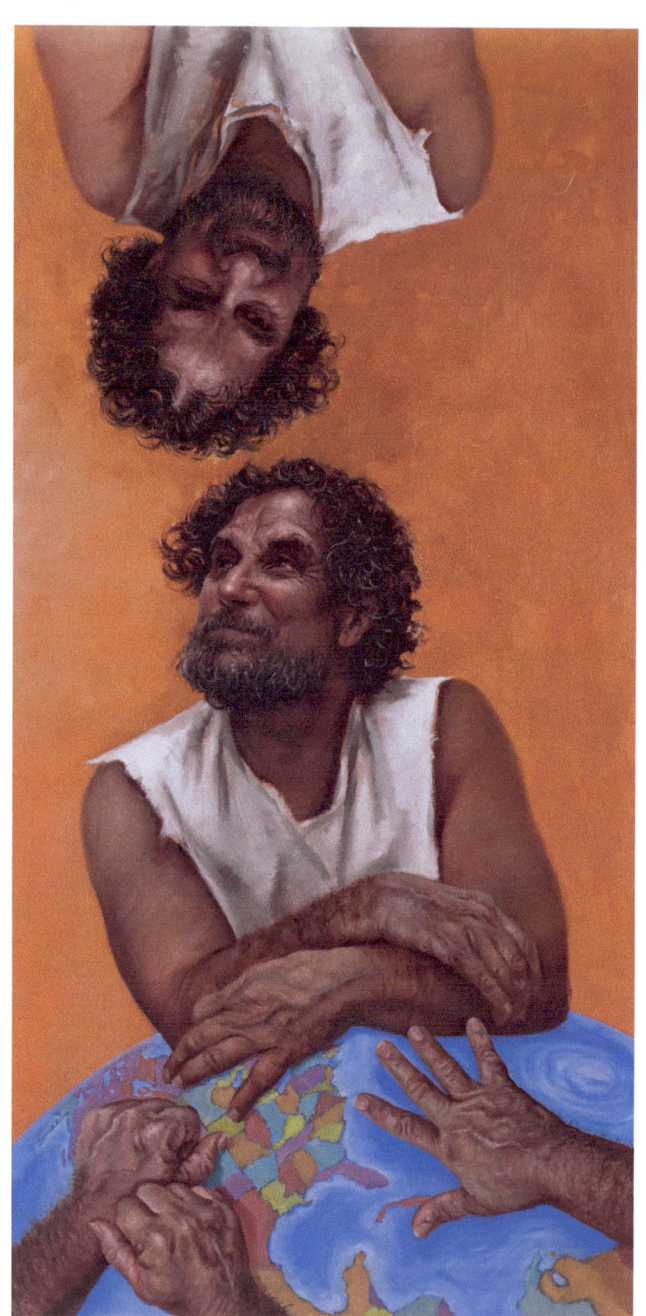

Fig. 71 "Naji's World"

"I

I have always been interested in Cleveland's beginnings and how it developed into a major industrial center by utilizing its geographical location and developments in transportation. This piece is a freehand ink drawing about the industrial history of Cleveland. It includes water and rail for transportation systems, components of the oil refining and steel industry and the many other industries that quickly grew alongside these.

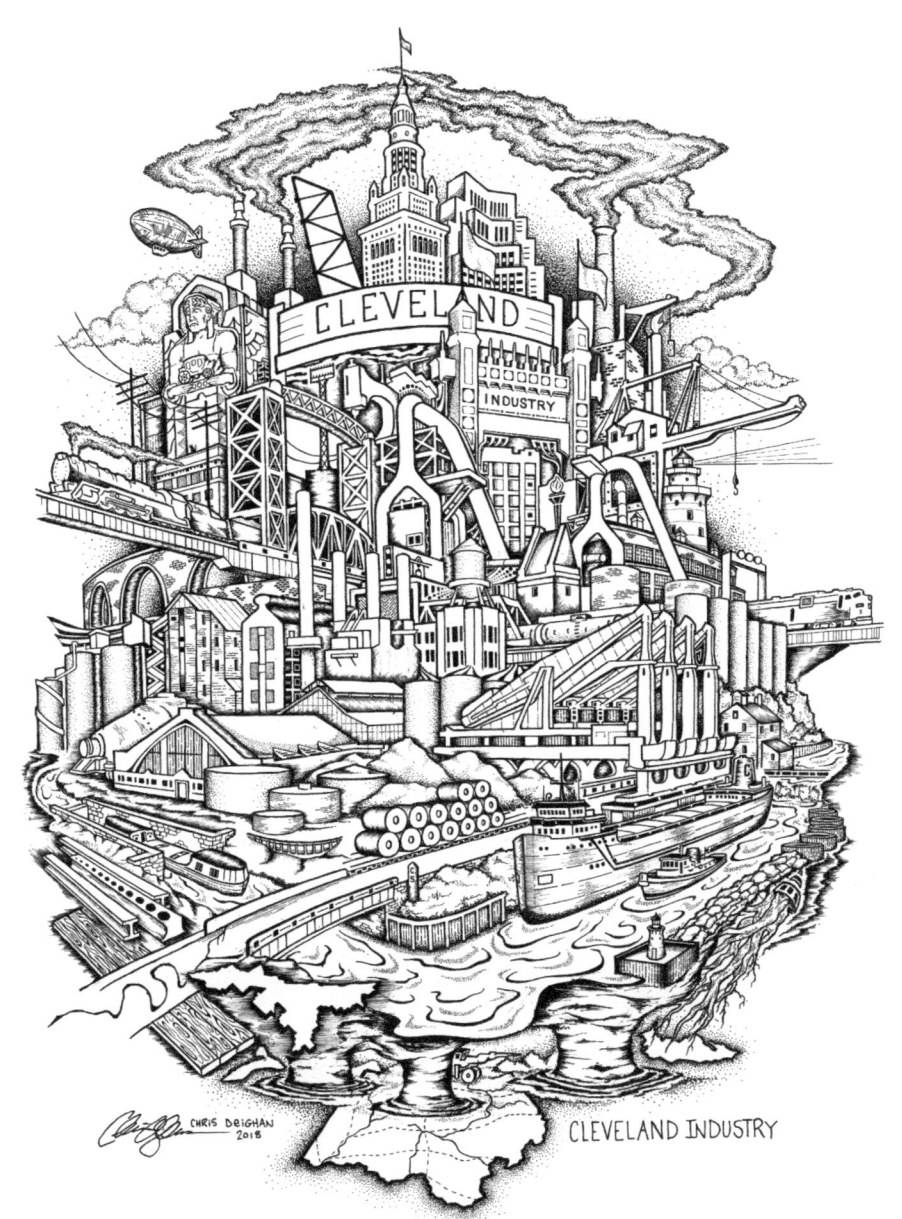

Fig. 72 "Cleveland Industry #2"

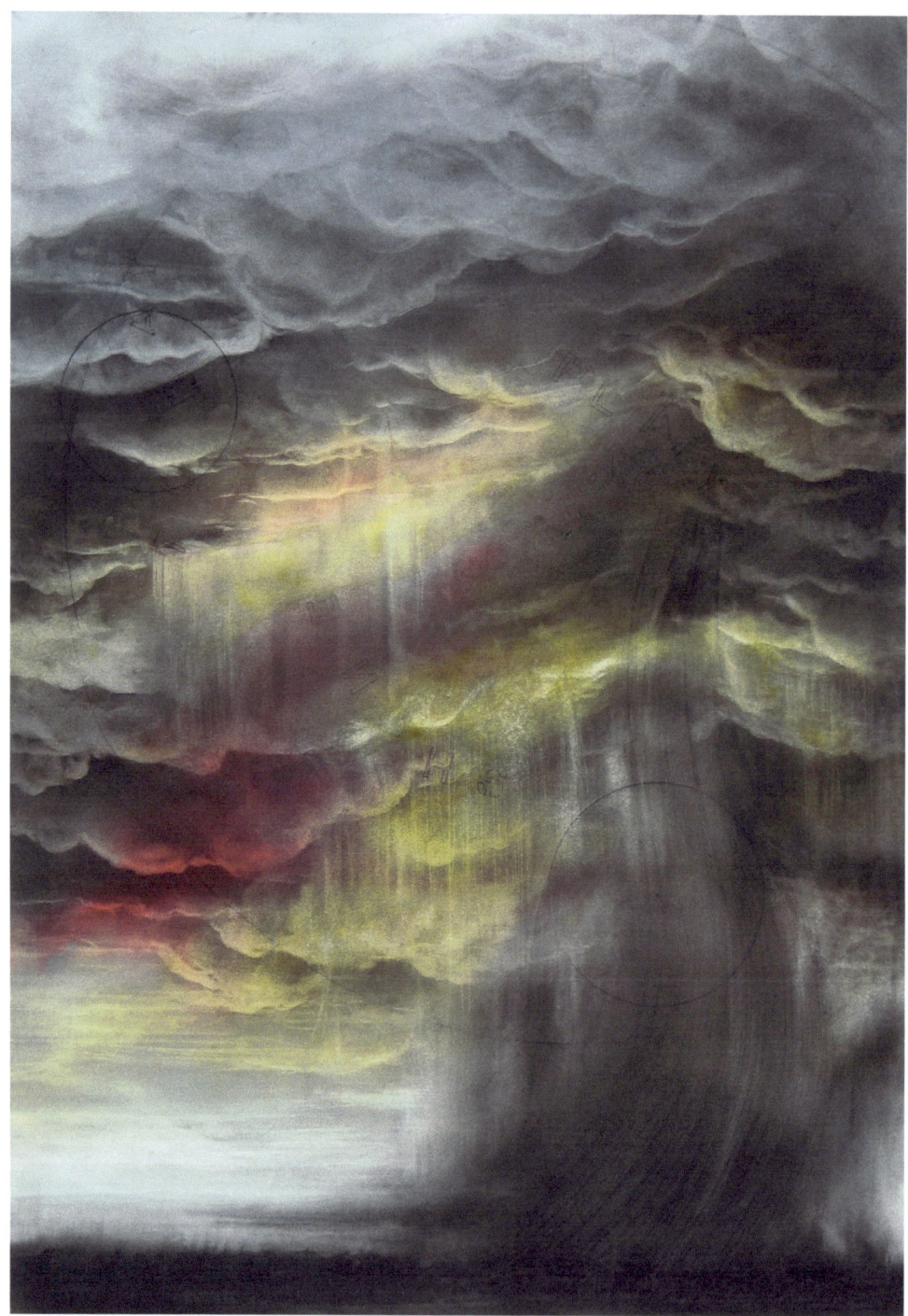

Fig. 73 "Shine"

"R

Ranking fifth on the list of dreariest cities in the USA, natives of Cleveland get used to the visions of gray skies and clouds. The weather also creates a unique viewpoint and understanding that there is always light even if it is temporarily obstructed. This is what "Shine" is all about. To live in the world of possibilities we must find time to play and enjoy the contrasts in the world, our neighbors, friends, family, and ultimately within ourselves"

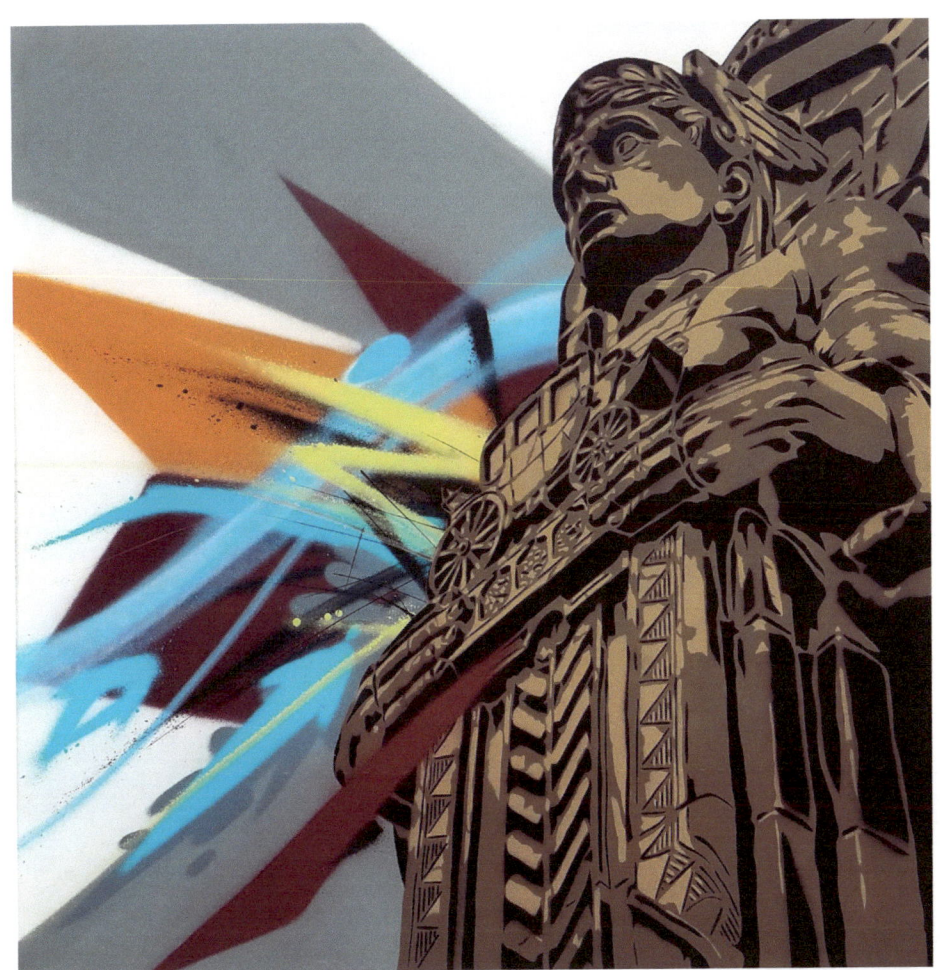

Fig. 74 "Lead the Way"

"I spent my first few years as a child living a Bernie Kosar's pass away from the Lorain-Carnegie bridge. I remember traveling over it often to go in and out of downtown. I was actually terrified of being on bridges as a kid (Fun fact: it's called Gephyrophobia) but those statues just seemed to make that bridge a little more stable and eased my mind a bit."

BOB PECK

"The Guardian statues always felt so majestic to me as a kid, like they had magical powers as they look down on you. They've always prompted or reminded me of the statues in the movie "The Never Ending Story". Maybe I thought they would shoot lasers from their eyes or that they would come to life in some degree. That memory has always remained in my mind as juvenile as it sounds, although now as an adult I see them as a great addition to Deco Art period and a Cleveland landmark. The kid in me still wants to see the lasers."

RICH CIHLAR

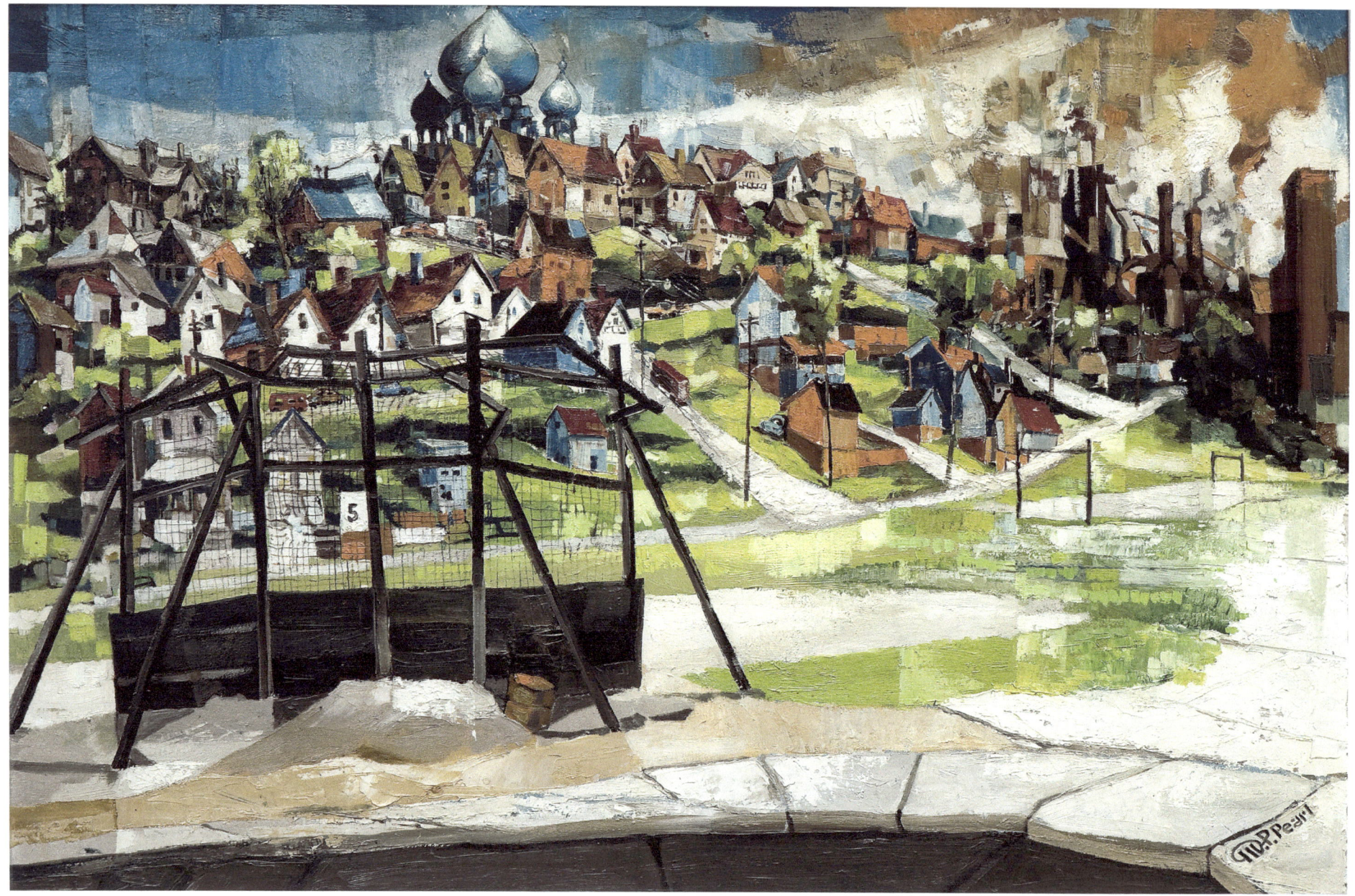

Fig. 75 "A Place to Stay, A Place to Pray, and Creeping Pollution"

"A

As a photographer I see potentially great compositions everywhere. But that's not enough. The goal is to find unique light which presents my view of the city through photos that are both memorable and iconic. Any time this happens it's been a great day of shooting."

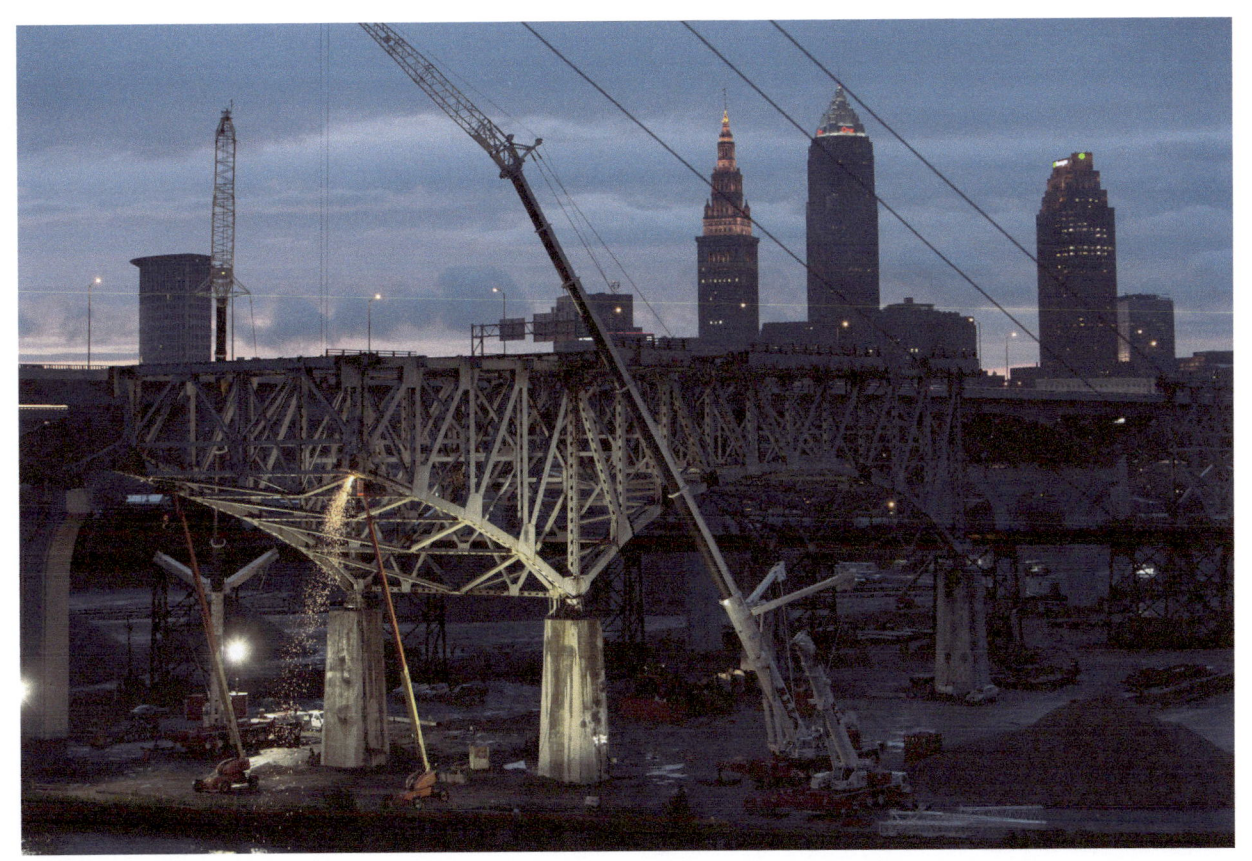

Fig. 76 "Innerbelt Bridge Demolition"

"I

I love that Cleveland is located on the coast of Lake Erie. I've lived close to it for many years and regularly take walks along it's shores. As do all bodies of water, it holds a lot of mystery and inspiration to me."

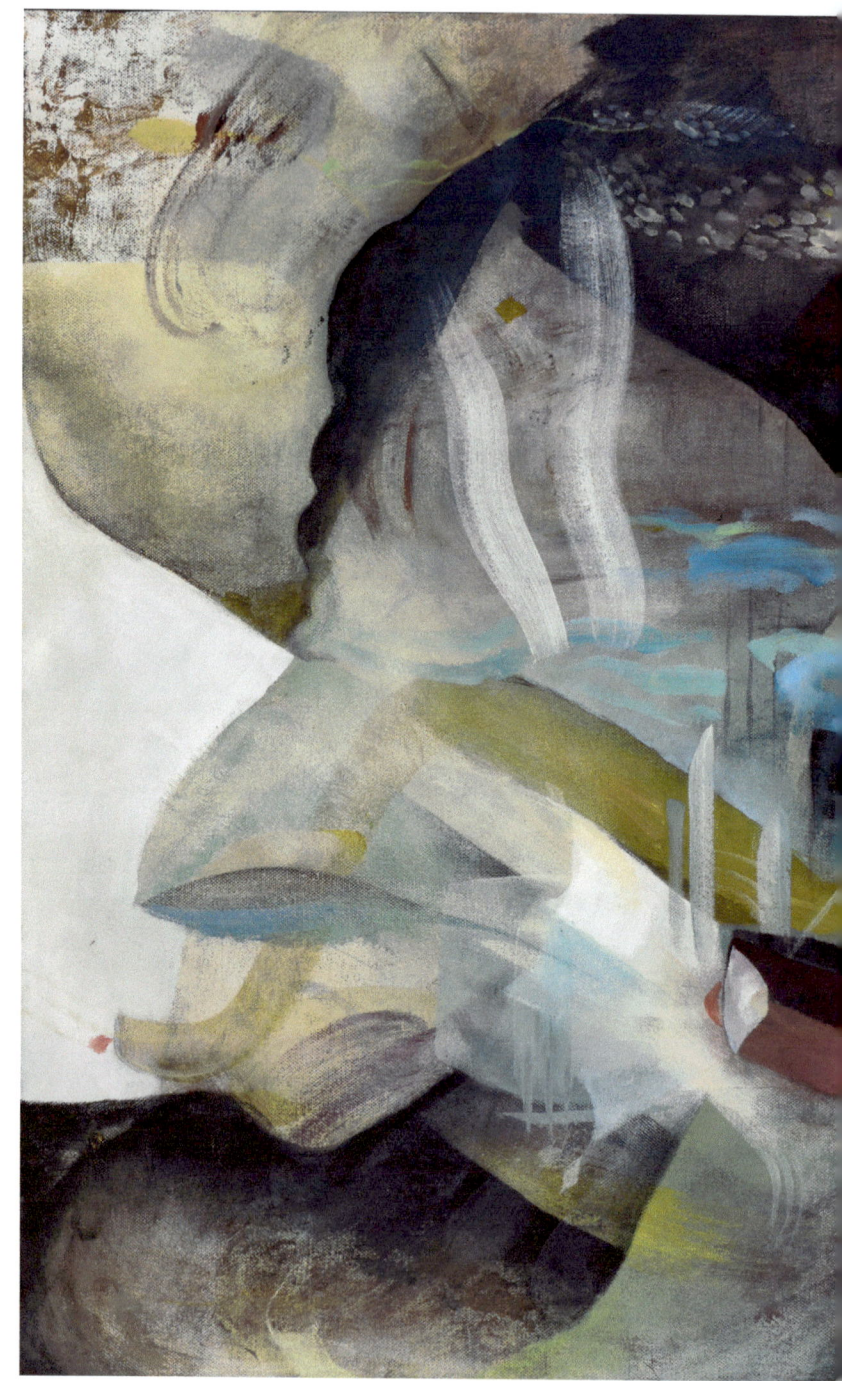

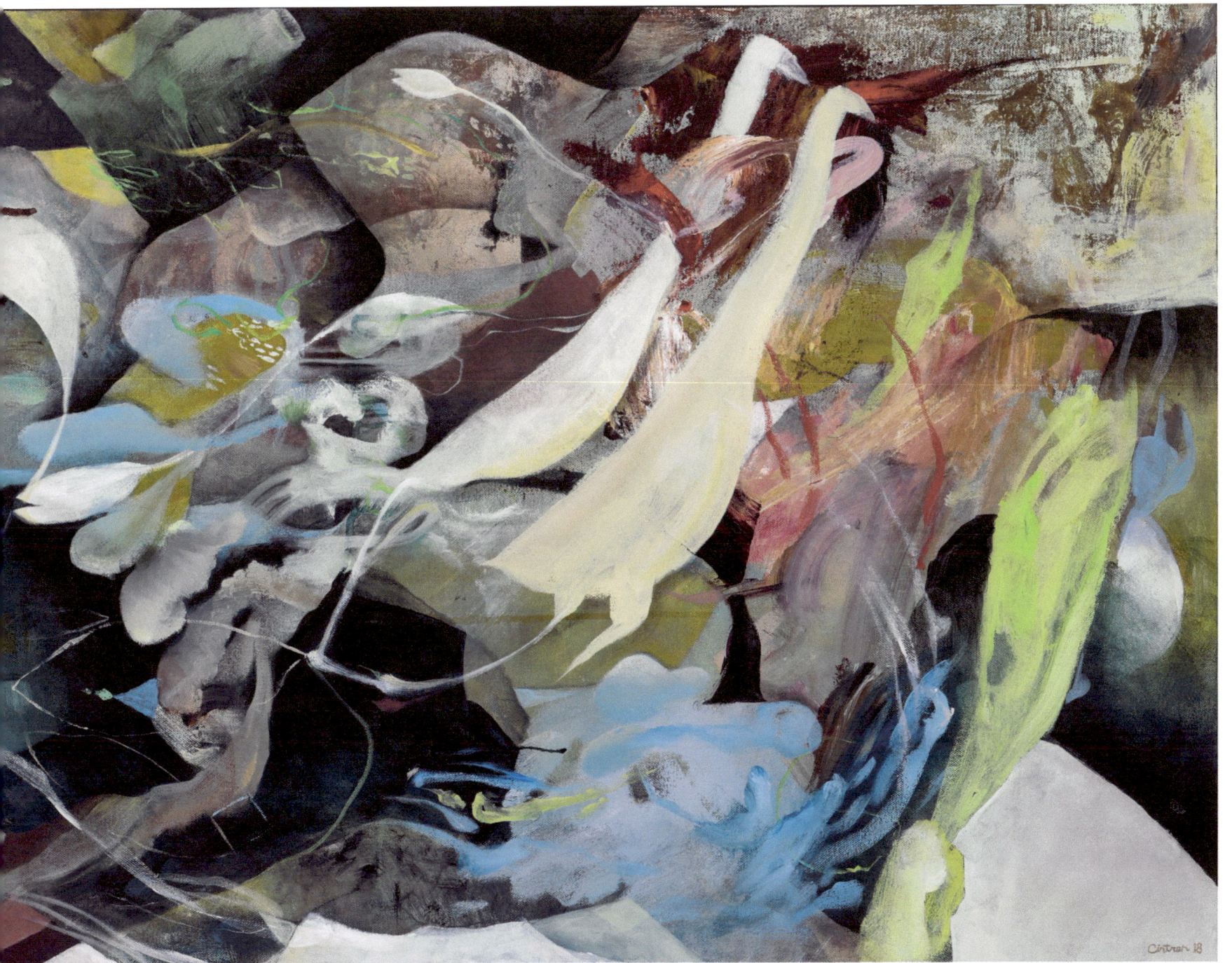

Fig. 77 "Under the Lake"

"I I began kayaking the Cuyahoga River in 2017 and this was one of the images from an early morning sunrise paddle. I love the sunlight hitting the edges of the buildings, bringing the city to light as it still is mostly asleep. The moodiness in the clouds as well as the peacefulness of the water draws you to a calm, relaxing realm.

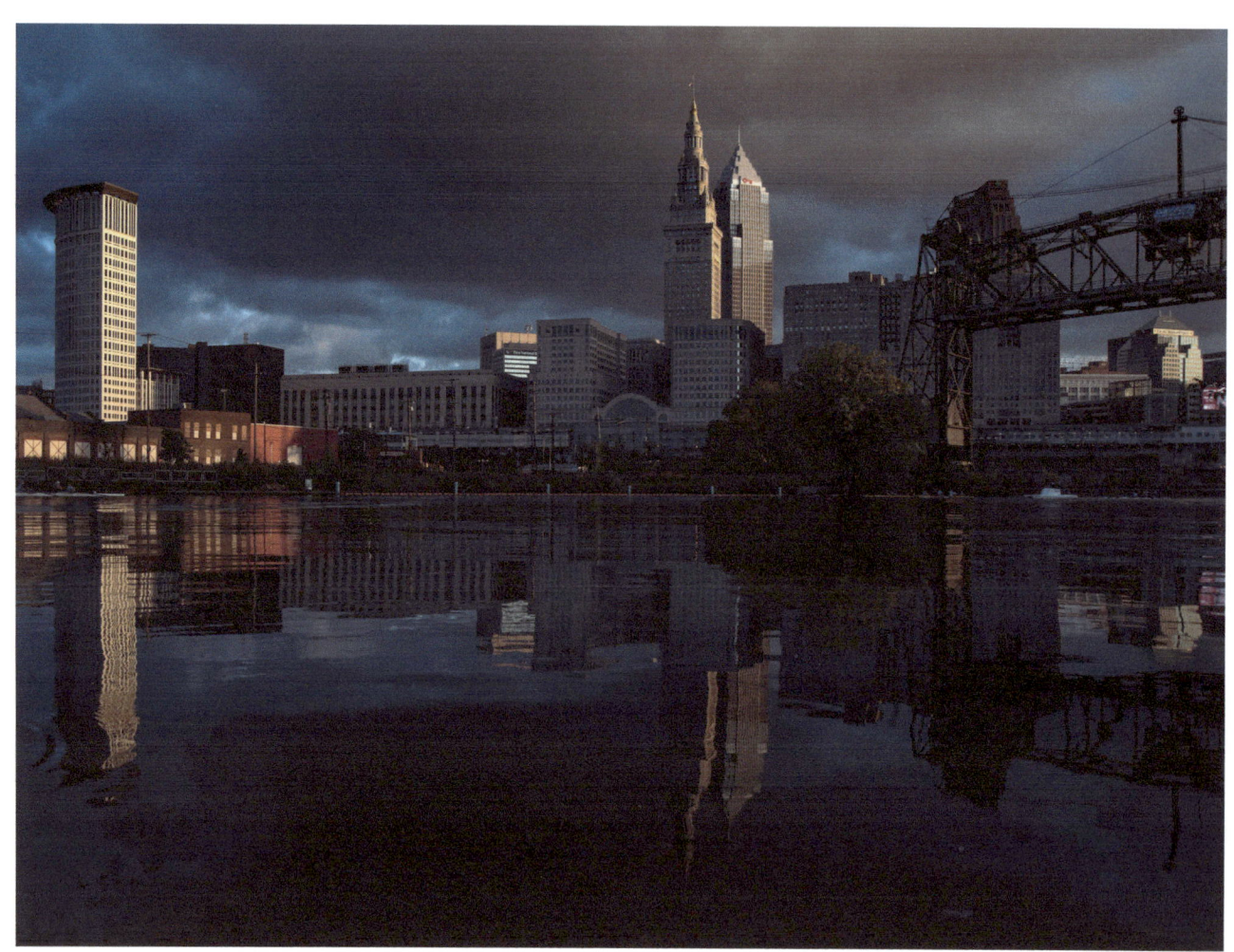

Fig. 78 "Reflections"

"M

My painting "Black Walnut"
is inspired by what grows
and is able to thrive in the
industrial areas of Cleveland.
Often people look over these
areas and consider them
wastelands, but they can be
where bits of life still survive,
even if they have to grow
through fences, rubbish and
other poor conditions.

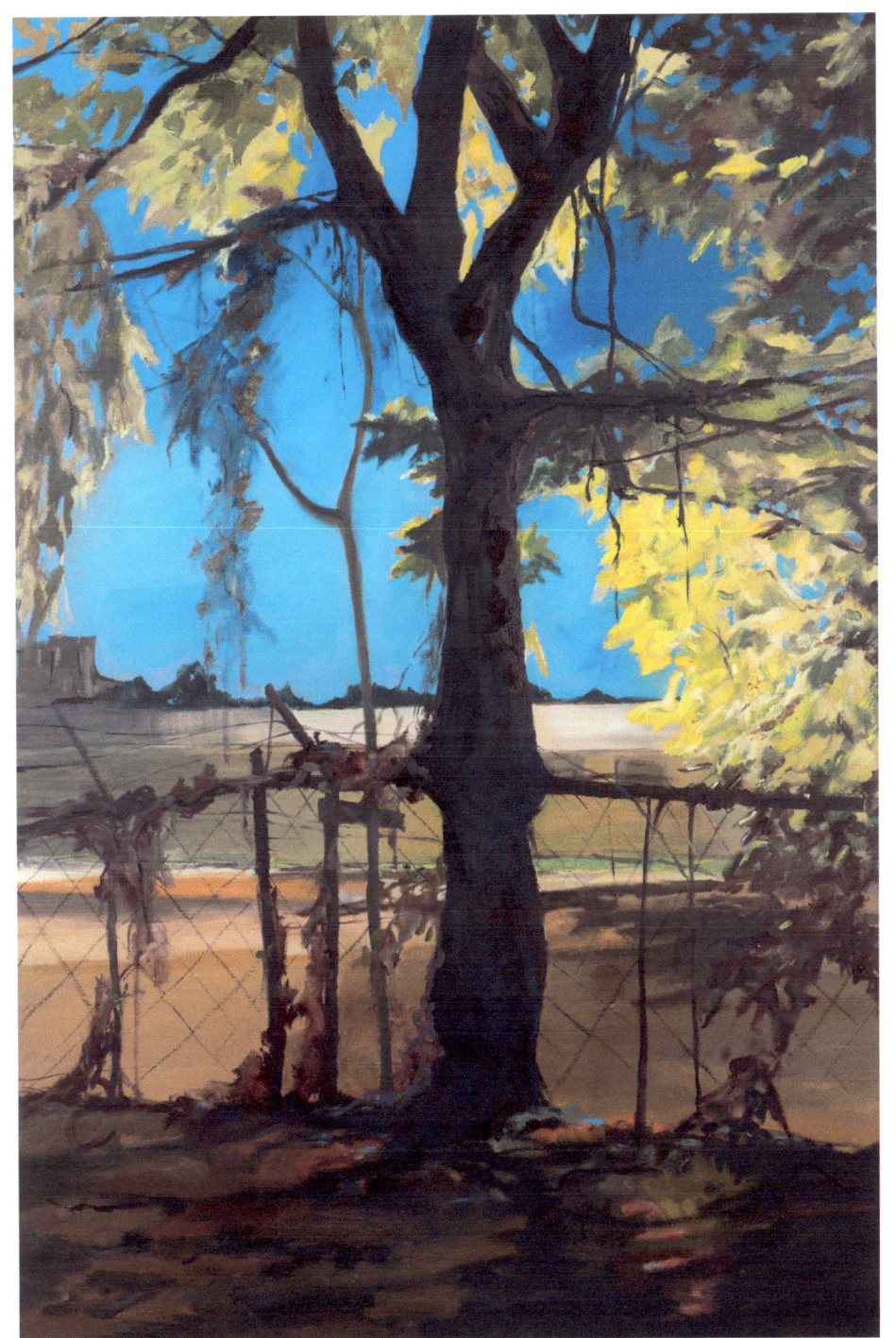

FIG. 79 "Black Walnut"

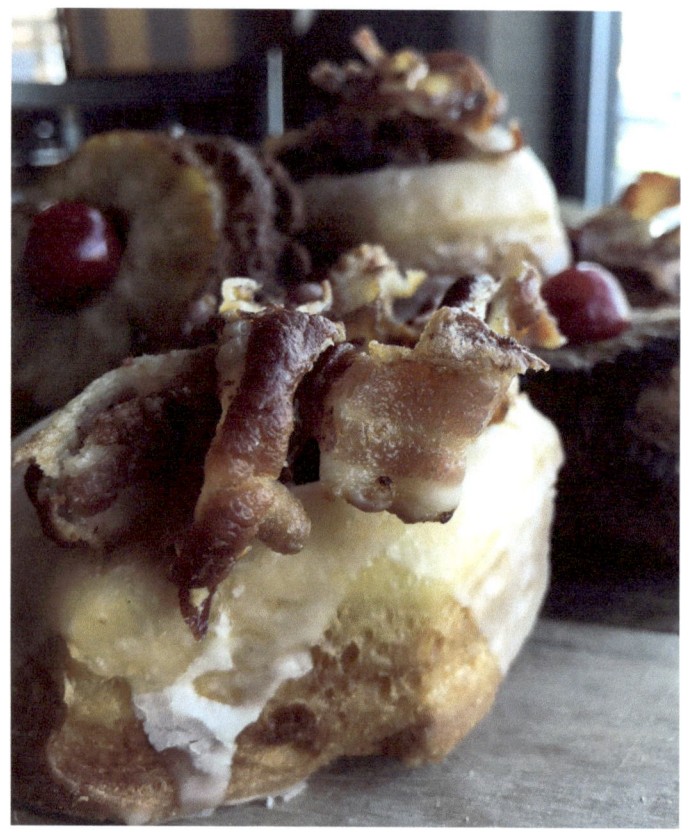

Fig. 80

"C

Cleveland's food passion lies in its heritage and nationalities. Part of the heritage of this working class city is appreciating life's simple pleasures. When you're growing up where much of the city falls under the description of blue collar, where mom and dad are both working to provide for latchkey kids, you're cooking what you know at home and indulging the things most convenient to you. Working in professional kitchens all over this city, you notice a reflection in the demands of the clientele. Fads come and go in this world but the palettes of this city remain truthful. You're not going to survive in our food culture pushing people to spend uncomfortable amounts of money to try small bits of food who's description on a menu could be considered a dare. This city is not afraid of the maraschino cherry on top of the sundae. We want luxurious amounts of ice-cream on French fries and donuts with bacon and kielbasa with mustard. We want goopy sweet strawberry cassata cake from Corbos. We celebrate the food that you truly desire. Our food is fuel to get through life's grey days and is met with jealous eyes by anyone not sitting at one of our tables."

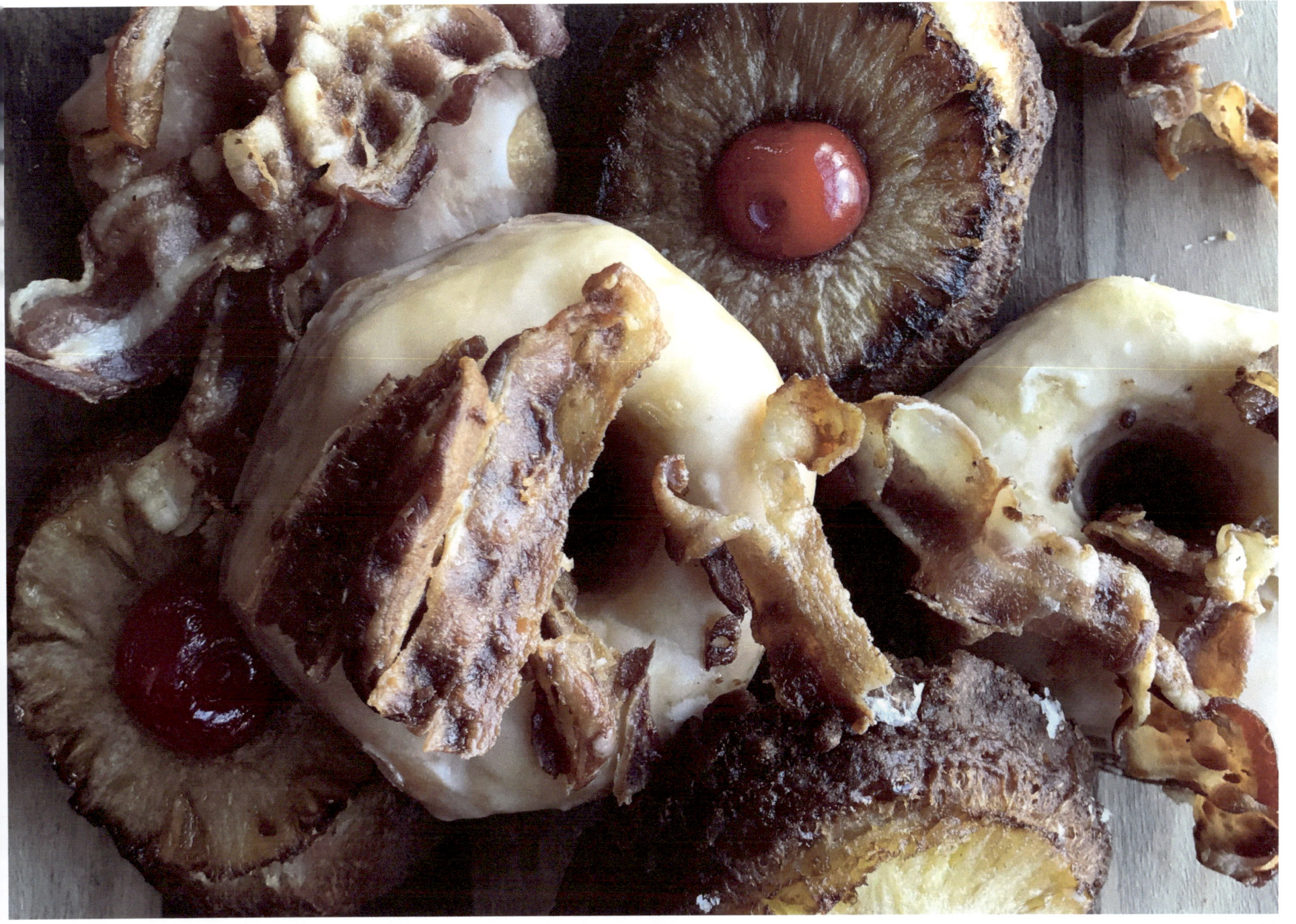

Fig.81

94

"I'm inspired by the gritty and seldom celebrated spaces and corners in this beautiful, hardscrabble industrial city. These places, teem with humanity and precious moments of secret drama which are only made possible by the city's diversity of peoples and culturally rich history."

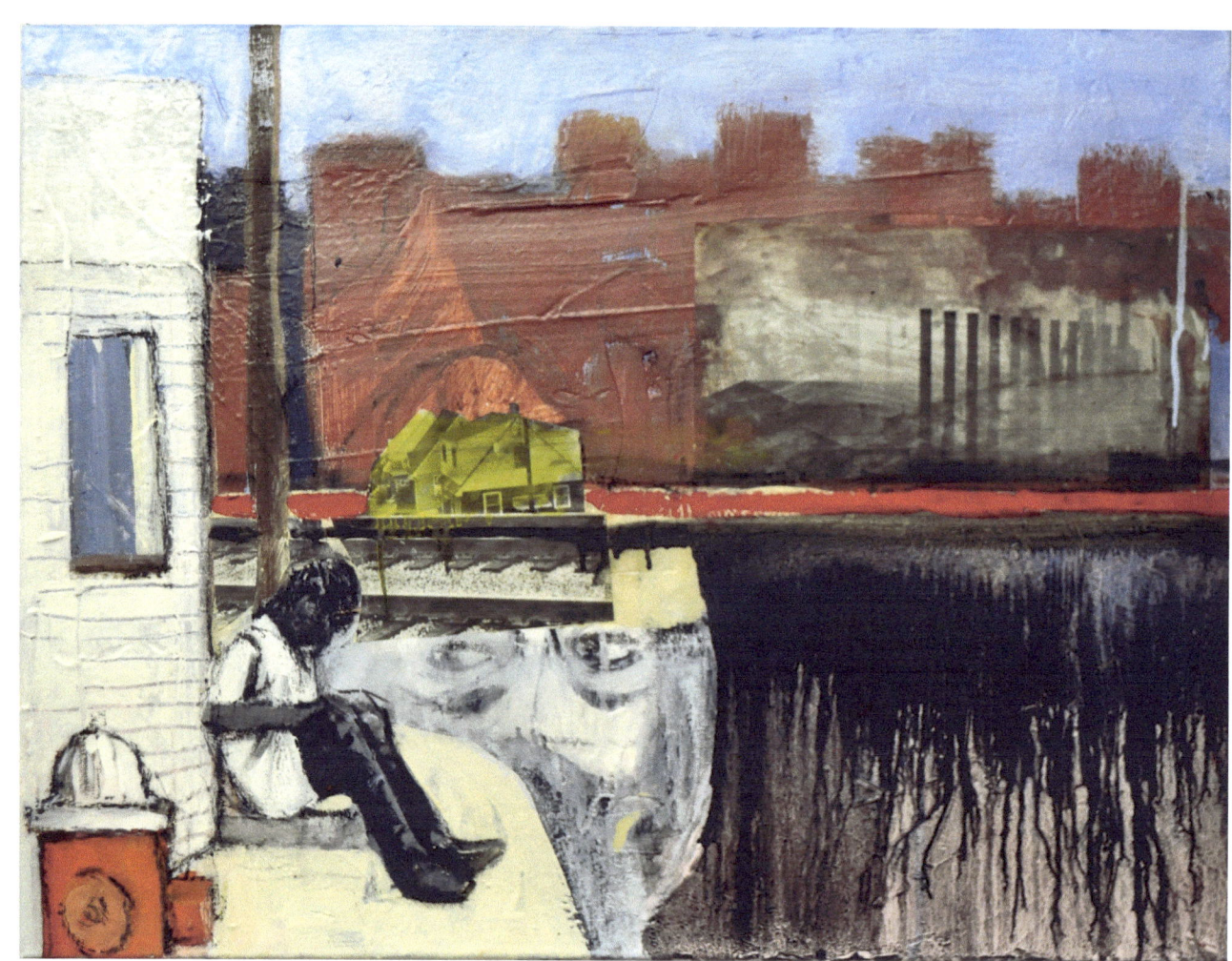

Fig.82 "Valley of Revelations"

"The illustration is based on a photograph I took at Huntington Beach in Bay Village in 2016. I grew up in Bay and spent a lot of time at Huntington, especially on the ever-interesting rock piers during the summer. Over the years, the massive rocks have shifted and become more difficult to navigate. I tried to capture that in the piece as well as the ambiguous nature of the relationship of the two figures."

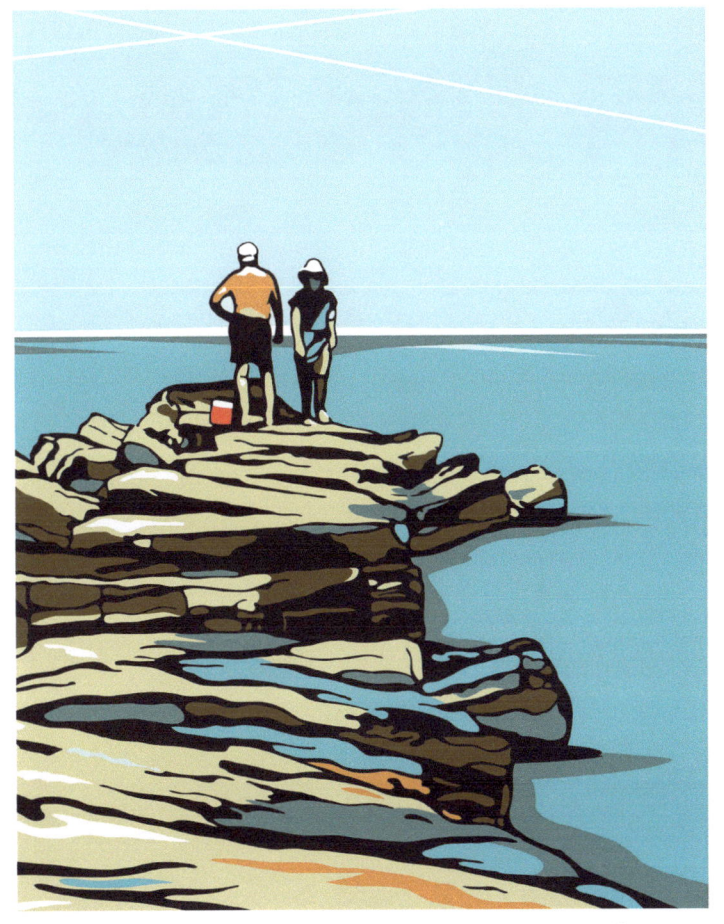

Fig. 83 "On the Rocks"

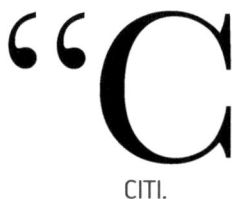

"CITI.

The collective struggle for working class emancipation has never been separate from a new experience of individual existence and capacities, wrested from the constraint of old bonds of community.

- Jacques Ranciere

THE EMANCIPATED SPECTATOR

It is possible to give a concrete and detailed analysis of any utterance, once having exposed it as a contradiction-ridden, tension-filled unity of two embattled tendencies in the life of language.

- M.M. Bakhtin

THE DIALOGIC IMAGINATION

I must tell you of this . . . generalities will abound. I come from a savage place, and we don't have much time.

- T.S. Eliot

in a letter to Ezra Pound

Cities are hard. You do not realize it till you are away from your own. Once you find what works for you, once you "know" it, "IT" changes. This "IT" works on two levels (there are more, but for the purposes of this small book, lets keep to the two). People change, and the landscape itself changes. Perhaps both react to changes in the other, change inspite of each other, change to better each other. But since change is not an either/or proposition we find ourselves beyond this point.

We exist in opposition, our very creative essence (which I will define as an essential trait of humans) is in direct opposition to landscape. What is interesting about this dynamic when we discuss the Now - is how we have visited a life threatening devastation with our essential creative (opposition). We attempt to be revisionist in our response to it. As if we did not as a populace wish, or at the very least, benefit from the advancement.

The word advancement is problematic when used in this way for it sets our diametrically (thank you Ritesh) superior to the landscape - perhaps this is the fork in the road for the natural surface has been altered by our building (advancement) on it. It goes without saying that we have been altered by what we've built.

WORKING/CITI.

Lets extend the metaphor:

Perhaps at this moment we are trapped by what we've built, so the altered landscape (cities) are actually prisons, a punishment for our creativity. For want of convenience is a direct effect of our ingenuity. Humans seem to always look for ways to get what we need easier. So someone decides or perhaps more precisely the better "Fisherman" fishes for all, and the better "Planter" plants for all etc. They each agree on what each is worth and trade accordingly so and so on. Years later, maybe even 100 years, or 1000 years someone consolidates "Fishing" (all the fisherman under one grouping), these fisherman brings the catch to the "ONE". The "ONE" makes the group trade gives each "Fisherman" their portion based on how much they bring in. So and so on.

(for the purposes of poetics we have rendered quotations to depict a meta-textual meaning)

As we build and our skill sets begins to individualize we find ourselves out of touch with the steps between us getting our needs conveniently and the labor it takes to get these needs to met. The more convenient, the more it begins to "cost", the "ONE" becomes an industry and this industry begins to see great amounts to trade, and begins to charge more to make the deals for the "Fisherman", industry then passes the growing cost to the convenient seeking individual who decides to find another "ONE"/industry who might offer the fish, and plants for less. Convenience.

So and so on.

Taking us to the Now.

We are so closed off to anything, or skill other than our "chosen" ones that over time, as systems automate, as our need for convenience grows we have created invisible labor.

THE NORMAL

Our appearance is tied to our ability to earn a living. Aside from the well documented role our ethnicity/race/gender play in appearance, it is attractiveness that continues to be a controlling tool of a patriarchal, and colonial, but aging civilization. Since we are living in a digitized industrial age attractive[ness] has continued to equate "normal". Our society/West controls what is considered normal (this control was inherited from a distinct colonial presence). We/West have become very good at the ways in which the "normal" is inferred.

(It is important to not divorce ourselves from the prevailing status quo, for the purposes of implying that we are part of our own oppression for whatever reason/ or cause agent- I will refer to the "West" as we, or our "society)

The primary method for this control is increasingly visual for our society is increasingly visually defined, and simply because over time we have become savvy enough to understand that the totalitarian decree does not control nearly as well. From our very first breath the conditioning begins.

Lean

Light

Tall

Blue/Pale eyes

Strong chin

Over time these attributes have come to define what our society/West views as "normal" and as an aside what is "good".

Hetrosexual

Monogamous

White

English speaking

Patriot

Christian

The picture of the young, slender blonde- her face pointed just so toward the camera, her eyes blank, but twinkling like a child. The fair maiden of a storybook. She is our patriarchal inheritance (even though she is subjected to this very same patriarchal oppression). She is the model of beauty- considered non- threatening. Docile. She is given to us from the moment our memory is no longer kept by our mothers. It is not that she is not beautiful. She is, but we all do not look like her, she cannot be the standard/ideal in a Just world.

It is at this moment that our sense of self is threatened. Controls are set in motion, we begin to feel a difference. As we grow this difference begins to play out. Clusters/social[ize] form- the slim children with fair (or close) features are grouped together. It is perhaps more sinister, and at the same time purely innocent, but it occurs, and we've all been subjected to it, in whatever form this is "IT" may take. And yes, there are instances of difference, but the dictum holds true -

Attractive is _____

The less you possess these characteristics, the less you may have.

[GENERALITIES ABOUND, AND I AM DISTINCTLY AWARE OF THEM.]

Just how long has this mode of control existed, how does it connect to cities? How embedded has it become?
When did we get to the point where we could no longer trace its inception?

Let us posit that it may have taken 2000 recorded years to get to this buildup of convenience, this control of the normal, and over this time we have learned methods of self protection, unconscious cloaks of rebellion. Perhaps these "cloaks" have also begun to be built in, predictable responses of our convenience? Our learned inclination is toward the individual, and this individuality is loved and loathed. We covet difference, and we abhor it, because it is outside of our knowledge base. Our human inclination is to be noticed, to appear different. So this difference is expressed in our uniforms (if I may) and points toward an individual identity (ies).

We are now living at a time where these uniforms can be co-opted, and sold back to us as symbols of identities we already have. The culture of selling cannot be traced. Of course we know when the industrial age hit, and of course we know when humankind began to discern value and commodity. We exist at a time where there has been centuries of invisible labor, years revving up to the commodification of identity. Selling us the uniform of the "normal". The NOW has become a culture of systems, and by proxy a system of symbols that allows for a lightning fast dissemination of information. A digital consequence. This "speed" is beyond our ability to process it fast enough. The symbols begin to have no discernable substance, no message. This causes us to feel unsure of which symbol is which individual, is which identity, which uniform. So we consume symbols like vocabulary, stacking words just in case. What was once earned rebellion is now commodified product.

Of course we still intuit this, and rhetorically push against it. Some of us manage to keep it out most of "IT", but the system of commodified symbols invades history. Since we can no longer trace its origin, we hack at it with revisions, and those revisions become the myths we except as truth. Our learned consciousness. Are we to assume that there is nothing one can do? Are we to take these "systems" of control as another inevitability that must be navigated for convenience sake?

Take it a thousand steps further -

the systems of the "normal" convenience continue to create a culture of wanting. A culture that is ripe for crime, corruption, and alienation since the city/landscape has been built passed its functional capacity to be inherently just. Since it is populated in hierarchies, and because of a divisive culture of consumption/convenience the "poor", those without the means to ignore the daily pressures of living are still bombarded with the "normal", and its tools of visual control the city becomes a utopia of "daydreams". It turns the "poor" into the bottom an hierarchy of humanized consumer prey.

This jacket will make me _____.

This phone is all i need to _____.

and,

Why can't I have _____.

They have _____.

The desperation of working, and only earning enough (perhaps) wage to barely survive, or worse yet never knowing work, and a wage to survive - leaves one in a state of constant want. The constant want leads to a "needing" desperately, an escape. This "escape" is as real, and painful as a bullet wound. For some, the sure method of escape is drugs. Over time the drug laws are built, and transform into a system of control- a protection tool of "normal", a way for the "ONE" to keep "FISHING/PLANTING" consolidated, a way to turn more of a profit. The tool is prison. Where in the Now you may become free labor as more and more cities, municipalities, and governments turn to privatization as a means to bring down the cost of maintaining the convenience of an overbuilt landscape. Since it has been built beyond its capacity to function. There are two main areas where the industries of privatization are easy to implement - schools, and prisons. The prison population is hired at a near slave wage to do jobs that use to provide a living wage. We no longer can see the invisible labor all around us until our individualized skill, the one we have "chosen" becomes a part of that invisibility. The savings that comes from this imprisoned workforce allows for even more consumption/convenience. It removes a potenial earner from a home/family dynamic, and through the process described in the page before feed the cycle, a cycle so vast, and ancient that we can no longer trace its origin.

Cities have grown past our ability to sustain a populace with its landscape. They have become a tool in the circle of convenience even as they were/are monuments to our ingenuity, testaments to our ability to command landscape for our own convenience. They have become prisons, the citadels of our "Normal".

"Work like you don't need the money.
Love like you've never been hurt.
Dance like nobody's watching."
- Satchel Paige

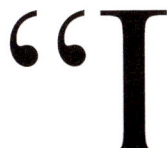

I chose Satchel Paige as my artistic representation for Cleveland because of his contribution to the sports world, his influence of African Americans in sports, and his larger than life personality.

He came from a reform school after a run-in with the law as a juvenile. Was scouted, recruited and played around the world. Opened up the doors for many talented African American ball players in the Negro Leagues. Until he finally took Cleveland's offer to pitch for the Indians after impressing them with his ability to throw 3 strikes perfectly over a cigarette that was put in place of a home base. He was the one who held the mound the last time "The Tribe" won a World Series. Sadly most don't know about this talented figure in history, but I hope that by having this piece on display will encourage others to do further research into the man who won the Cleveland Indians its last World Championship title."

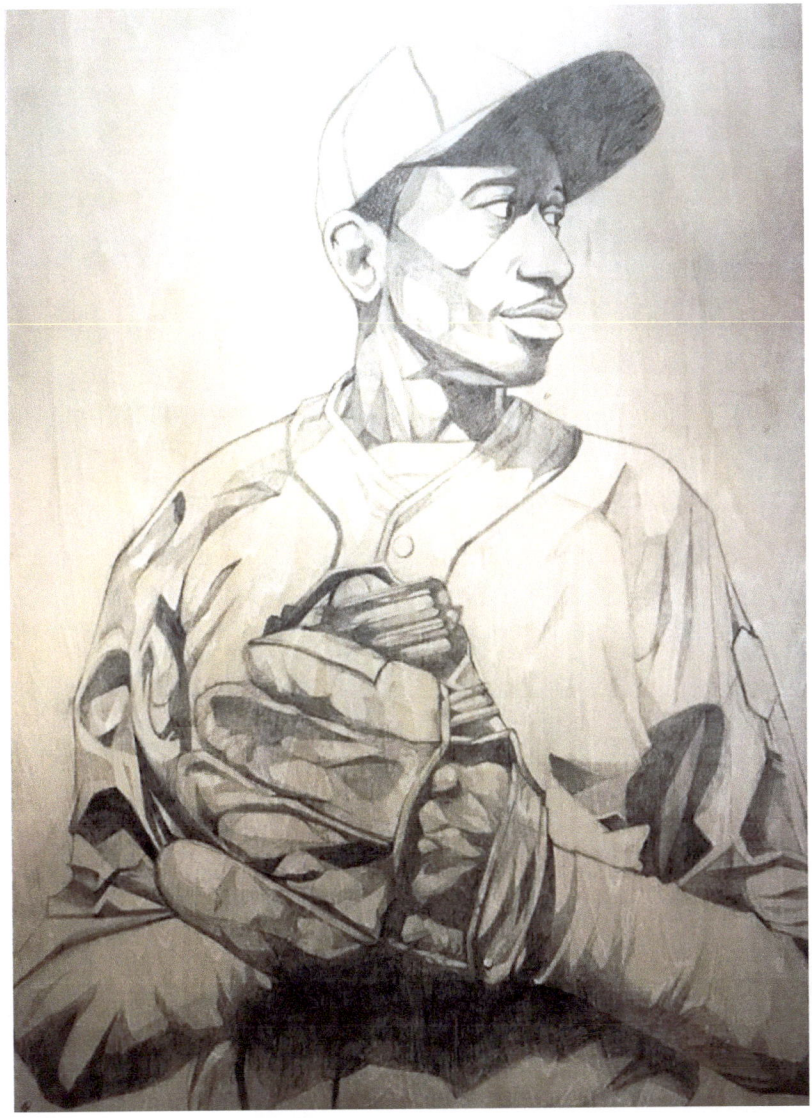

Fig. 84   "Satchel Paige"

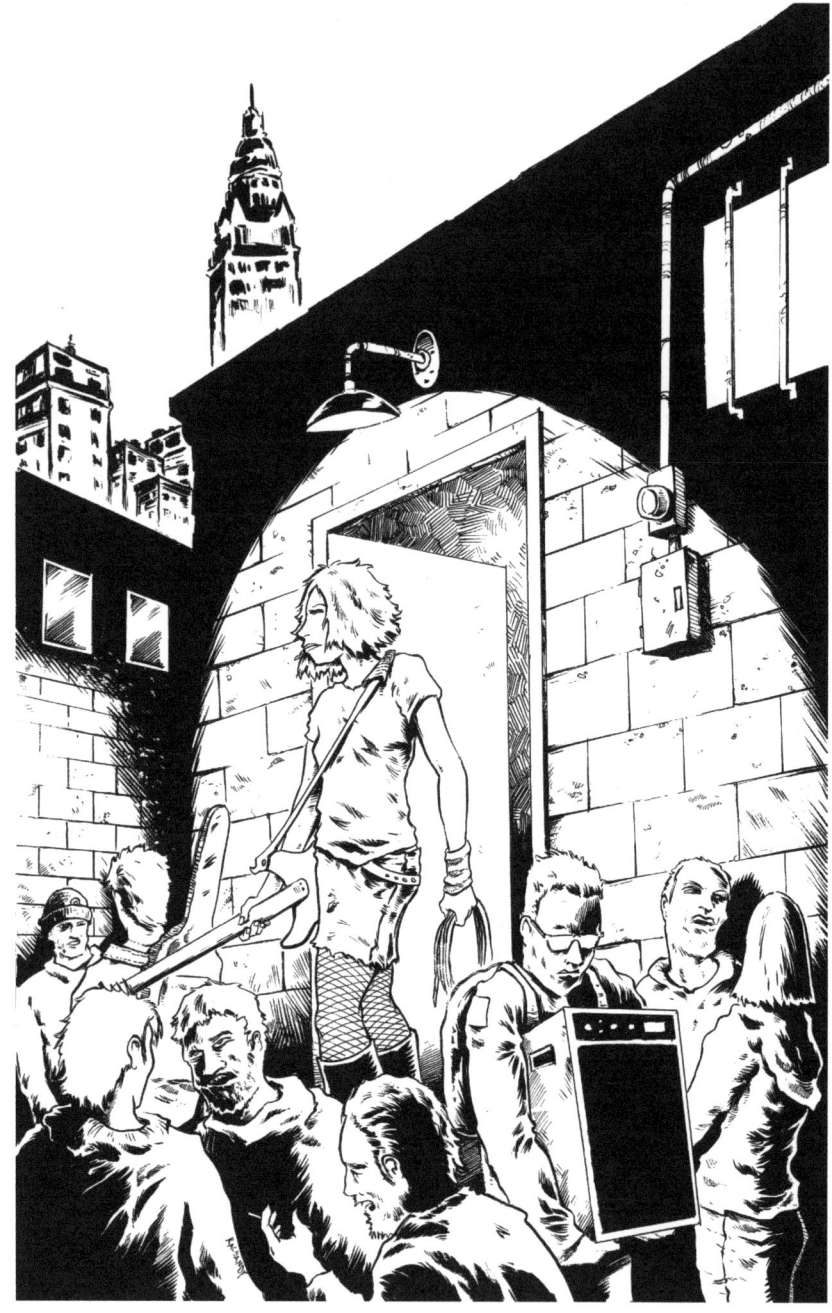

Fig. 85 "Julie"

"W

While I was growing up and pursuing art and illustration, many of my friends picked up instruments and formed bands. They drove all over playing numerous shows and open mic nights around the city. I spent my time at these shows watching the members of the bands and the people who came to see them. This drawing is meant to capture these people, in between sets, doing what they love for very little return."

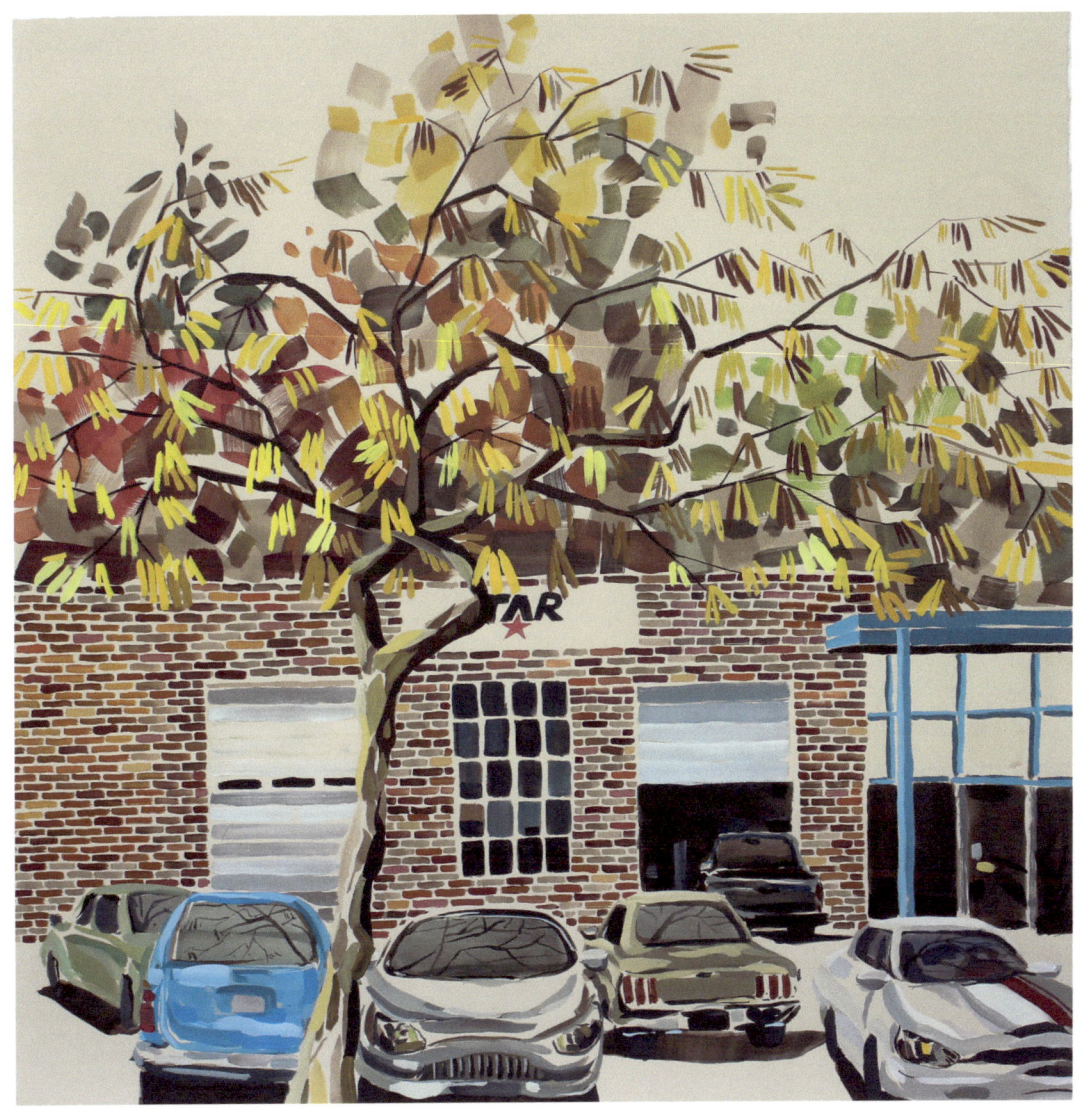

Fig. 86 "Star"

"C

Cleveland has been a source of inspiration for my entire artistic career the landscape of this city is quintessential to the narrative of a modern Midwest American city."

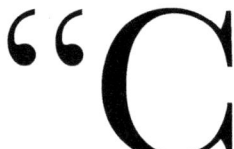

"Cleveland is where my art community lives and where I exhibit, make and teach. This region is a rich resource, both for the great art that is made here, and for the natural objects I collect and use in my work. My work resonates with these connections to this place and its extraordinary people."

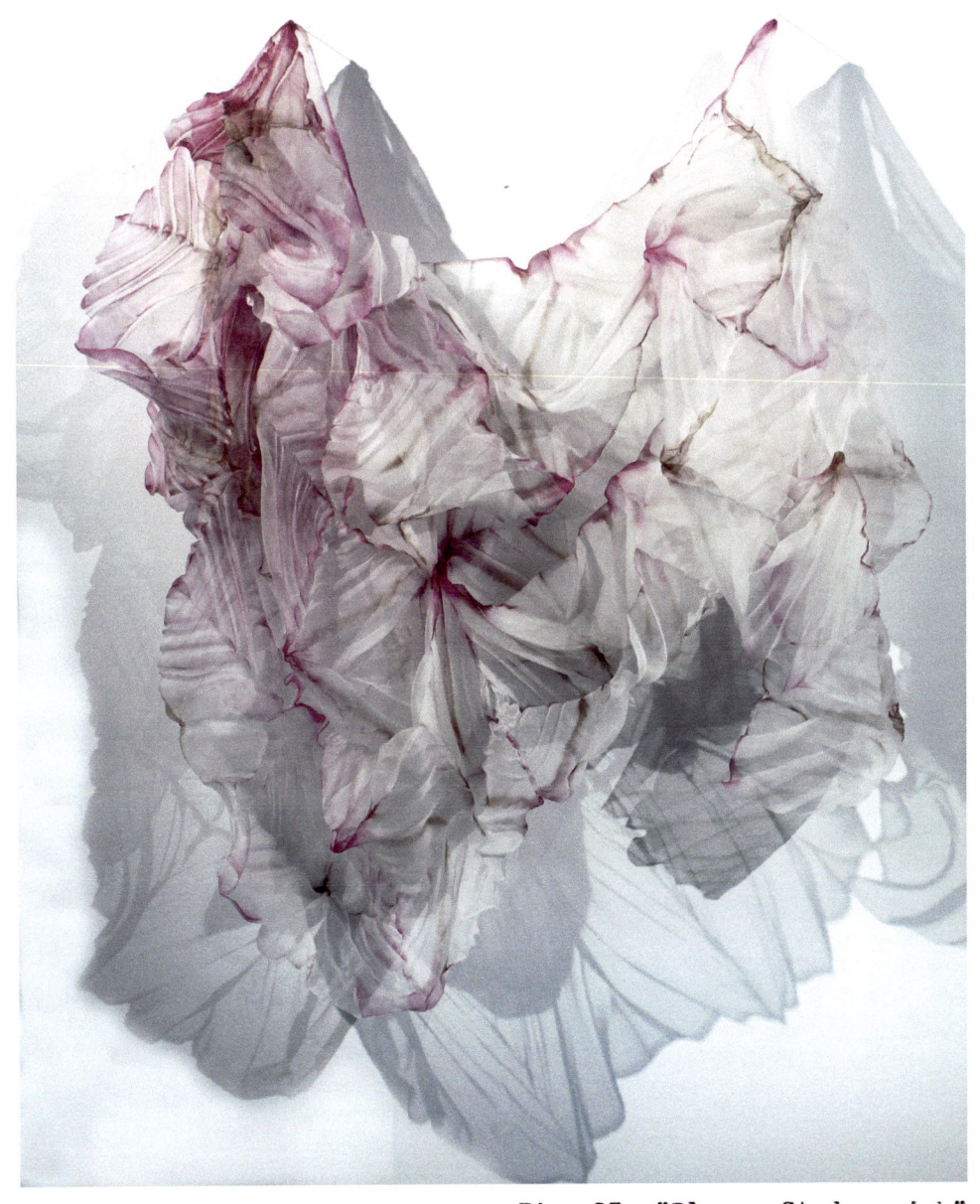

Fig. 87 "Planar Study, pink"

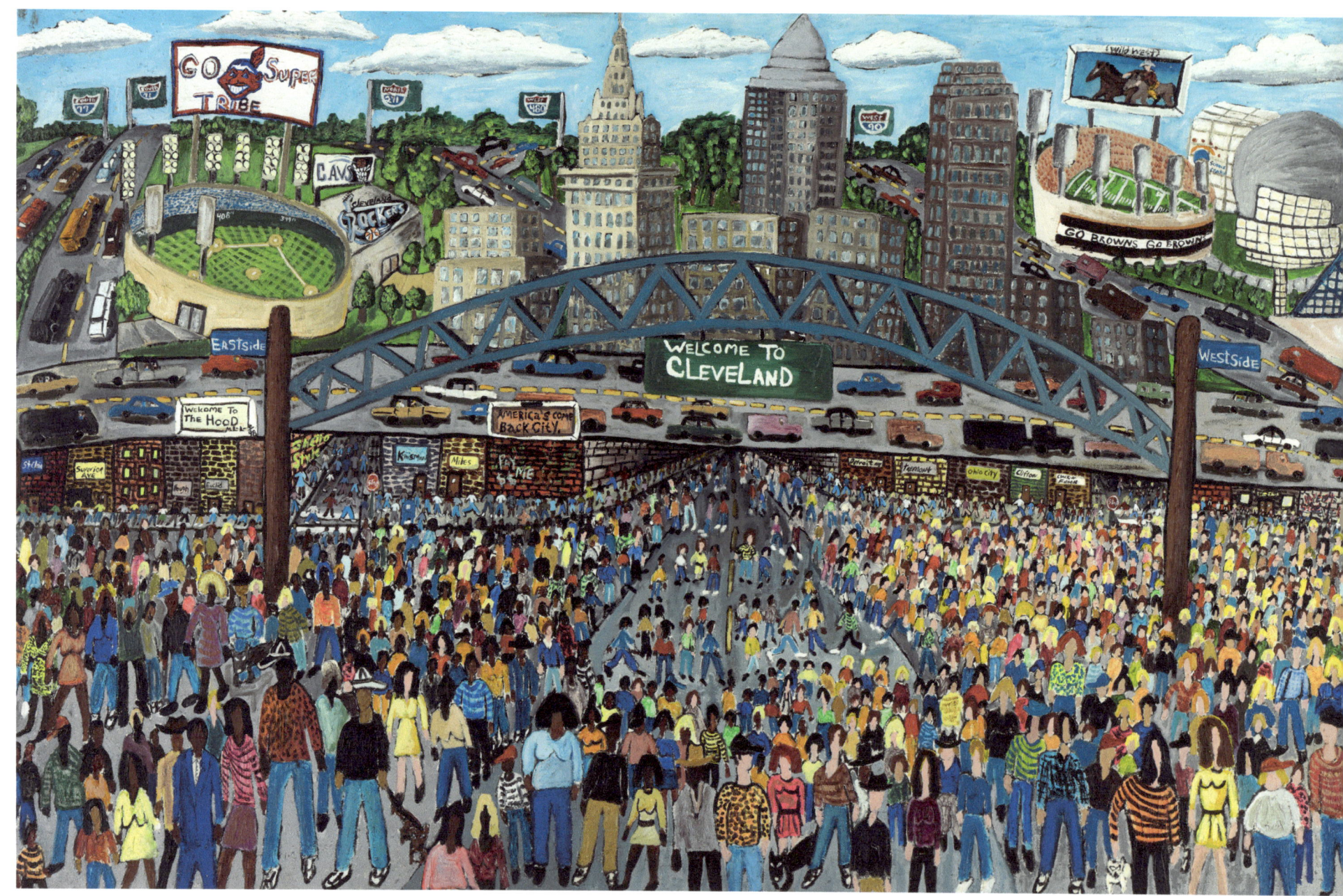

Fig. 88 "My Hometown" ©Cleveland Museum of Art

" **I**

 It was after I had come back from Los Angeles, California in 1992. And after seeing the kind of homelessness, crime and the division between rich and poor on a much larger scale. This is what inspired me to paint "My Hometown."

From that experience I grew a greater love for my Hometown the way people come together for the greater good of the city. We don't agree on all the issues all the time but we are a proud city with a great history and great people. "The Community" is a visual example of Cleveland's inner city communities. A slice of urban view point, from the corner stores and churches, businesses and messages being expressed in the community that help the city develop it's personality and culture. Cleveland is a melting pot of many cultures that have come together and helped the city rise to the international stage it is on. I love this town"

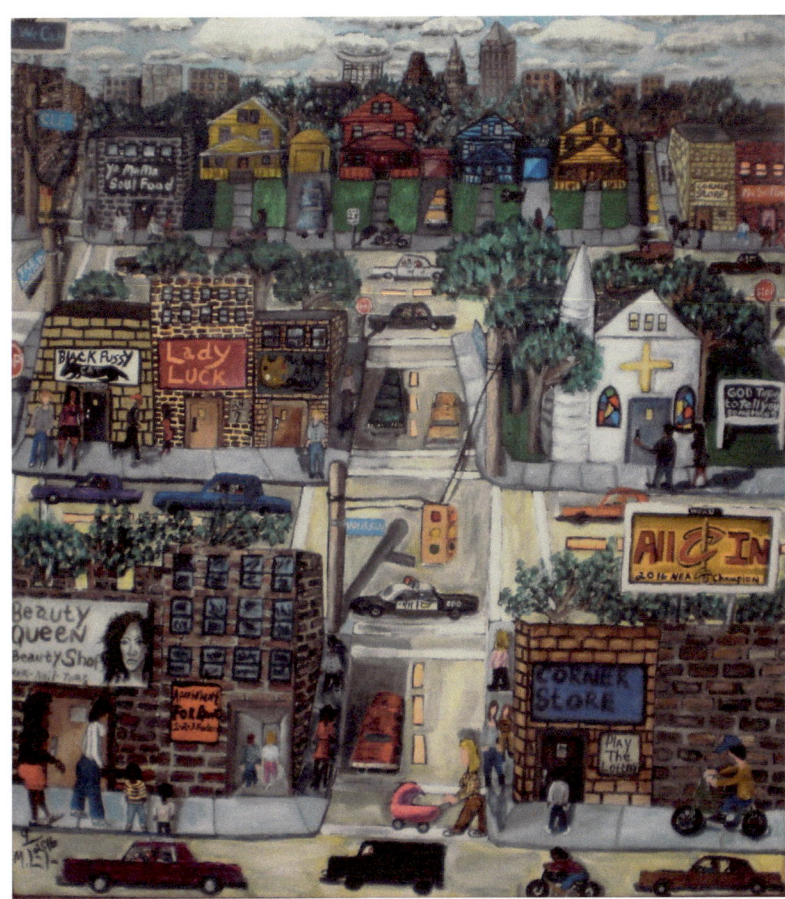

Fig.89 "The Community"

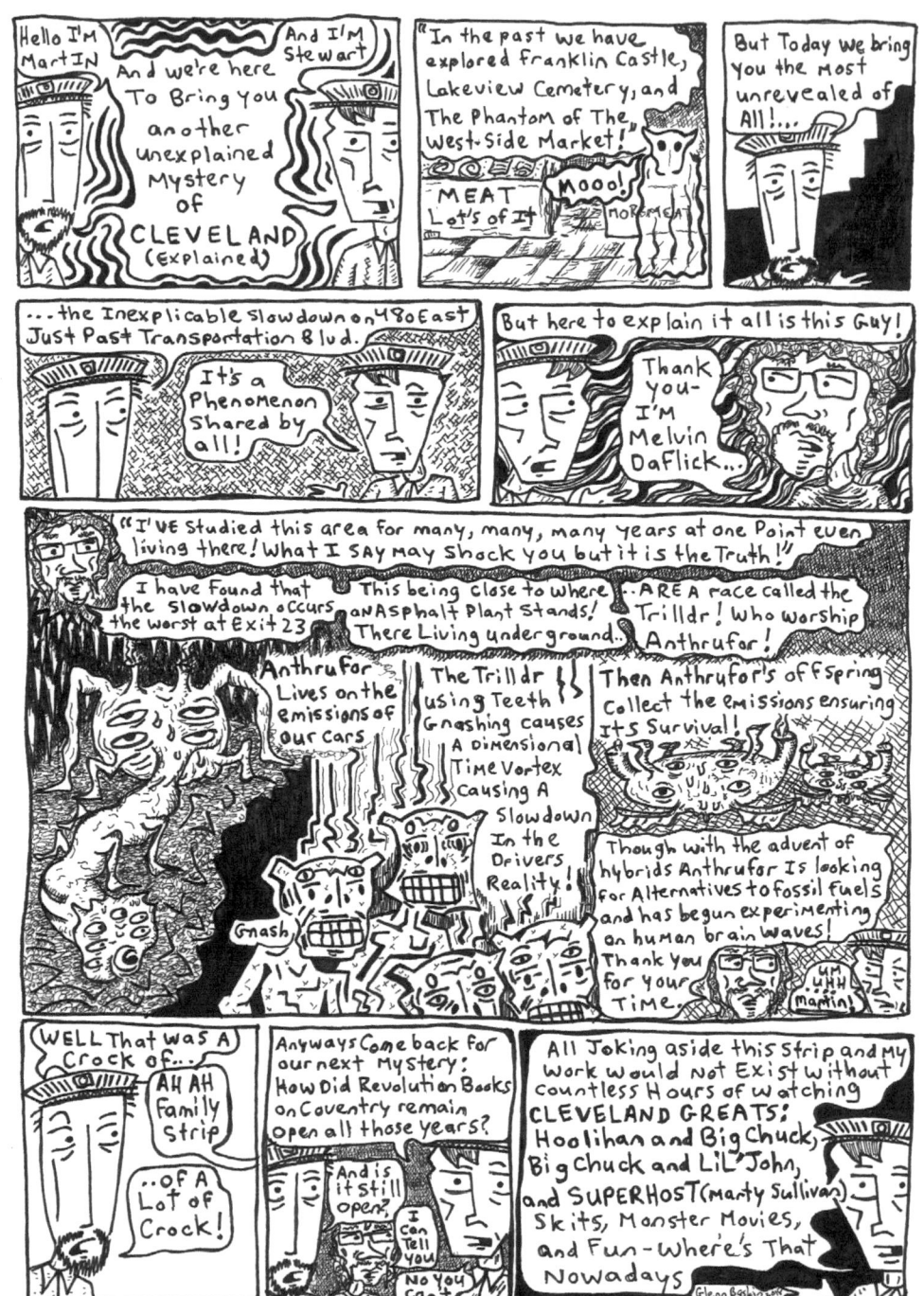

Fig. 90   "Cleveland Fixed Again"

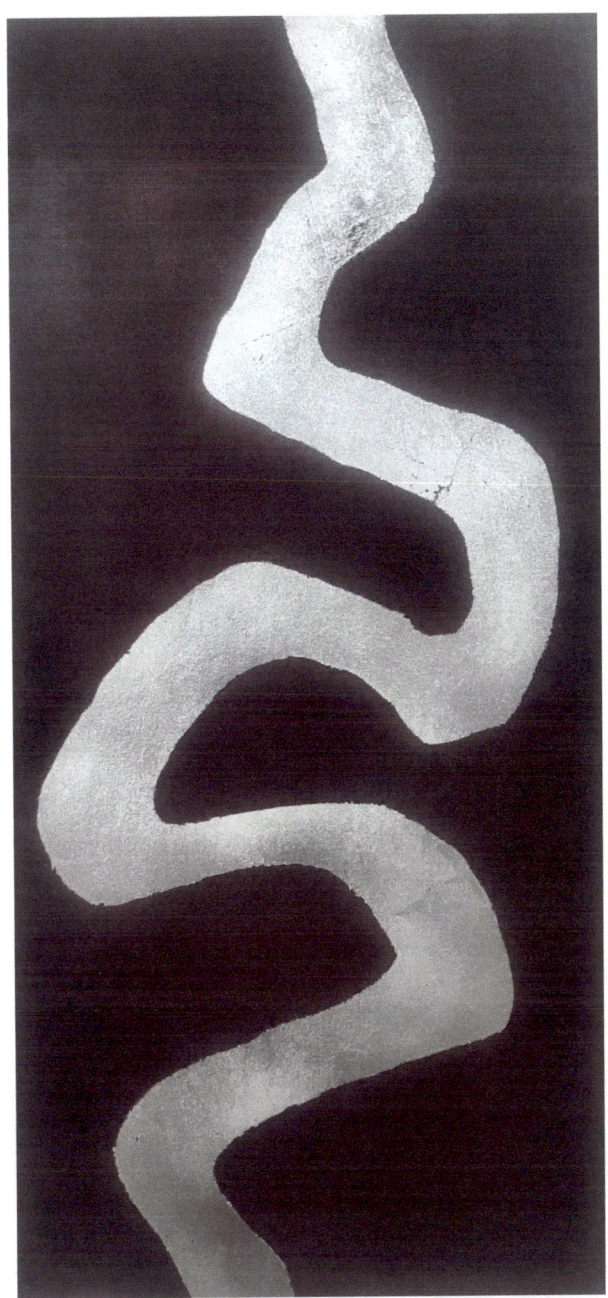

Fig.91 "Cuyahoga"

"M

My piece features the outline of the Cuyahoga River, in gold and silver. It shows the bends and curves of the river as it winds through the city and exits into Lake Erie. I think the shape of the river is as recognizable as any Cleveland landmark. I did the piece in two panels to create a yin-yang effect, referencing the fact that Cleveland is very much a divided city in several ways. The river creates a physical boundary reinforcing the divide of East and West. When meeting someone new from Cleveland it is inevitably asked if they are an East-Sider or West-Sider, and there is pride and prejudice on both sides of the river.

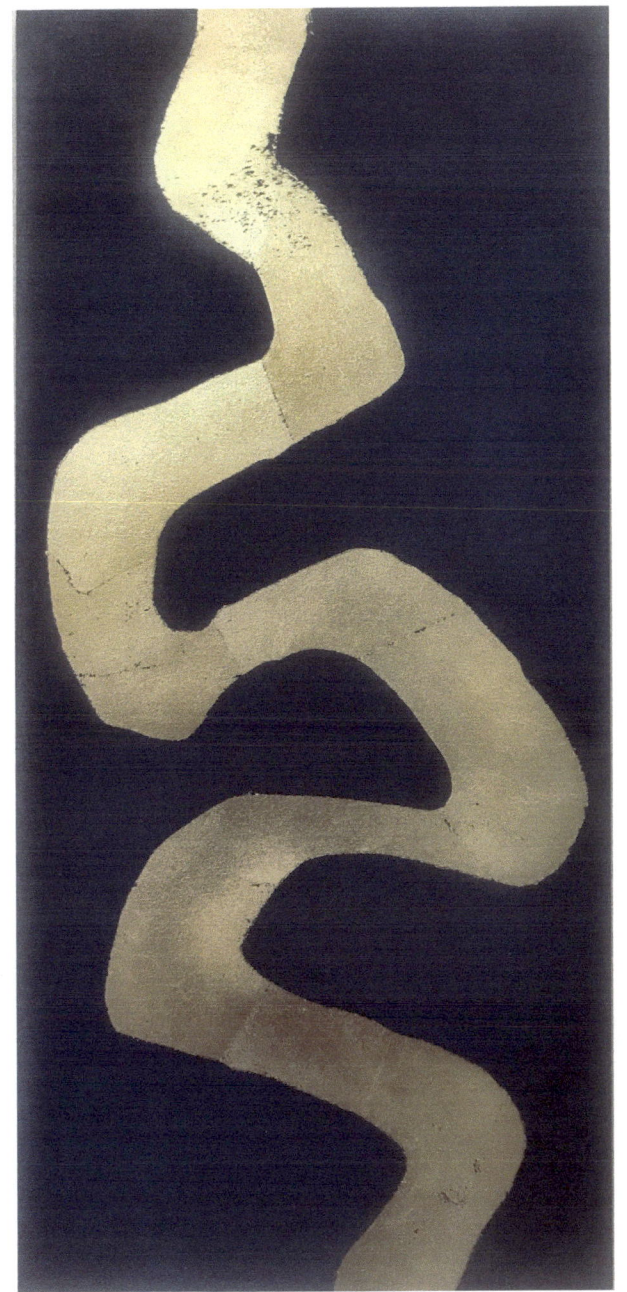

Fig.92 "Cuyahoga"

"T

The settings of my stories--
even if they are imagined--
always look like Cleveland: the
old housesand storefronts,
the trains, the shapes of
local oaks and maples, even
elements of Cleveland graffiti.
It's just what comes out
when I draw."

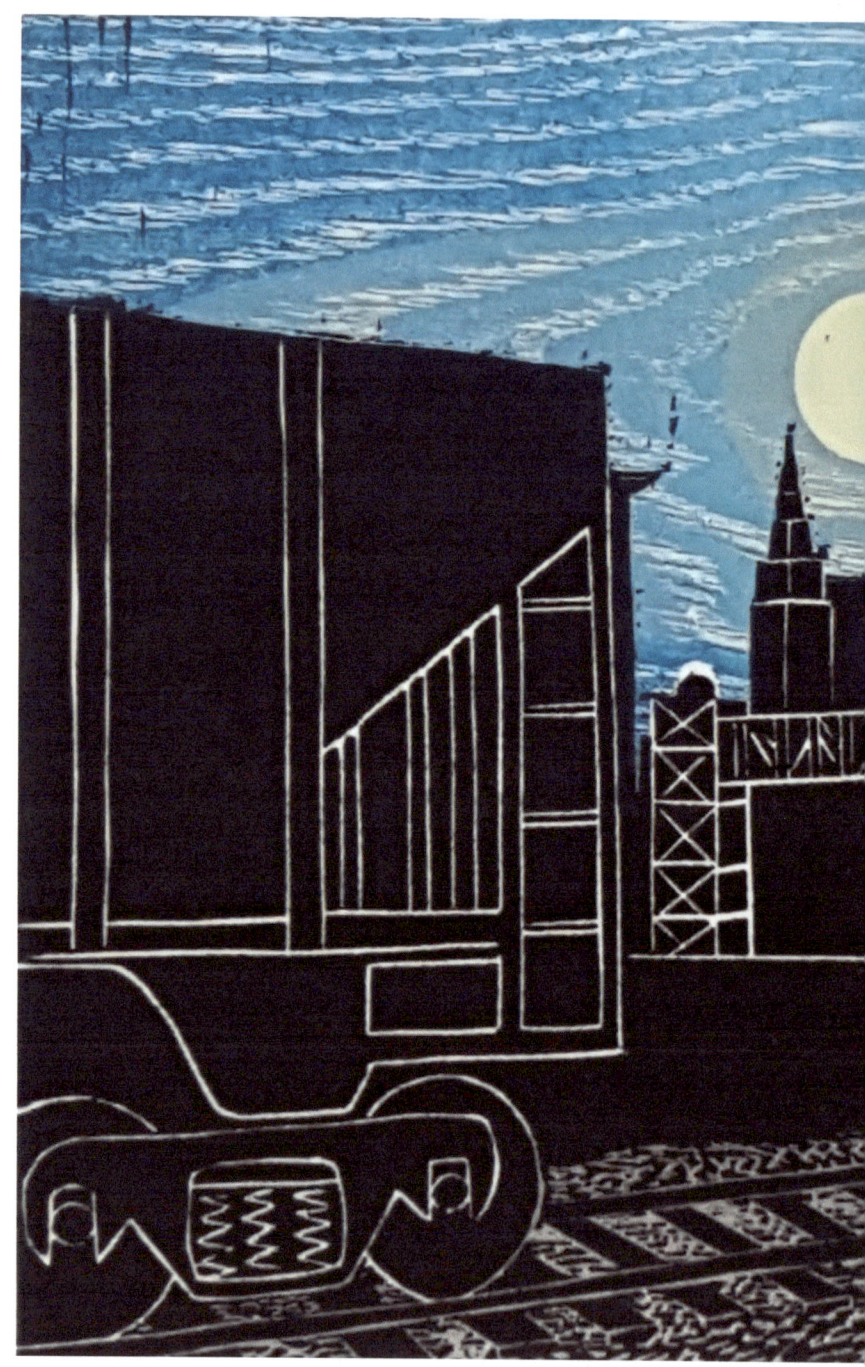

Fig.93 "All Over Town"

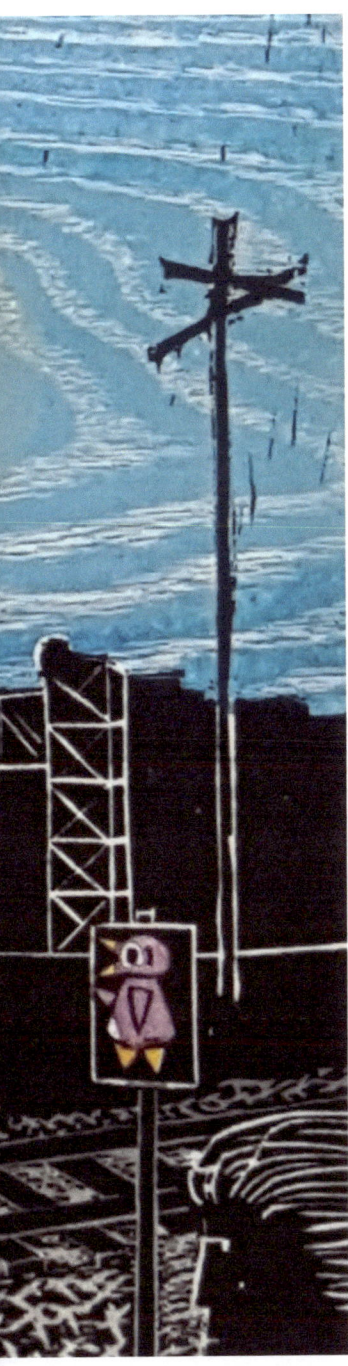

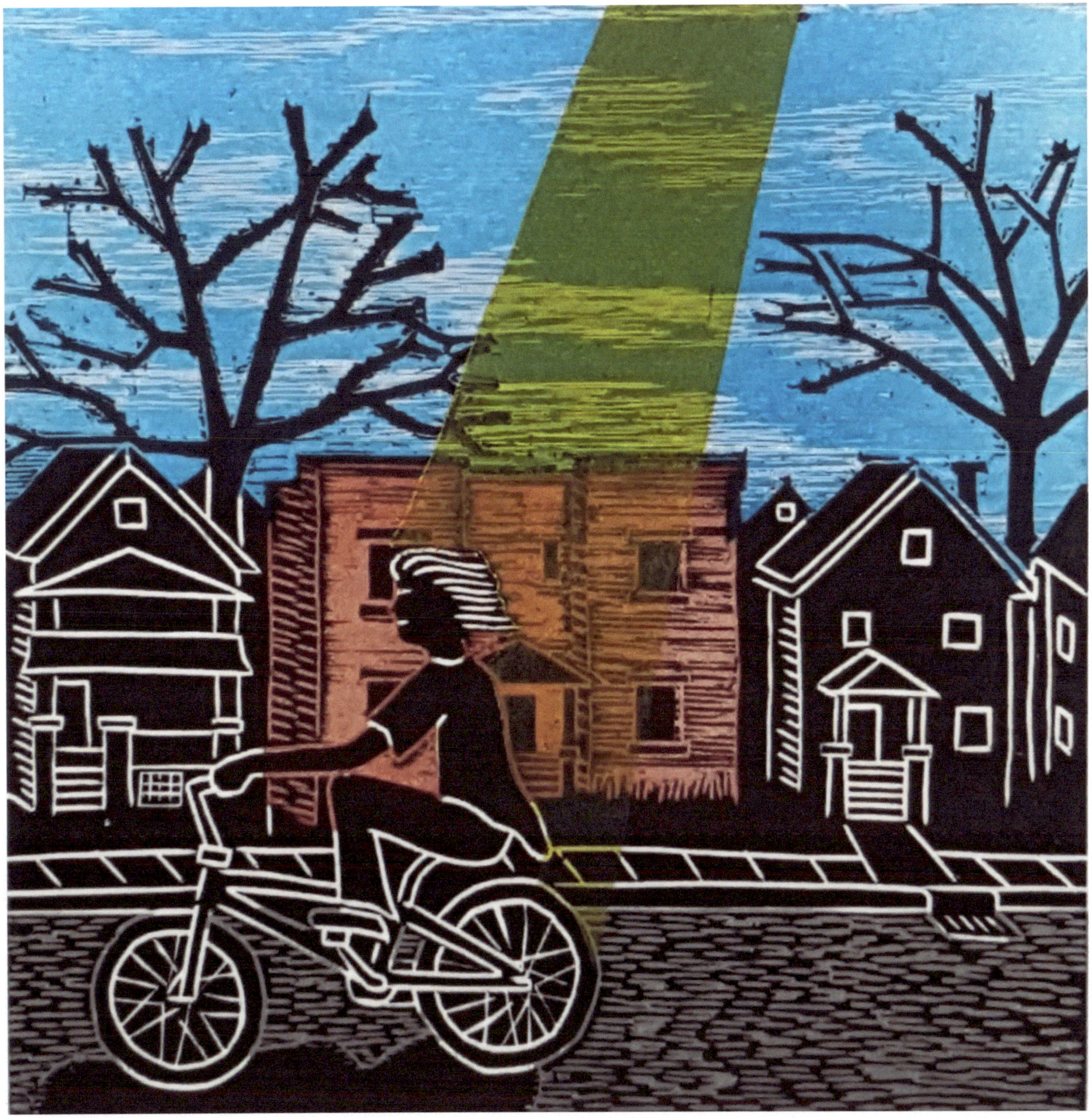

Fig. 94 "He Wanted to Finish the Job"

114

"I

I focused on the steel mills. I wanted to capture the beauty of their aesthetic presence in our current cityscape, a means of commemorating what our city is rooted by, but also as a signifier that this industry is part of our past, encouraging people to now look forward to new horizons for this city."

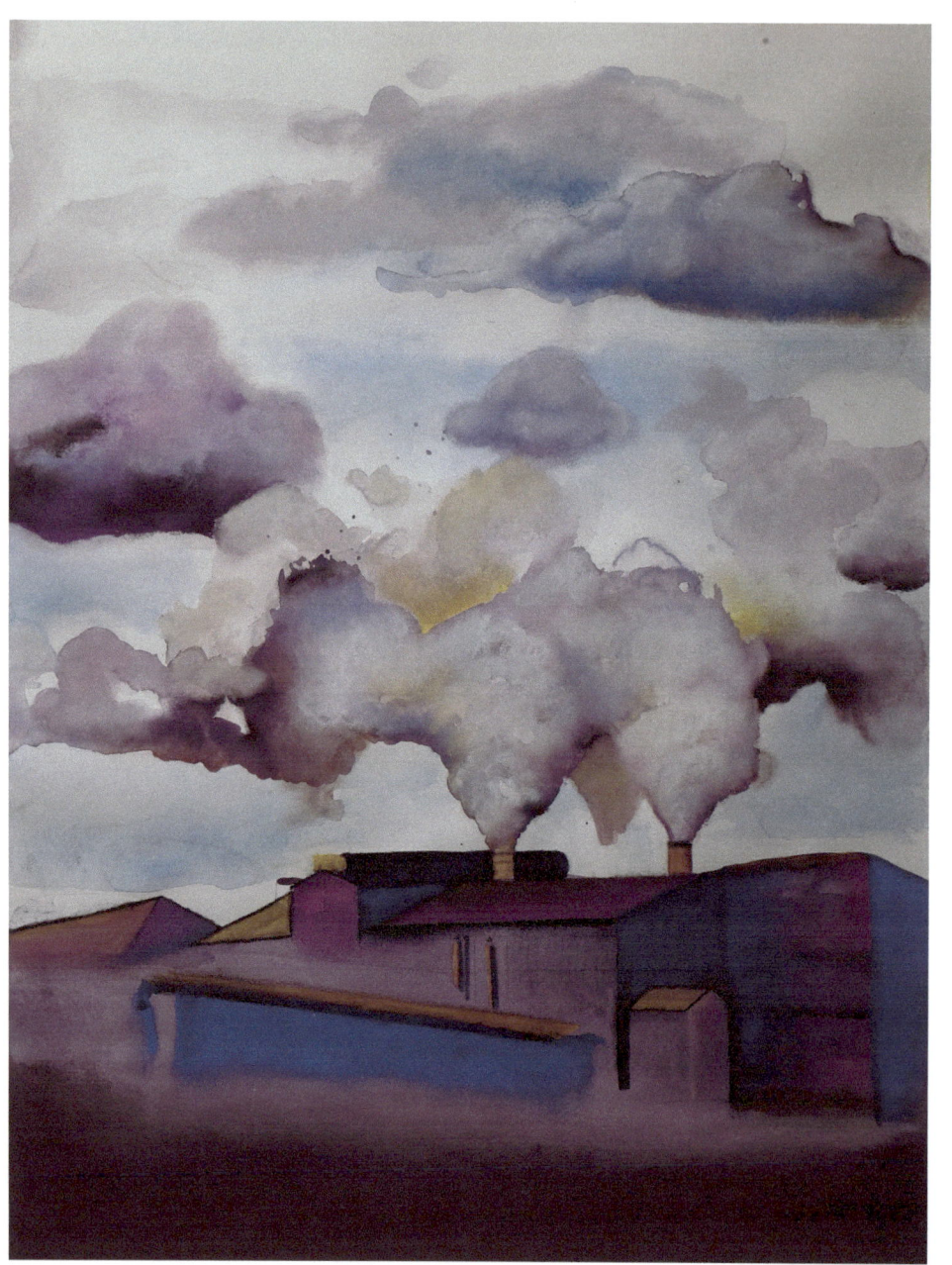

Fig. 95 "Untitled"

"**L**oci of Potential/Sites of Transition integrates trajectories and methods of production that I have spent a career exploring. My rhythmic return to drawing interfaced with my natural inclination to create experiential environments by sculpting space. This work also developed by mining the rich, complex vein that only an urban environment can offer. Cleveland is fully charged with history, materials, and a sense of place. Using energy conversion as a focal lens, this installation of drawings/sculptures aggregates my concentration on the industrial environment, my investigations of the creative process, and cycles of renewal and decay."

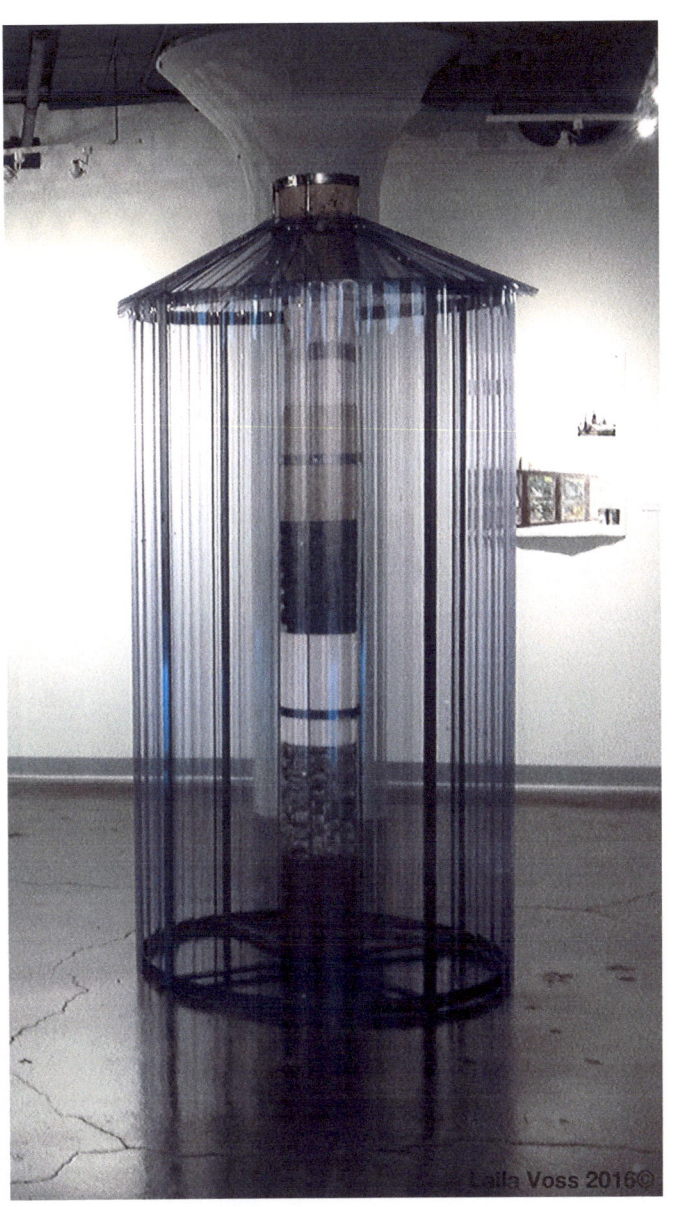

Fig. 96
"Loci of Potential/Sites of Transition"

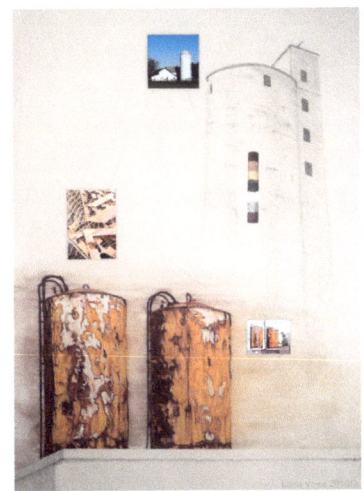

Fig. 96b

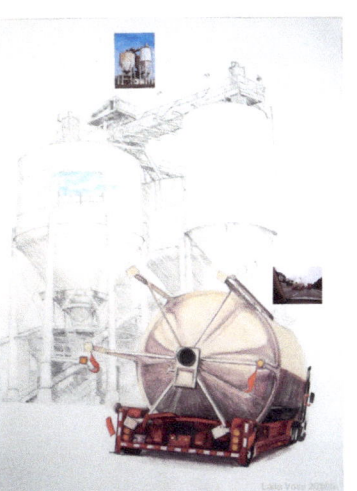

Fig. 96c

"B
Between the city and the Metroparks, there's always something new to see. As an abstract/landscape painter, it's great to have both industrial and rural settings for inspiration."

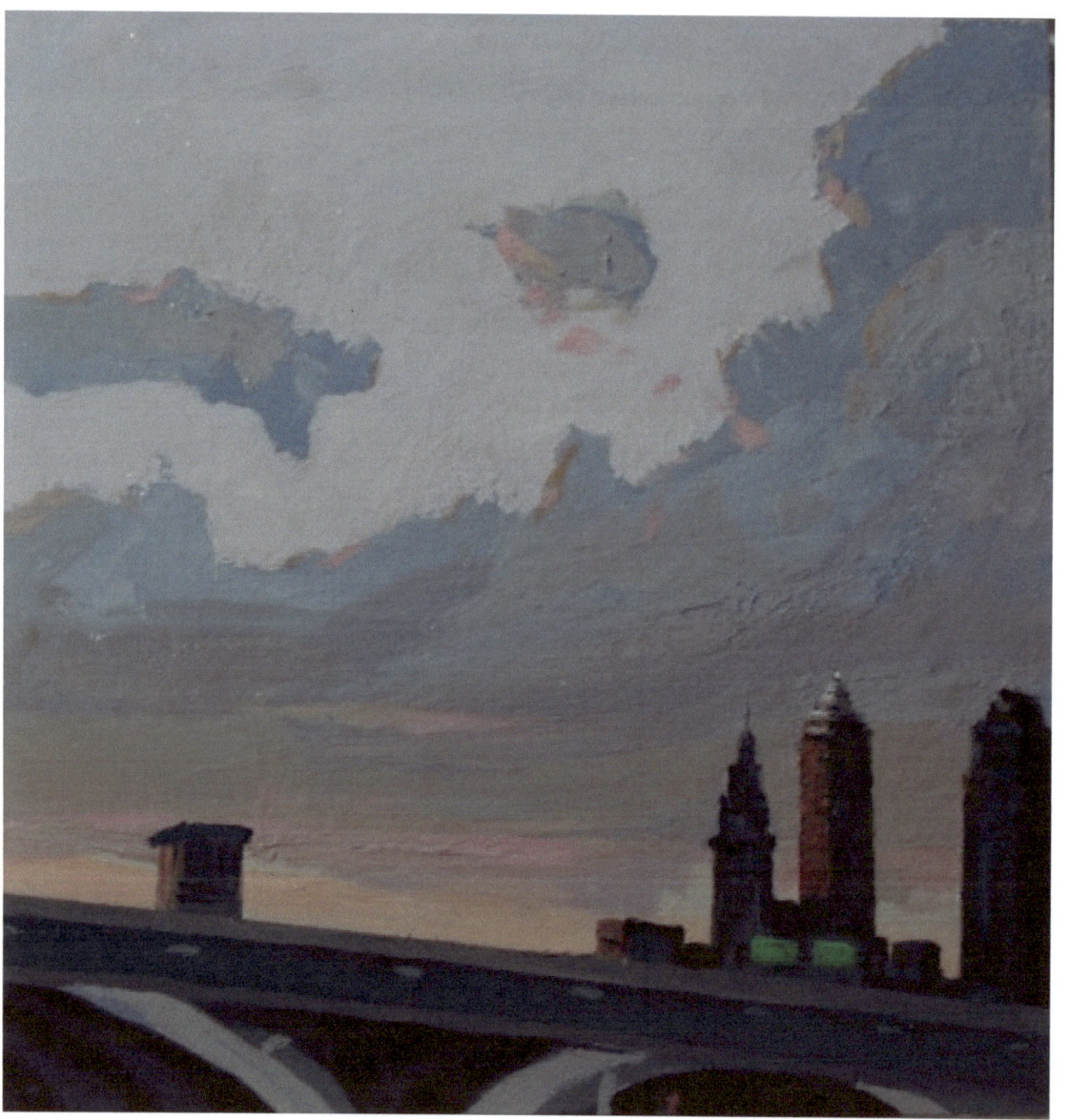

Fig.97 "Sunset Bridge"

"The portraits I create focus on hardworking Clevelanders who I am surrounded by. These people are artists, barbers, bakers, bartenders, and musicians, to name a few. They all apply a blue collar work ethic to their profession - a true sign of what it means to be from Cleveland. The passion and resiliency of this new working class is what inspires me in my own studio practice every day."

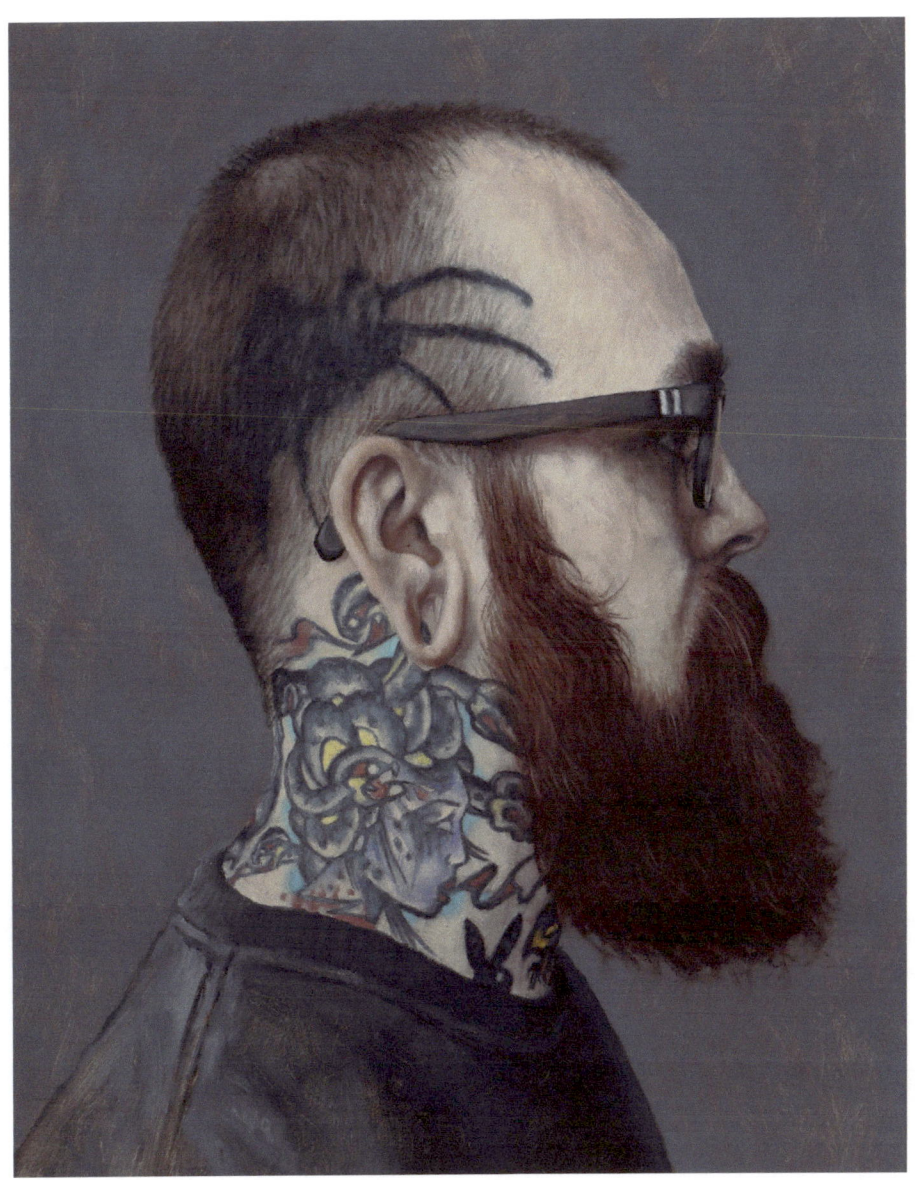

Fig. 98 "Red"

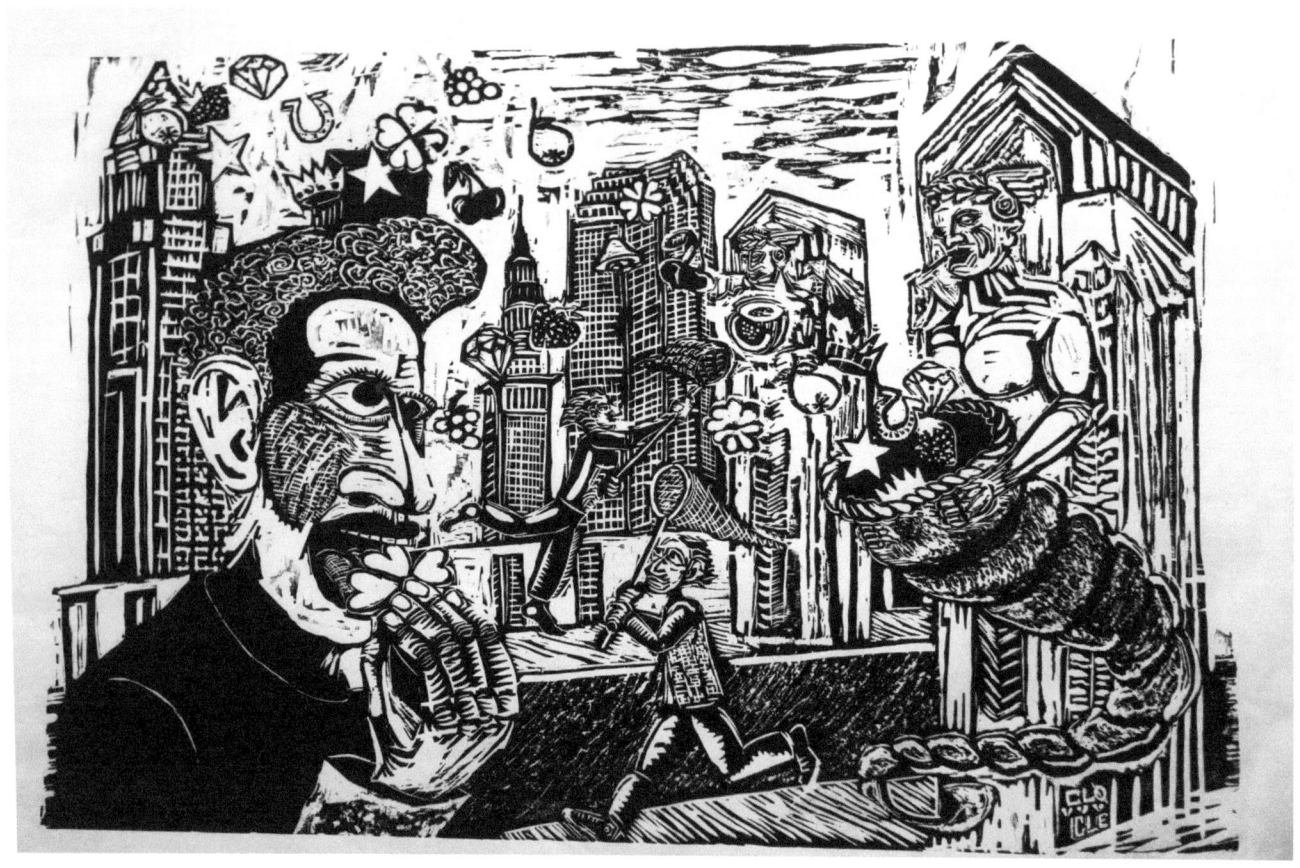

Fig. 99 "CLE Feeds Me"

"I

I appreciate what Cleveland gave me: precious friends, an education, many learning and traveling opportunities, the discoveries of myself, and plenty of space and chances to work and expand; no place was ever so generous to me as The Land."

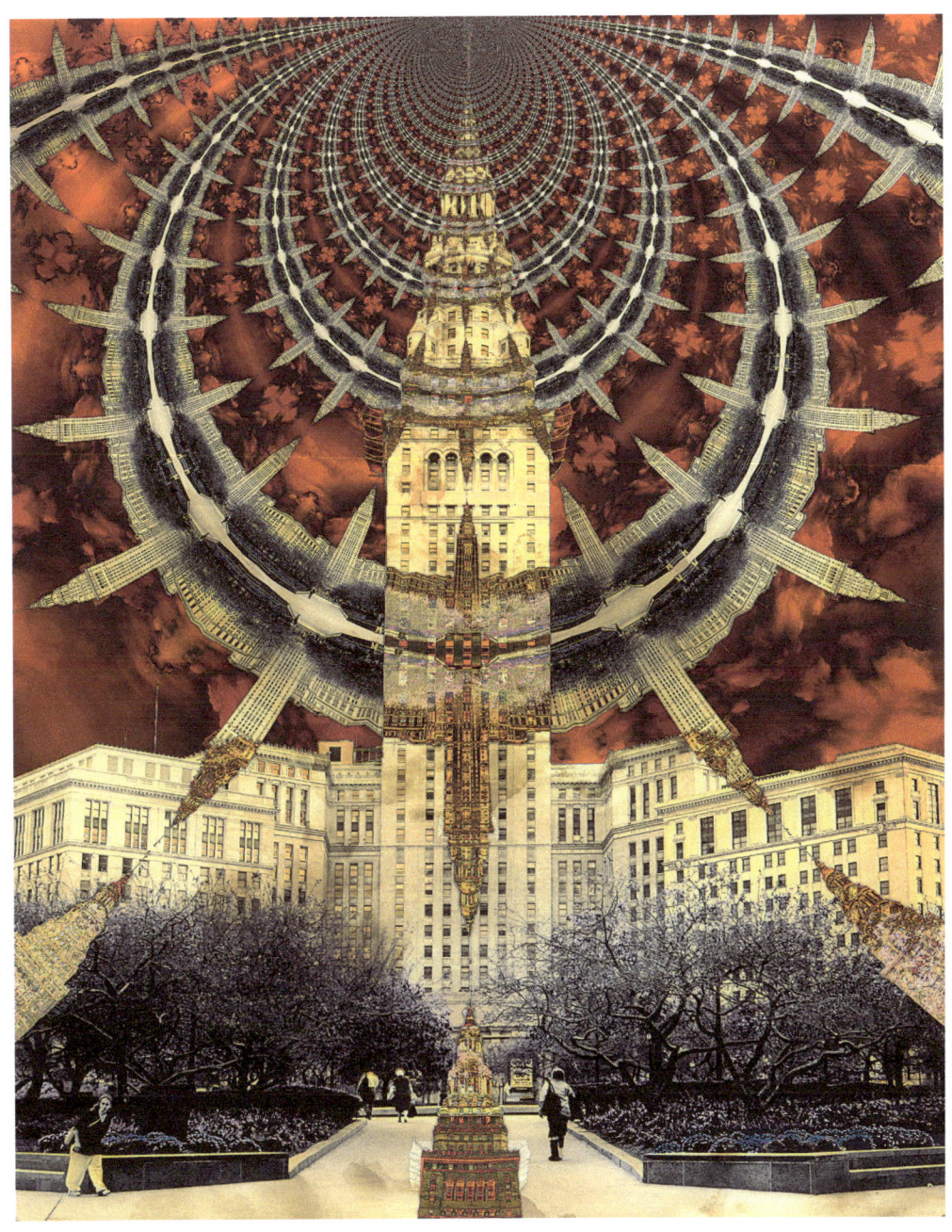

Fig. 100 "Terminal Spin"

"F

For me, Cleveland is the framework of my life. All of my memories and most important moments exist, forever, within it."

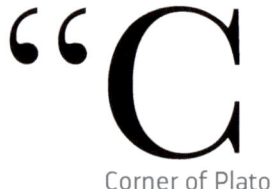

"Corner of Plato

The French Impressionists described their paintings as executed "en plein aire." But it's been a long time since I last went outside and painted things in the plain air. I live in East Cleveland, within a mile or so of the buildings and streets depicted in several recent paintings. Like a normal 21st century artist I photographed these scenes out of a car window with my phone, then painted them at home, where the air usually smells like coffee.

The little building depicted in "Corner of Plato, Mural on East 152nd St." attracted my notice many times, as I travelled on East 152nd Street to tend to business in North Collinwood, or on route to the highway. Maybe the squat, angled structure was a gas station at one time, or a fast food franchise. Somebody sealed it up behind big panels, and somebody else (I assume) painted a picture on one side, showing a boy touching a butterfly with his forefinger. That was two years ago – more recently the panels disappeared, so the building is a little hard to recognize. It's still there (at the corner of a street named Plato), with broken windows and some red and blue sections, in the middle of a rough vacant lot paved with grass and gravel, behind a sagging hurricane fence.

Making that painting felt strangely familiar. It seemed almost to paint itself. I drew with black pastel on primed canvas, then painted the buildings with white latex paint and off-white

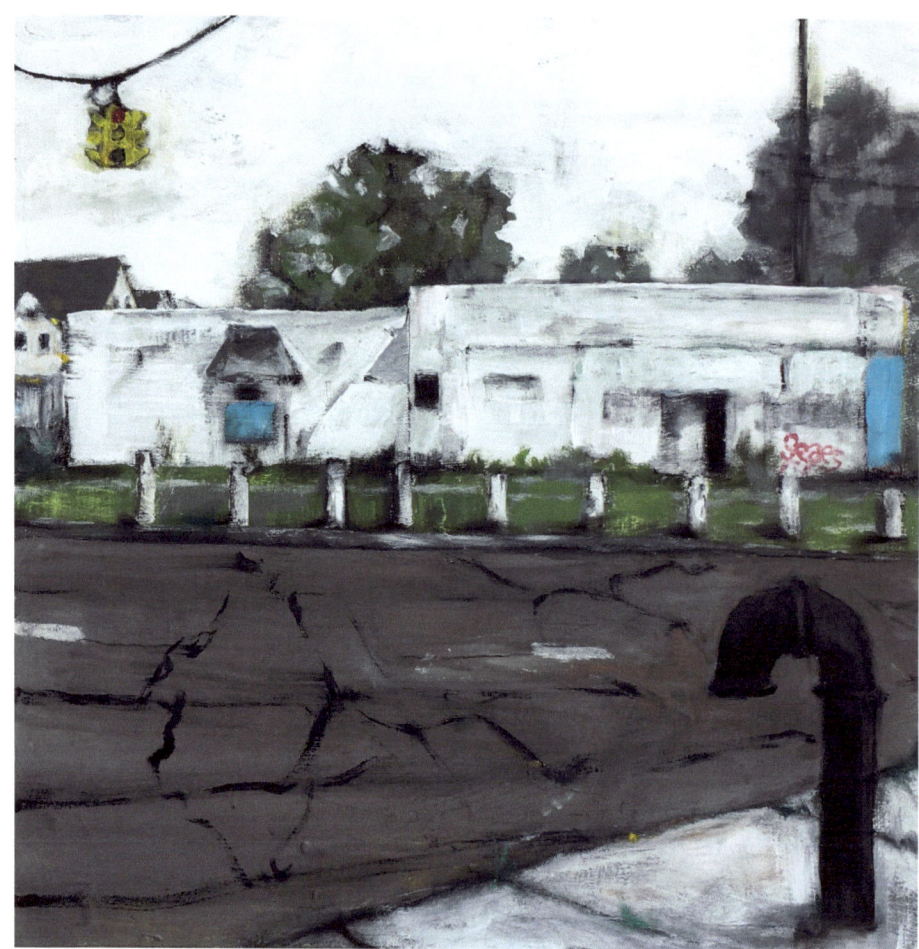

Fig. 101 "Hayden and Shaw

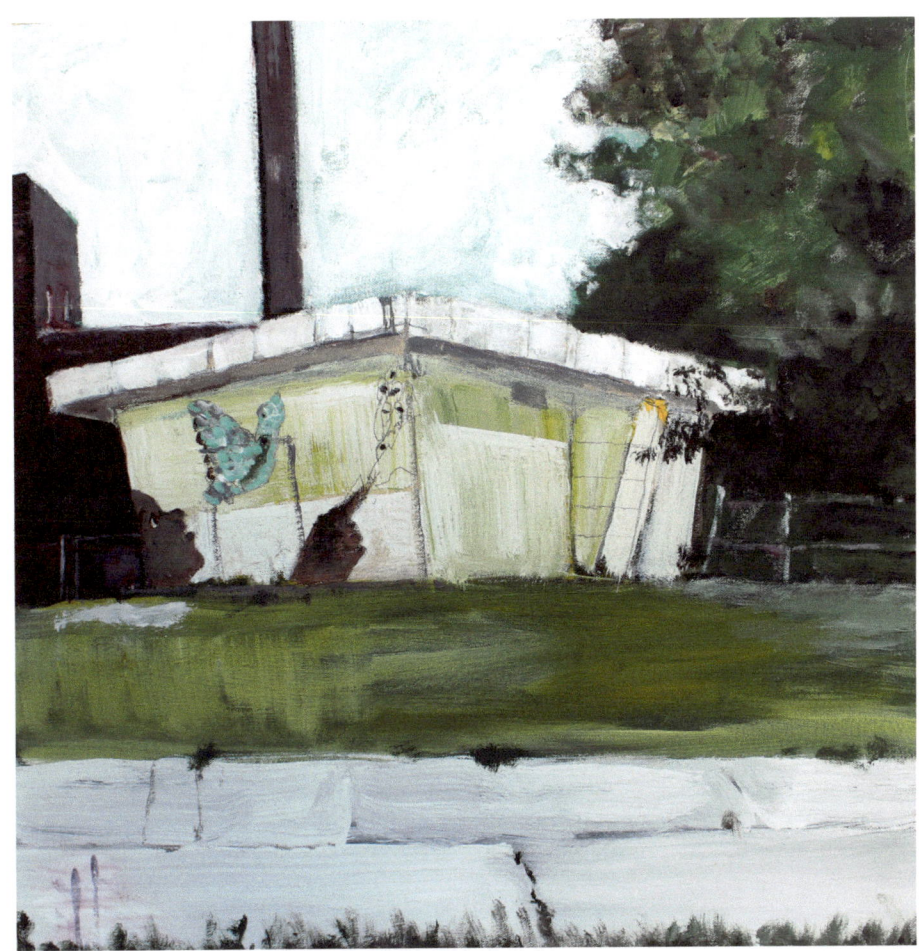

Fig. 102 "Corner of Plato, Mural on East 152nd St"

acrylic colors. The trees, the sky, the fence, the brick-brown red of the chimney and finally the grass in the foreground came along fast and clean – all with scarcely a false move, which is not my usual, error-driven M.O. The last time I made a work anything like this was when I was a boy, painting one summer in the mostly deserted, falling-down town where my grandmother lived, in the far corner of Iowa. I stretched canvases and painted the sheds and crumbling storefronts on Main Street, standing at a portable easel in the hot dust with the stray dogs.

I guess the self I was at that time had a hand in painting the two works reproduced here. The first of these ends up being about wonder and innocence and loss, with its boy and butterfly and its breezy technique. The other work, which shows an abandoned shopping center just north of Hayden Avenue at the intersection of Shaw, is more pessimistic. The Shaw-Hayden area at one time saw considerable bustle and activity, and maybe will again someday. But East Cleveland is at low tide. The wreck of the not-distant past washes awkwardly up along the curbs, dragging over the potholes. I took a liberty in this second painting, moving a weird-looking standpipe from elsewhere in the city into the foreground of my version of the view. I intend it as a sort of sentinel, or a gate, hinting at the powers of the earth beneath, where the waiting legions of the future foregather.

"T

The industrial crucible of
Cleveland is my genesis. Now in
it's post smog days, what lives
on? Cold cobalt Lake Erie, the
wheeling gulls through grey skies
over a shining new city — call it
beautiful melancholy."

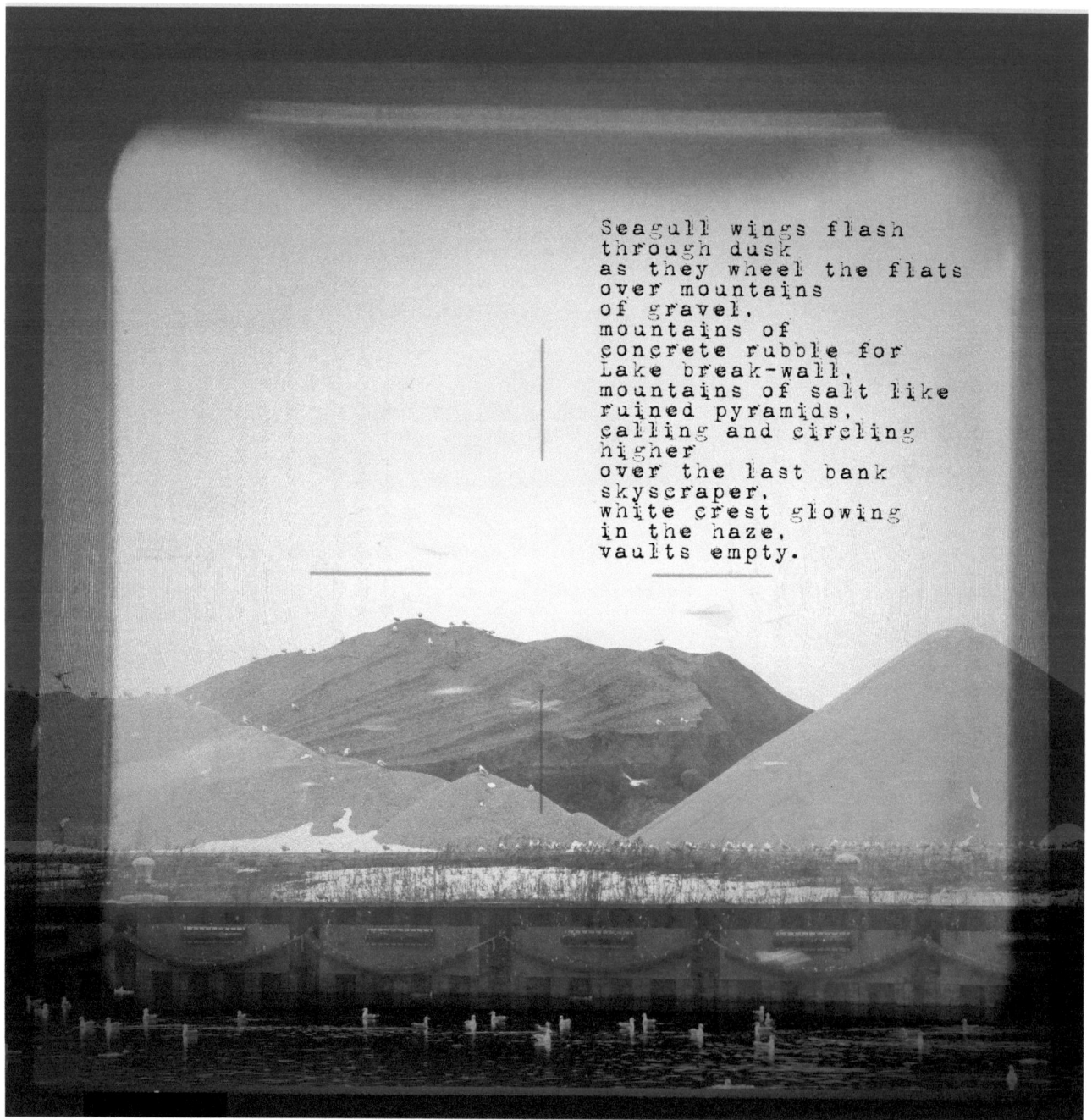

Seagull wings flash
through dusk
as they wheel the flats
over mountains
of gravel,
mountains of
concrete rubble for
Lake break-wall,
mountains of salt like
ruined pyramids,
calling and circling
higher
over the last bank
skyscraper,
white crest glowing
in the haze,
vaults empty.

Fig. 103 "Rusted Heart #6"

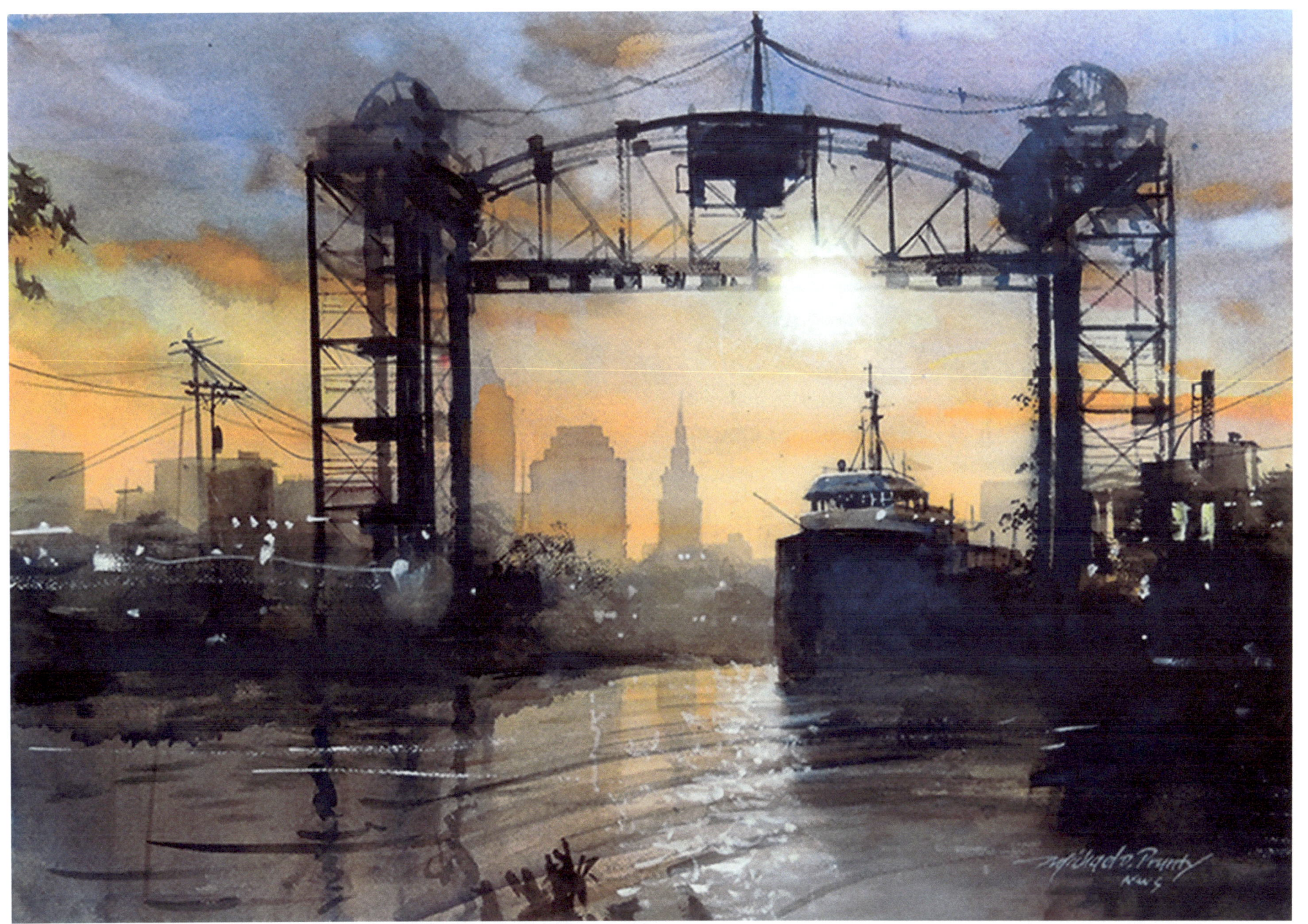

FIG. 104 "Columbus Road Lift Bridge"

"I

I get most of my inspiration from the parks here. There is a section of the MetroParks where Hogsback Lane and Valley Parkway intersect that have inspired at least a half-dozen paintings already. I have been fortunate to have been a Cleveland resident my entire life and gracious to have had a successful art practice over the last several years. I am extremely thankful for my supportive family and friends and the thriving arts scene!"

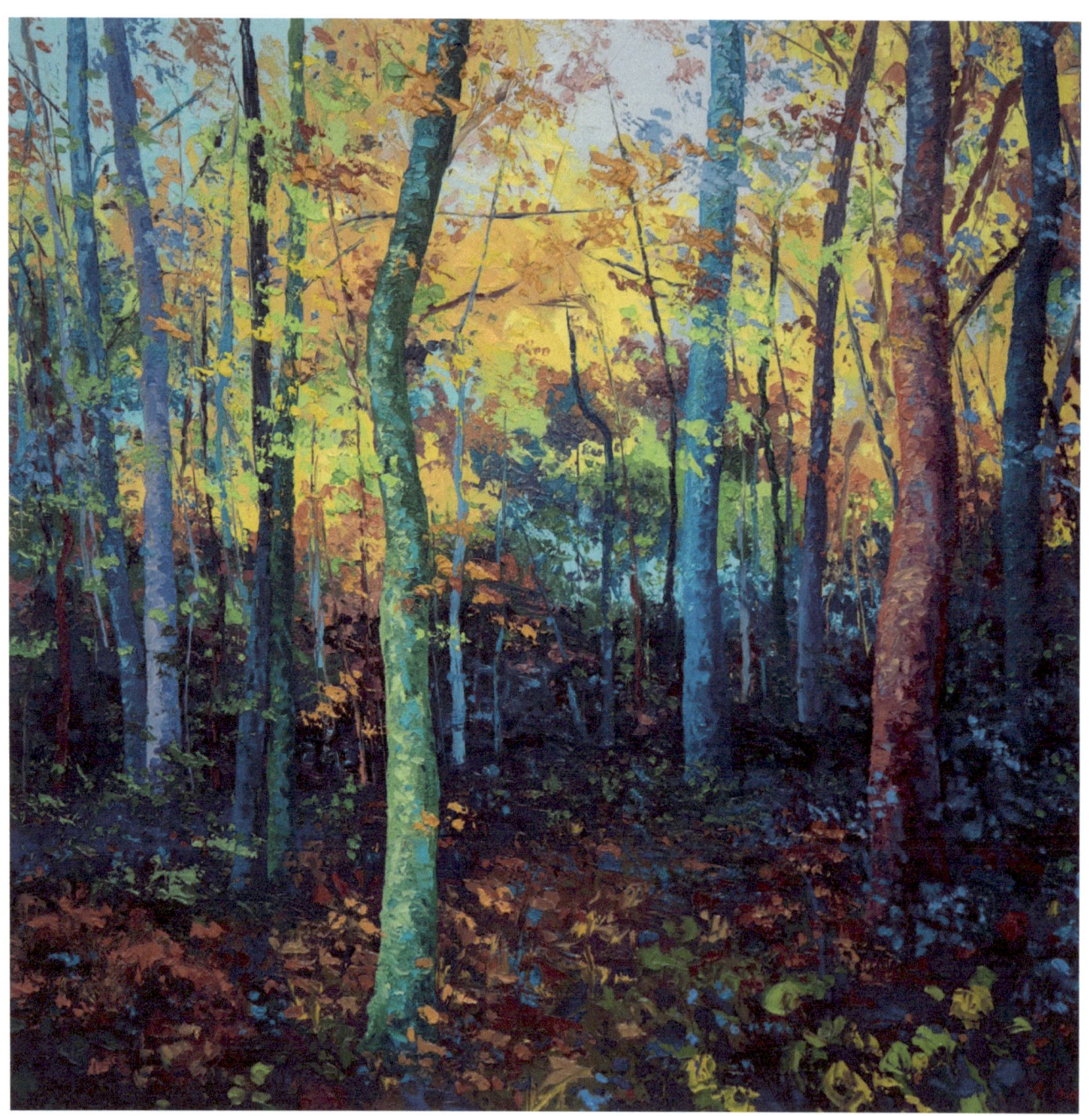

Fig. 105 "Hogsback Lane 1"

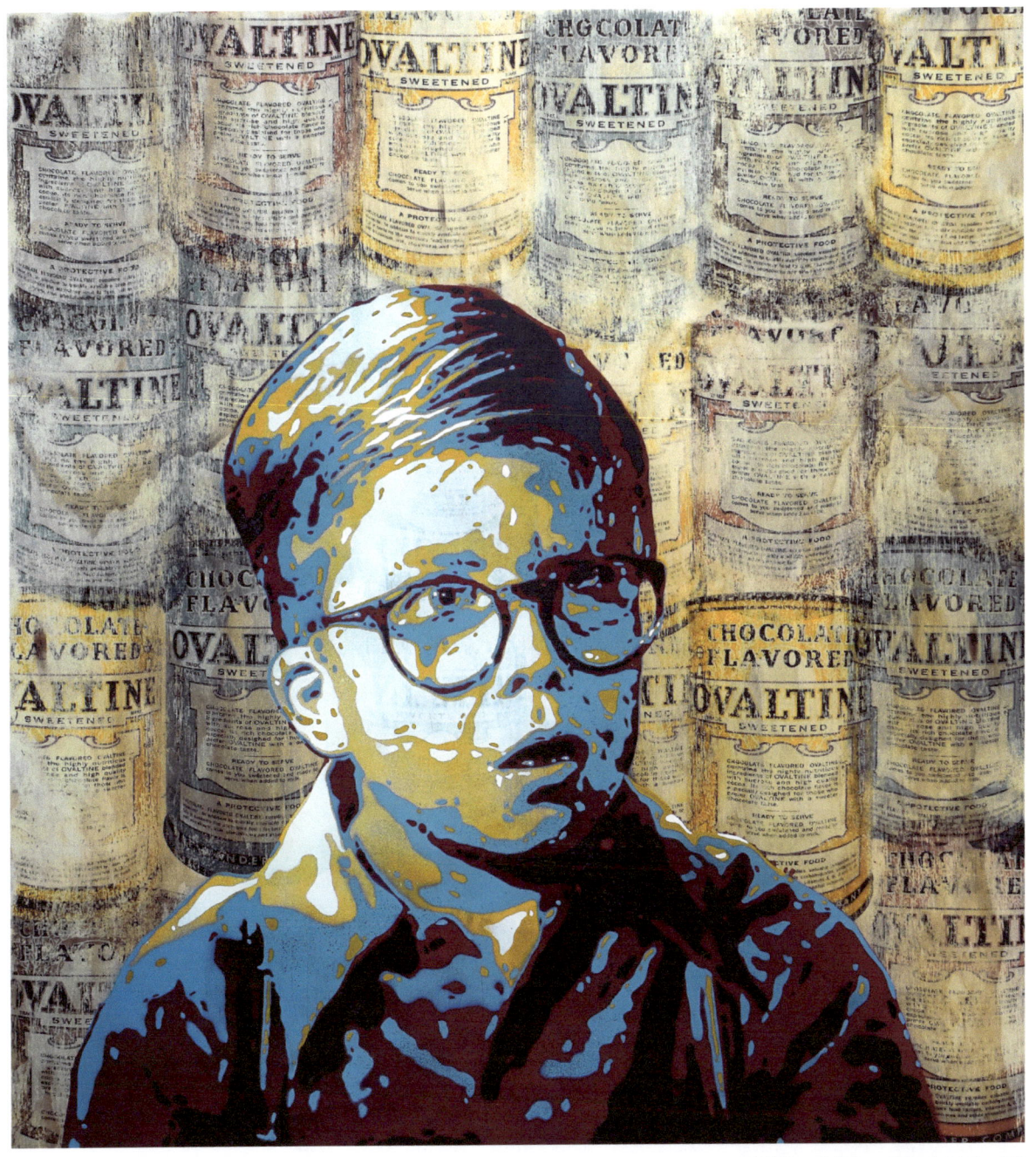

"I

I was born and raised in Cleveland and don't intend on ever leaving. I love the mix of culture, art, music, sports and food. The blue collar, down to earth vibe along with the endless events and activities make this a unique city. The strides in the last 25 years have been incredible making Cleveland a true comeback city."

FIG. 106   "Untitled"

"T

The self-professed "vinegar-obsessed" Chef pioneered this passion in the vast cellar of his century home, fermenting more than 300 gallons of single-origin, single-varietal, and barrel-aged wine, beer, and malt vinegars to launch Tavern Vinegar Co. in 2008. Tavern Vinegar is available online and in specialty shops around the country, including Publican Quality Meats in Chicago, Room Service in Cleveland, and Revival Market in Houston.

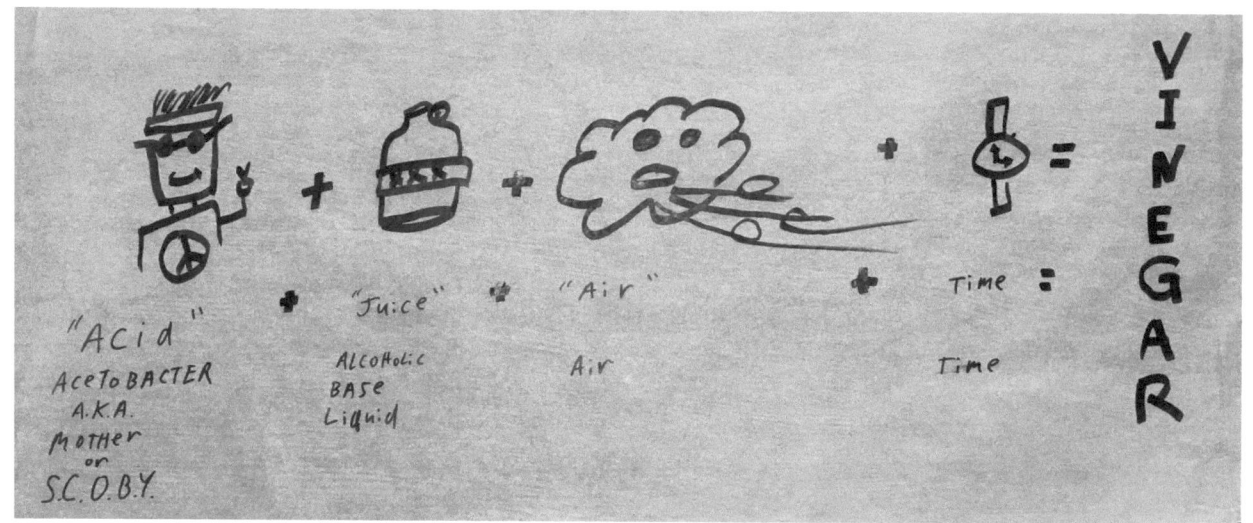

Fig. 107   "Untitled"

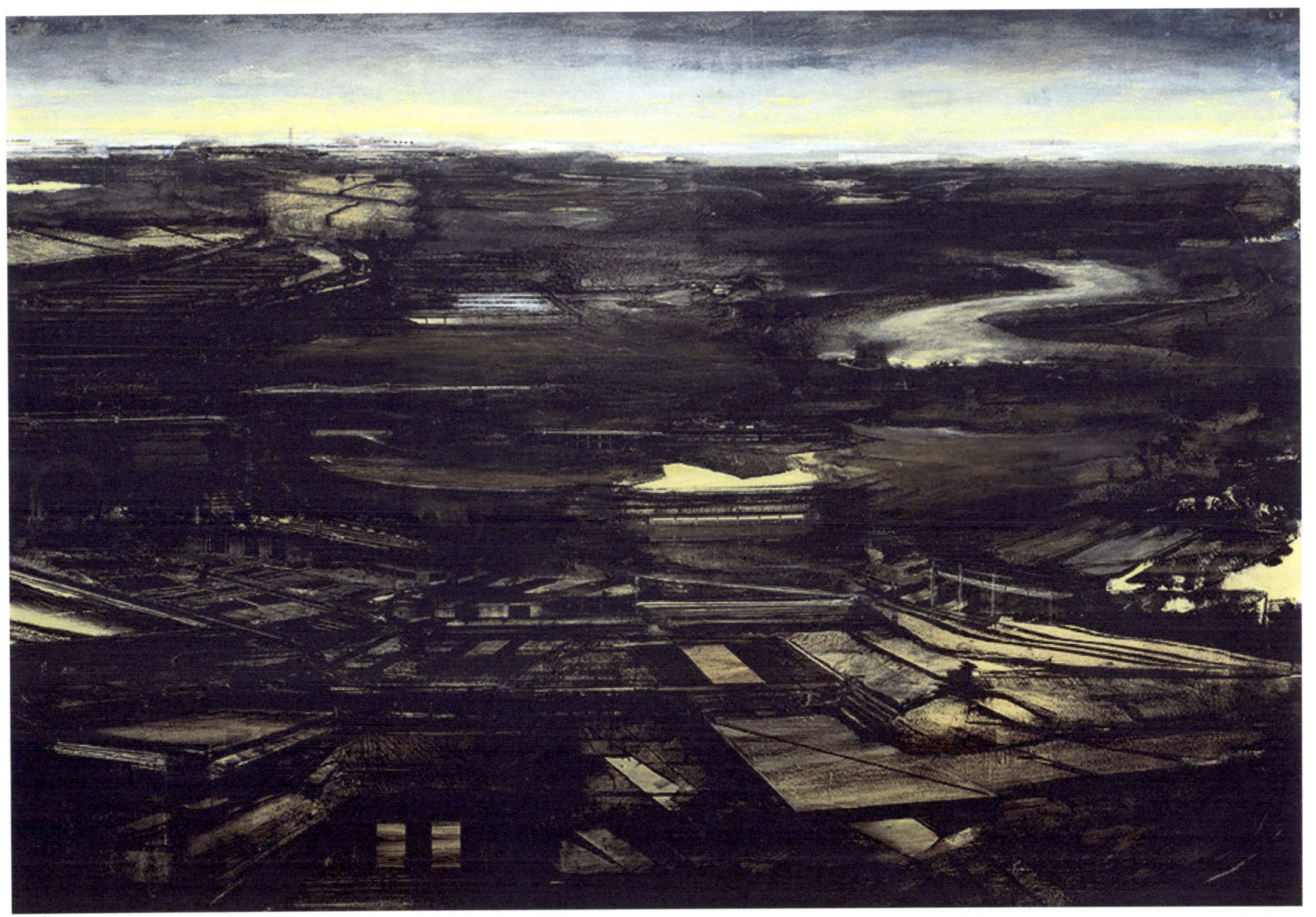

Fig. 108 "Promethian Web #2"

HERBERT ASCHERMAN, JR.

After 34 years of operation, I closed my Cleveland (Ohio, USA) portrait and social affairs studio in April of 2009. I am still active as a portrait, landscape and street photographer. Projects I have undertaken in the past several years include: * 250 - 8 x 10 platinum landscapes from my annual visits to the Forest at Fontainebleau, France * 350 portraits of villagers and their retail stores in the town of Kodaly, Kerala (southern) India* 750 platinum portraits of Northern Plains American Indians. Recent exhibitions (I hosted 6 one-man exhibitions in 2016) include a 65-image 40 Year Retrospective. I lead a group (50-years-old and older members) on the art and aesthetics of photography, publish on historical photographic subjects, curate exhibitions of Alternative Process Photographers, serve as editor of the Northern Ohio Bibliophilic Journal, curator for the Art at the School Gallery, and collect books on photography (over 2200 in my library). Throughout my career I have lectured to more than 200 organizations internationally and have exhibited in 150 venues in the US, Europe, India, Australia and Japan.

GLENN BASKIN

80 Proof Comix has been around since the late 80's in various forms/names. In 2007 it began a true storyline (Days of Bewilderment) featuring past characters put in a new situation. Taking bits, pieces, fragments, and experiences from working in the DD/Mental Health group home setting, I've worked on creating a comedic realistic look at the staff that work at these homes and some of the situations they face (without getting on a soap-box). Unfortunately the storylines in the comic that are less believable are more than likely true. Website: www.80proofcomix.blogspot.com/

MARY JO BOLE

Bole's work is skewed by a lineage to Victorian leftover culture experienced through her equally decaying hometown of Cleveland, and her adoptive, Columbus, with formative stints in The Netherlands and Lithuania. She has used earthly materials & processes: the impermanence of permanence, seen in stone, metal monuments in the Victorian crumbling cemeteries. She has made components of her work at existing or self-organized artist residencies and in relating industries. Website: www.maryjobole.com

COURTNEY BONNING

Courtney Bonning serial entrepreneur and pastry chef. Originally from Cleveland's west side, she moved to Napa Valley, CA and Seattle, WA, gained some perspective and moved back to beautiful Cleveland! Courtney is an alumni of Kent State University and The Culinary Institute of America. Courtney dominated and competed on Food Network's Cupcake Wars and Sweet Genius and won many other awards for her pastries. Courtney is currently a partner at Bigmouth Donut Company and is the proud former owner of BonBon Pastry & Cafe as well as the mastermind behind Cafe 55. Courtney can also be found preforming as Chef Chef BonBon at Cleveland Public Theater with the touring New York production of Conni's Avant Gard Restaurant when she's not napping.

MARK BRABANT

Mark Brabant is a freelance graphic designer, co-publisher of CLE DOG magazine and award-winning screen print artist. He exhibits and sells his work in shops, galleries, and art festivals around the midwest. He is a life-long Clevelander who currently resides in Avon. Mark's work can be seen at www.hoveringobject.com

JUDITH BRANDON

From the turbulent to the sublime, Judith Brandon is known for her signature craftsmanship and multilayered works on paper. Her work is a highly intuitive fusion of the emotional, natural and spiritual worlds. Harmonizing layers of ink, incised geometric patterns and hidden imagery with masterful drawing, the viewer is at first taken by the initial impact of the overall dynamic imagery. Upon closer attention we become engaged with subtle formations of cities, landscapes, geometry and text within spiritually nuanced themes. Her artistic language is eloquent and persistent and has garnered numerous national awards.
Website: www.jmbrandon.com

STEVE CAGAN

Steve's major work is in what is often called documentary, but what he prefers to call activist or socially-engaged photography; He has been centrally concerned with exploring strength and dignity in the everyday struggles of grassroots people to resist their pressures and problems, and contributing to those struggles through a photographic practice developed in close collaboration with those communities. Web site: www.stevecagan.com.

TIMOTHY CALLAGHAN

Timothy Callaghan is an artist living in Cleveland Ohio. He is the recipient of a 2015 Ohio Arts Council Individual Excellence Award. His paintings are in numerous private and public collections through out the state. He received his BFA from the Cleveland Institute of Art and an MFA from Kent State University in 2005. Callaghan has had numerous solo exhibitions at William Busta Gallery in Cleveland and has exhibited in group shows in New York, Philadelphia, Washington D.C., and Elmhurst, Illinois Additionally Callaghan authored One Painting a Day, a Quarry Books publication in 2013. Website: www.timothycallaghan.com

JOHN W. CARLSON

John W. Carlson, is an international artist based in Cleveland. John is a painter and educator and has been conducting workshops and classes in drawing and painting for over ten years. John has been accepted into numerous juried shows including the prestigious Butler Midyear Show at The Butler Museum of American Art and recently juried into The Ohio Arts Council Riffe Gallery First Juried Show in Columbus OH. In 2004 his charcoal drawing "Viewpoint" was purchased by the Erie Art Museum and entered into their permanent collection. John's work, "Visitation" was purchased and entered into The Massillon Museum's permanent collection in 2017. Website: www.johnwcarlsonstudio.com

DAVID CINTRON

David Cintron was born and raised in Cleveland, Ohio. He studied at Kent State University where he received a BFA in Graphic Design with a minor in Studio Art. Since 1990, David has been working as an artist, musician and designer in Cleveland. His visual art is created in a variety of mediums including paint, ink, print, collage and photography. David's current body of work consists of painted gestural abstractions inspired by the outside natural world as well as the inner spiritual world. Through dialogue between creative process and composition, works are intuitively and organically developed. Website: www.davecintron.com

REBECCA CROSS

Rebecca Cross employs the traditional techniques of Japanese shibori (a shape- and color-resist immersion dye process), a liquid and aleatory process from which subsequent compositional decisions derive. She is interested in the interplay between the ephemeral nature of life, the permanence of beauty, and the persistence of memory. Represented by Hedge Gallery in Cleveland, Ohio, Cross exhibits her work nationally and internationally. Website: www.rebeccastextiles.com

SARAH CURRY

Sarah Curry was born and raised in Cleveland and received her B.F.A. from Kansas City Art Institute with a major in Illustration. Her love of teaching both children and adults at The Cleveland Museum of Art inspired her to attain her Master's degree in Art Education from Case Western Reserve University. She received the Northeast Ohio Educator of the Year from The Ohio Art Education Association in the fall of 2017. She is a Regional Director for the Ohio Youth Art Governor's Show, an Adjunct Professor and Cooperating Teacher at Case Western Reserve University and a Reader for the Advanced Placement College Board. She is one of the founders and board members of Artful Cleveland, a non-profit organization providing studio space to artists and educational classes to the community. Her work is currently represented by Hedge Gallery in Cleveland, Ohio. She has spearheaded over ten public art installations in the Cleveland area collaborating with local artists, students and community members. Website: www.sarahcurryartist.com

CHRIS DEIGHAN

I am a 30 year old artist from Cleveland, Ohio. I have been drawing since I was 5 and have always like to create fictional cityscapes and landscapes. Website: www.artfromchris.com

EILEEN DORSEY

Eileen Dorsey was born in Cleveland, Ohio and studied art at Kent State University where she received a Bachelors in Fine Arts. Her work can be found in the collections of the Cleveland Art Association, Cuyahoga County Administration Building, Southwest General Hospital, and University Hospitals Case Medical Center. Dorsey has owned and operated the Eileen Dorsey Studio and Gallery located in the 78th Street Studios arts complex in the Gordon Square Arts District of Cleveland's Westside for the past 8 years. Eileen won Cleveland Scene Magazines Best Artist of 2018. Website: www.eileendorsey.com.

GARY AND LAURA DUMM

Laura who is primarily a painter, married cartoonist/artist Gary Dumm in 1971. In 1976 he met Cleveland's Harvey Pekar and embarked on a 30-year-plus collaboration producing that author's autobiographical comic "American Splendor." But his favorite artistic collaboration has been with his wife, and master of color, Laura. In 2013 they created and installed a 60'x 8' mural in Ohio City entitled "Our Love Letter To Cleveland." In 2013 they had a show that dealt with subjects like greed, GMO's, pollution etc. in a Pop-Art Surrealistic style. They are currently working on a series of large environmental paintings using classic horror monsters as the central figure. Laura says she will never retire and will paint till the end and Gary contends that he will continue drawing comics and cartoons until they pry the pencil from his cold, dead fingers. Websites are: www.dummart.org www.dummart.com

ELIZABETH EMERY

Elizabeth Emery earned an MFA from Alfred University and a BA in Art History from the University of Pennsylvania. Her work has been exhibited nationally and internationally and is included in public collections including The Cleveland Clinic, Progressive Insurance, Columbus Metropolitan Library, American Greetings,

Rockefeller Collection (Dresden, Germany), Metro Health, Westin Hotel Cleveland, Cleveland Artists Association, and Schein-Joseph International Museum of Ceramic Art. In 2017 and 2015 Emery received Ohio Arts Council Individual Excellence Awards, and in 2015 she received a Dave Bown Award of Excellence. In 2018 Emery was selected as one of 18 local, national, and international Artists-in Residence for FRONT International: Cleveland Triennial for Contemporary Art. Website: www.emeryspeaking.com

HILARY GENT

Hilary Gent has spent the last 8 years staging public exhibits, launching art walks, and planning elaborate receptions for individuals and organizations – all of which have transformed the way residents and visitors view our region. She was one of the first visionaries to plant roots in a forgotten century

warehouse, creating unforgettable art events through her space, HEDGE Gallery. What started as an underground activity attracting a few hundred people every quarter has grown to become a monthly art mob of thousands, called THIRD FRIDAYS, which according to Scene Magazine is "The Best Arts Event" in Cleveland.Hilary has been recognized by Scene Magazine's special section on People as someone who makes Cleveland the best place in America. She has earned awards and grants for her efforts to collaborate with nearby agencies, resulting in programming that has stimulated the entire Gordon Square Arts District. Website: www.hedgeartgallery.com/

MICHAEL GILL

Michael Gill came to printmaking as a writer, looking for ways to give stories to his own kids as they were learning to read. Therefore all his projects start with the words, but

evolve in the long process of making the woodcut pictures. He prints and teaches at Zygote Press and the Morgan Conservatory. He has had solo shows at William Busta Gallery, Tregoning and Company, and BAYarts, and his works are in collections at the Cleveland Clinic, Baker and Hostetler, Bainbridge Island Museum of Art (Seattle), Columbus College of Art and Design, Baylor University, and Cleveland Public Library Special Collections. He is editor and publisher of CAN Journal.

MICHAEL GREENWALD

Michael is a Cleveland based who's work has been exhibited extensively in both group and solo shows for over 20 years. His paintings are represented in numerous collections across the country. Born in Oxford, England and raised in Cleveland, Michael has lived in New York, California and Tokyo, Japan and is an avid traveler. He studied anthropology and sculpture at Skidmore College and glass blowing at the Cleveland Institute of art. Michael lives in Cleveland Heights and works at his studio in downtown Cleveland. Website: www. GreenwaldStudio.com

DEREK HESS

Derek Hess' unmistakably distinctive, emotionallty charged prints and drawings have been a force in both the music and art worlds for more than 25 years. Derek began creating promo flyers for live rock shows in Cleveland, OH in the 1980s. He soon began producing color silkscreens which gained the attention of a multitude of concert promoters and bands, and which are now in the permanent collections of the Grammy Museum, The Rock & Roll Hall of Fame, and the Louvre. In addition to countless album covers, apparel designs, and gallery shows all over the world, Derek has been featured on TLC, MTV, Fuse, VH1,

Alternative Press, Newsweek and Juxtapoz to name a few. The award-winning 2014 documentary Forced Perspective chronicles his art, life, and struggles with dual diagnosis. Derek has since become an outspoken voice for mental health and addiciton awareness, and has advocated for those who suffer with those issues by founding ACTING OUT!, which sponsors an annual arts festival and professional conference that aims to explore, without judgment, issues that arise in the junctions between mental illness, addiction, and creativity. Website: www.derekhess.com

RON HILL

Over the last 35 years, Ron Hill has been a cartoonist, illustrator, caricaturist, creative director, author, editor and high school teacher. Born in Cleveland and a graduate of the Art Institute of Pittsburgh, he is an award-winning editorial cartoonist for six Cleveland-area,

weekly newspapers, as well as an in-demand caricature quick-sketch entertainer. Ron is a member of the National Cartoonist Society, the American Association of Editorial Cartoonists, and the Northern Ohio Illustrators Society, and currently a managing partner at Act 3, LLC, a print,web and video design studio. Website: www.Act3creative.com, www.RonHillArtist.com

LESLIE EDWARDS HUMEZ

Leslie Edwards Humez is a Cleveland pop-surrealist who once upon a time had a day job in the publishing trades. She is the resident sculptor at Gallery Plus in 78th St. Studios and owner of PS...Preservation Silk, which produces luxury scarves from antique saris. Her fanciful sculpture is occasionally seen around town, and some of her imaginings have been exhibited on four continents. She teaches sculpture, thrives on collaboration, and often connects the dots between the literary and visual arts by translating metaphor, allusion or word gags into three dimensions. Leslie and her husband, metalsmith Nick Humez, brainstorm before breakfast and share no delusions about the scarcity of rational thought. They live in modest digs on the shoulders of the Grand River, and bend over backwards to humor their rescued ginger cat, Bob. Website: www. ClevelandArtSculpture.com

NINA HURYN

Nina Vivian Huryn grew up in Cleveland, Ohio and graduated from The Cleveland Institute of Art. Pieces of trash and objects she finds when walking around the city take on a new meaning when they are incorporated into the images on one of her tooled leather and wood assemblages. The technique Huryn has developed through the years draws the viewer in to examine the illustration, rarely realizing that the substrate is leather. To view a gallery of her work, link to her Etsy store, and read her blog please visit www.ninahuryn.com.

RYAN KACSANDY

Ryan Kacsandy is an illustrator and painter from the Cleveland area. When he's not working in restaurants or spending time with his family he draws webcomics with his friend. He is currently working on a horror comic titled the Saturday Night Slasher, but he also works on a self published book called the Abominations of Science. Website: www.thesaturdaynightslasher.com

LORI KELLA

Lori Kella was born in St. Joseph Michigan in 1974. She received a BFA from the Cleveland Institute of Art, and her MFA from Cornell University in 2001. Kella has exhibited in prestigious venues such as Galerie Drei and the Rathaus Galerie in Dresden Germany, The Print Center in Philadelphia, MOCA Cleveland, The Cleveland Museum of Art, Artspace in Raleigh, NC, Target Gallery in Alexandria, VA, and William Busta Gallery in Cleveland, OH. Lori Kella has received four OAC Individual Fellowships Awards, a full fellowship to attend Vermont Studio Center, and a Creative Workforce Fellowship from the Community Partnership for Arts and Culture & Cuyahoga Arts and Culture. Lori Kella lives in Cleveland, OH and she is currently a part-time Assistant Professor at Kent State University's School of Art. Website: www.lorikella.com

GEORGE KOCAR

George F. Kocar is an award-winning painter/illustrator who has had over fifty solo shows and over five hundred juried and invitational exhibitions across the United States. In the 1980's through the 2000's, he was a freelance illustrator who illustrated a weekly column for the Cleveland Plain Dealer. He had numerous illusion clients most notably The New York Times, The Washington Post, PLAYBOY, ESQUIRE, PSYCHOLOGY TODAY and numerous publications throughout the United States. His work is featured in AMERICAN ILLUSTRATION 2 and 3, and OUTSTANDING ILLUSTRATORS TODAY 2. His work is widely collected and is in numerous public and private collections most notably The Butler Institute of American Art, BP America, American Greetings, The Rock and Roll Hall of Fame and Museum, Ashland University, among others. Website: www.gkocar.com

SCOTT KRAYNAK

Born in the great city of Cleveland, Ohio, Scott has loved art and nature since going camping and canoeing and taking art classes at the Cleveland Museum of Art as a kid. Today Scott is a Park Ranger and professional artist, who has been represented by numerous galleries throughout the country, and has had extensive exhibits of his work from coast to coast. Scott's work is in permanent collections throughout the world. Though interested in creating and working with many different types of subject matter and mediums, Scott's main purpose and passion for his art is celebrating the natural world, from landscapes and bears to the little creatures often overlooked like lizards and salamanders.   Among other books like Animal Crackers, Scott also illustrated the newly released Truck Farm, based on King Corn director Ian Cheney's film of the the same name, and is one of the artists in the Harvey Award nominated graphic novel, The 27 Club. Of all of Scott's creations and accomplishments, The heART of Cleveland book stands out as his proudest and most personally fulfilling achievement. Website: www.scottkraynak.com

TIMOTHY LACHINA

Working as a graphic designer and art director for over thirty-five years have only sharpened my eye to see things differently. Life lessons have only encouraged me to see deeper meanings in things. I have logged hundreds of miles backpacking in places like the Grand Tetons, Yellowstone, the Appalachian Mountains or the high desert of the southwest. The sense of grandeur and silence is overwhelming in these places. With senses stimulated, these feelings and emotions will never leave me. With this awareness, I've tried to apply this way of thinking with finding common objects and make a compelling image. My ongoing body of work is themed as "structures in silence". Industrial landscapes, the desert, or water ways, or abandoned America scenes become looming elements that when confronted, the beauty of these structures is shown.

AARON LANGE

Aaron Lange is the creator of the underground comic series Trim, along with other titles published by the Comix Company of Vancouver. His art and writing have appeared in publications such as Mineshaft, Cinema Sewer, and Hustler. He is currently working on a book about Peter Laughner and the nascent Cleveland punk and underground scenes.

ROBERT LEDYARD

Robert Ledyard has been drawing and painting since early childhood. He received no formal instruction and learned almost everything from his mother and grandfather. He has published several comic books titled ORT with Diluvian enterprizes. He lives in Akron, Ohio with his family.

MICHELANGELO LOVELACE SR.

Michelangelo Lovelace Sr. born and raised in Cleveland, Ohio. As a child he began drawing to escape the hard reality of inner city life. In 1992 he moved into the Hodge Artist Complex Studio Apartment where he intermingle with other artist from all walks of life. While continuing to cultivate , develop his art. Lovelace was mentored by the late Rev. Albert Wagner for 13 years before his passing in 2007. In 2013 because of hard work and persistence, Lovelace won a Community Partnership For The Arts Fellowship, followed by a 2015 Cleveland Art Prize For Midcareer artist in the painter category. Then in 2017 winning a Ohio Art Council Individual Excellence award. Michelangelo Lovelace Sr. continues to paint about urban inner city life.

LIZ MAUGANS

Liz Maugans is the Director of YARDS Projects, and curator of the Dalad Collection at Worthington Yards in Cleveland's Warehouse District. She co-founded and is the Former Executive Director of Zygote Press, a non-profit printmaking studio also located in Cleveland, Ohio. She founded the Collective Arts Network, a quarterly journal, online resource and arts consortium that works to promote Northeast Ohio artists and organizations to a greater audience. She is founder of the Artist Trust, an open access collective arts project and artist registry to better connect Cuyahoga County Artists of all disciplines to each other and the greater community. Maugans was instrumental in bringing the Rooms-to-Let Project to Slavic Village and acts as a consultant and participant of the temporary installations that take place in foreclosed houses. Maugans chairs the Community Advisory Committee for FRONT International Triennial and is an active Board Trustee of the Collective Arts Network. Website: www.lizmaugans.com

RAY MCNIECE

Ray McNiece is the author of nine books of poems and monologues, most recently Love Song for Cleveland, a collaboration with photographer Tim Lachina. The Orlando Sentinel reporting on Ray's solo theater piece "Us — Talking Across America" at the Fringe Festival called him "a modern day descendant of Woody Guthrie. He has a way with words and a wry sense of humor." He toured Russia with Yevgeny Yevtushenko, appeared on Good Morning, Russia and performed at the Moscow Polytech, the Russian Poets' Hall of Fame where he was dubbed 'the American Mayakovski.' He has toured Italy twice with legendary beat poet Lawrence Ferlinghetti.

CHUCK MINTZ

Photography is Chuck's third career. He has degrees in Electrical Engineering, and has done course work in photography at Maine Media Workshop, Parsons, ICP and Cuyahoga Community College. He is a Life Trustee of Jewish Family of Cleveland advisory boards of the Cleveland Print Room and the Artists Archive of the Western Reserve and is a recipient of the Ohio Arts Council Individual Excellence Award for 2015 and 2017. Website: www.chuckmintz.com

BILLY NAINIGER

Billy Nainiger was born in Cleveland, OH and has been an aspiring artist since kindergarten. He is a graduate of The Cleveland Institute of Art with a major in illustration and minor in photography. Along the years his subject matter and styles have changed from the abstract to the realistic and everything in between. He is currently a mixed media artist that uses spray paint, pastel, cut up paper and found objects. The last few years he has been busy with solo shows with a pop art influence based on such themes as The Beatles, the films "The Big Lebowski" and "A Christmas Story." He is currently working on a solo show for September of 2018 based on Quentin Tarantino films. Billy is also a Cleveland Fireman and co-owner of E11even 2 gallery located at 78th St. Studios in Cleveland.

MICHAEL NEKIC

I was born and raised in Cleveland and have been working in the arts for the last 45 years. Initially a black and white fine art photographer, I transitioned from film and traditional darkroom processes to digital work in 1995 with help from my brother Mark, who gave me a copy of Picture Publisher. He convinced me that I could generate imagery, through the use of software in my computer, that would be impossible to create within the confines of a darkroom. A list of all of my Corporate clients and a history of shows and awards, along with many examples of my work for sale is available on my website: www.michaelnekic.com

FRANK OBLAK

I am a working artist currently living in the city of Euclid, Ohio, and my work in a varied in both mediums and themes, from illustration to sculpture, and from representational to abstract. Some of my artwork can be described as being dark, but at the same time I try to interject some humor into most of my work to keep it light and more universal. I hold degrees in Glass, Graphic Design, and Art Education, from both Kent State University and the University of Akron. Website: www.frankoblakart.com

FRANK ORITI

Frank Oriti was born in 1983 and raised in the suburbs of Cleveland, Ohio. He earned his BFA in Two-Dimensional Studies from Bowling Green State University in 2006 and returned to his hometown shortly after. For the next year and a half he worked at one of Cleveland's steel mills and continued painting in his spare time. In the fall of 2008, Oriti headed to Ohio University where he began creating work inspired by his past experience in the blue-collar work force. He graduated with his MFA in Painting in 2011. In 2013, Oriti was featured in The New York Times and was also the recipient of the Cleveland Arts Prize Emerging Artist Award. Recently, his work was featured in the prestigious BP Portrait Award in London's National Portrait Gallery. He currently lives and works in Cleveland, Ohio.

CLAUDIO ORSO-GIACONE

Claudio Orso makes woodblock prints, paper puppets, ceramic sculptures, and poems; coming from Turin, Italy, he has been living in Ohio for many years, got his MFA in printmaking at Bowling Green, and Zygote Press has been his art home in Cleveland, where he was also a resident artists at the Morgan Conservatory. He worked and taught art in a wide range of situations and events, national and international residencies, the Oberlin Big Parade and the Cleveland Parade the Circle, and a puppet opera performed by the Oberlin Conservatory orchestra. Since 2010 he has been coordinator of Apollo Outreach at Oberlin College, a college course workshop of media literacy focused on storytelling with young and elderly learners. Website: www.claudioorso.com/

MOSES PEARL

Pearl actively documented the people, architecture and flavor of life within Cleveland and the surrounding counties during his entire life. He did so with an individual gestural style that was appealing for its color, animation and joie de vivre. He was a talented draftsman and by his own admission began drawing compulsively by the age of 5 or 6. As a professional artist he was included in 19 Cleveland Museum of Art May Shows, where he won several awards. He was also accepted into 15 National Mid-Year exhibitions at the Butler Institute of American Art where he also won awards. Pearl valued education throughout life, both his own and what he could pass on to his many students over the course of a 30 year teaching career in the Cleveland public school system. His teaching extended into his family and influenced all of his children, two of which became accomplished artists in their own right.

STUART PEARL

Stuart Pearl is a Cleveland photographer who is active in the art community as a volunteer judge for several photography organizations and also Vice President of the Artists Archives of the Western Reserve (AAWR). His work has been exhibited in several Ohio museums as well as the Metroparks and he received "Best In Show" in the 2008 Butler Midyear Exhibit. Pearl's

photographs have been included in books of the Cleveland Museum of Art as well as other publications of that institution. As a volunteer photographer he has contributed work to the Cleveland Sight Center, Adoption Network, PBS Station WVIZ/WCPN Ideastream, Metroparks, and the Holden Arboretum. Website: www.pearlphoto.com/

BOB PECK AND R!CH CIHLAR

Bob Peck and R!ch Cihlar paint together under the name "Don't Panic!". Their abstract and pop art styles collide like a candy colored explosion of organized chaos. Each piece features a subject (by R!ch Cihlar) and abstract energy (by Bob Peck). Don't Panic! has been establishing its roots with live painting performances, murals, and gallery exhibitions around the city of Cleveland, and continues to thrive in the art scene. Bob's website: www. WakeMeWhenImProfound.com, R!ch's website: www.RichardCihlar.com

CHRISTINA SADOWSKI

Christina has been photographing Cleveland as well as the desert landscapes of Nevada for nearly a decade. Her photography professor in college told her to photograph what she loved and her work would always be interesting. She was born and raised in Cleveland and has always been passionate about the city. As a child, she used rolls and rolls of film photographing landmarks in the city. Years later, she realized photography was her artistic medium and began photographing the cityscape all over again. Most of her work shows a gritty, industrial side of Cleveland, that reminds her of the hard working class town it is. Her work can be seen in various shows as well as at e11even 2, the gallery she co-owns, within 78th Street Studios. Website: christinasadowskiphotography.com

KAREN SANDSTROM

Karen Sandstrom is a lifelong Clevelander who has been writing and drawing for about as long as she's been looking at Lake Erie. Her illustrations have been published by Boyds Mills Press (an imprint of Highlights), the Plain Dealer, Crain's Cleveland Business, Edible Cleveland and Ohio Authority. She earned her BFA in illustration from the Cleveland Institute of Art and her bachelor of science degree in journalism from Bowling Green State University. Website: http://www. karensandstrom.com

JONATHON SAWYER

As a proud Clevelander, award-winning Chef Jonathon Sawyer has worked tirelessly to help elevate the culinary landscape of his hometown with his distinctive restaurant concepts, including his newest venture, Trentina, an intimate, fine-dining restaurant focusing on the cuisine of Trentino in Northern Italy. His flagship, The Greenhouse Tavern,

is a French and seasonally inspired gastropub named by bon appetit as one of the "Best New Restaurants" in 2009; and Noodlecat, a mash-up noodle house focusing on local ingredients, sustainability, and top-tier ramen, with locations at Public Square and the historical West Side Market.

Prior to establishing his Cleveland businesses, Sawyer gained cooking experience across the country. The Pennsylvania Institute of Culinary Arts graduate began his culinary career at The Biltmore Hotel in Miami before working in New York City alongside Charlie Palmer at Kitchen 22. Chef Sawyer worked as chef de cuisine for his friend, colleague, and fellow native Clevelander, Michael Symon, and then became Chef Symon's executive chef at Parea in New York, receiving a three-star review from The New York Times. He moved back to Cleveland in 2007 to partner with a local entrepreneur to open Bar Cento, a modern Roman enoteca

in the Ohio City neighborhood. In 2010, Food & Wine magazine named him a "Best New Chef" and he's been nominated for a James Beard Foundation Award for Best Chef: Great Lakes in 2013 and 2014. In 2015 Chef Sawyer won the James Beard Foundation Award for Best Chef: Great Lakes. In addition, Chef Sawyer has made several national television appearances including Bizarre Foods America with Andrew Zimmern, Iron Chef America, Dinner Impossible, Unique Eats, and Best Thing I Ever Ate.

CORRIE SLAWSON

Corrie Slawson's work is a mixed media exploration of process rooted in the survey of land along her daily commute in Cleveland, OH. She builds landscapes that analyze development patterns related to population loss and land-use in places embedded with historical tension; imagery emerges through layers of printmaking, drawing, photography and painting. Her work has been exhibited in the US and internationally, including at The Toledo Museum of Art, Akron Art Museum, Centro Culturel de Tijuana and Galerie Module Drei in Dresden, Germany. She has also created projects for MOCA Cleveland, SPACES, Zygote Press and The Sculpture Center.Corrie received an individual artist excellence grant from the Ohio Arts Council in 2011 and has done international residencies in Tijuana, Mexico, Dresden, Germany and Champagne, France. She earned her BFA at Parsons School of Design (NY) and her MFA at Kent State University. Her work is represented by Shaheen Modern and Contemporary in Cleveland, and Metropolitan Gallery in Austin, Texas. Website: www.corrieslawson.com

PAM SPREMULLI

The only thing more cheerfully optimistic than Pam Spremulli is her art. Most well known for her unique interpretations of architectural landmarks from around the world and her Children's book "Letter Birds", Pam takes the familiar and makes it the exceptional. "The mouse is my brush, the monitor my canvas" is how she describes her technique, "and not to forget a little dab of fun!".Pam resides in Chagrin Falls, Ohio with her husband and two daughters. Website: www.pamspremulli.com

JUDY TAKÁCS

Born in New York City, raised and educated in Cleveland, Ohio, Takács is best known for her ongoing traveling portrait series and book, Chicks with Balls: Judy Takács paints unsung female heroes. A winner of nine Best in Show top awards over the past few years, her figurative work has been exhibited in solo, invitational and juried shows at the Butler Institute of American Art, Zanesville Museum of Art, Evansville Museum, ArtNEO Museum, Salmagundi and National Arts Clubs, and at art centers, colleges and galleries throughout the nation. Her paintings, projects and contributions to the figurative art world are noted on Wikipedia and Takács' goal as a painter is to depict a living, breathing soul whose presence invites viewers to linger, connect and think. Website: judytakacspaintspeople.com

NICK TAYLOR

Nick Taylor grew up in the suburbs of Cleveland and attended The Cleveland Institute of Art, Kent State (05), and Baldwin-Wallace College (08). Utilizing the city and surrounding areas (specifically the Metroparks) as inspiration, Nick explores the various types of landscape through color theory; often combining elements of abstraction and representation. Swatches of color often appear stacked or aligned, suggesting street signs, billboards, trains, old buildings, bricks, suburban houses, or patches of fields; breaking up the space similar to the patchwork of maps, fault lines, or natural phenomenon. The small scale work offers an intimate relationship to a place or moment. Website: www.nicktaylorart.com

BRINSLEY TYRRELL

Brinsley was Professor of Sculpture at Kent State University for 28 years, after which he was awarded the title Professor Emeritus upon retirement in 1996. Simultaneously, Brinsley's art career earned wide recognition and respect in the areas of sculpture, drawing, enamels and ceramics; his career continues to this day. In addition to his personal work, he has completed over forty commissions and public art projects, spanning more than 50 years. In 2011, Brinsley was awarded the Cleveland Arts Prize for Lifetime Achievement for Visual Arts. Brinsley has been an active supporter and participant in the cultural institutions of Ohio, having served as Member, Chair and President of the Board of Trustees of SPACES (Cleveland), a member of the Art in Transit committee for the Cleveland Regional Transit Authority, and on the Arts in Public Places panel for the Ohio Arts Council, among others. His work resides in dozens of corporate and private collections and museums, including the Gund Foundation, the Cleveland Clinic Foundation, the Akron Art Museum, Oberlin College and the Governor's Residence in Columbus, Ohio. Website: artistbrinsleytyrrell.com

JEREMY UMANSKY

Jeremy Umansky is a zymologist, forager, and chef/owner of Larder Delicatessen & Bakery. His interests include fungalytic enzymes, making charcuterie, and spending time with his wife Allie, daughter Emilia, and dog Baba Ganoush.\

DOUGLAS MAX UTTER

Douglas Max Utter was born in Cleveland, Ohio in 1950. After high school he studied Classical languages and literature at Case Western Reserve University, before moving to New York City where he spent three years painting and writing in the late 1970's. Following the death of his father in 1980 Utter returned permanently to Cleveland and married the sculptor L. Hyler. His painting began to attract notice in 1987 when he won the Cleveland Museum of Art's May Show Best Painting Award. In the 1990's and after, Utter's manner and materials have shifted several times, but his subject matter remains rooted in figural depiction and the mythological or biblical scenes central to the history of European painting. His work has been shown in Cleveland and New York, Phoenix and Augsburg, Germany. He also has published reviews and essays about the arts, from 1988 through the present. Over the years Utter received three Ohio Arts Council Fellowships, was awarded a CPAC Fellowship in 2011, and the Cleveland Arts Prize for Lifetime Achievement in 2013. Website: douglasutter.com

LAILA VOSS

Laila Voss is best known for multi-media installation, performance, and sculpture in the United Sates and abroad. Her work has been featured in several major art institutions and is included in both private and corporate art collections. Voss has been the recipient of grant and residency awards such as the Ohio Arts Council Individual Excellence, the, Cleveland Neighborhood Summit Volunteer of the Year Award, and the FCCA Prague, Czech Republic. She has completed a number of public art projects in the Cleveland area, curated exhibitions, directed galleries, has taught at numerous NEO educational intitutions, and serves on a non-profit board. Since 2016 Laila Voss has been Executive Director at Art House, Inc. She received her BFA from Ohio University and her MFA from Kent State University.

RA WASHINGTON

Is a composer/ writer living in Cleveland's West side and the author of 28 books most recently CITI (Red Giant Books) and The Paris Notebooks (Nightballet Press). He currently composes for the afrofuture outfit, Mourning [A] BLKstar.

EVIE ZIMMER

Evie Zimmer is an American artist creating and teaching in Cleveland, Ohio. Evie's work has been described as a "strange loop" of process and product. Her oil paintings radiate an inherent energy field not unlike traditional mandalas with acidic colors transforming into soothing pastels, and geometric patterns melting into exotically organic shapes. Recently, Evie's paintings have become more floral and symmetric yet still maintain her unique and recognizable abstract style. Evie is quite active in the arts community both locally and nationally. Her work has been shown, sold, and published across the country including New York City, Art Basel Miami, Palm Springs, Ca., various publications and online shows, and digital billboard displays in Baltimore and on Sunset Blvd in Hollywood. Evie is constantly creating new work from her studio where she welcomes visitors and students. Website: eviezzz.wixsite.com/eviezimmer

DIANE ZIZKA

Diane Zizka is a visual artist who grew up in Cleveland and has been immersed in art since she was a child by the influence of family members. She also received formal training at Cleveland State University where she earned her BA in studio art 2017. Being the daughter of a factory worker has influenced her appreciation of the grittier aspects of Cleveland and the nostalgia it brings. Zizka works in a wide range of mediums such as painting, sculpture and photography and currently resides in Las Vegas, Nevada, where she continues her artistic practices.

CLEVELAND ART HISTORY REFERENCES

Ohio Art and Artists   Edna Maria Clark   Garrett & Massie   1932

Ohio Indian Trails   Frank Wilcox   The Gates Press   1933

The Henry G. Keller Memorial Exhibition   Cleveland Museum of Art   1950

The William Sommer Memorial Exhibition   Cleveland Museum of Art   1950

Carl Gaertner Memorial Exhibition   Cleveland Museum of Art   1953

The Ohio Canals   Frank Wilcox/William McGill   Kent State University Press   1969

Ohio Indian Trails   Frank Wilcox/William McGill   Kent State University Press   1970

The Several Dimensions of William Sommer   Hunter Ingalls   Columbia University   1970

Federal Art in Cleveland 1933-43   Karal Ann Marling   Cleveland Public Library   1974

A Study in Regional Taste: The May Show 1919-75   Cleveland Museum of Art   1977

The Memories of an American Impressionist: Abel Warshawsky   Ben Bassham   Kent State University Press   1980

Paul B. Travis: Africa 1927-28   Ann Boger   Cleveland Museum of Art   1982

Print-a-Month: Cleveland Printmakers 1932-36   Margaret Campbell   John Carroll University   1982

Cleveland Institute of Art: The First Hundred Years   Nancy Coe Wixom   CIA   1983

August F. Biehle, Jr: Ohio Landscapes   Dr Ellen Landau   CWRU   1986

Henry Keller's Summer School in Berlin Heights   Rotraud Sackerlotzky   Cleveland Artists Foundation   1991

William Sommer: Cleveland's Early Modern Master   Elizabeth McClelland   John Carroll University   1992

F. C. Gottwald and the Old Bohemians   Cleveland Artists Foundation   1993

Fine Arts in Cleveland: An Illustrated History   Holly Witchey/John Vacha   Indiana University Press   1994

Triumph of Color and Light: Ohio Impressionists and Post-Impressionists   James Keny/Nannette Maciejunes   Columbus Museum of Art/Keny Galleries   1994

The Encyclopedia of Cleveland History   John Grabowski/David Van Tassel   Indiana University Press   1996

Transformations in Cleveland Art 1776-1946   William Robinson/David Steinberg   Cleveland Museum of Art   1996

A Brush with Light: Watercolor Painters of Northeast Ohio   Cleveland Artists Foundation   1998

Carl Gaertner: A Story of Earth and Steel   Cleveland Artists Foundation   2000

Paul Travis 1891-1975   Henry Adams   Cleveland Artists Foundation   2001

Drawn to Perfection: Jean and Paul Ulen and the Slade School Legacy in Cleveland   Marianne Berardi/Christopher Bedford   Cleveland Artists Foundation   2003

Great Lakes Muse: American Scene Painting in the Upper Midwest 1910-60   Patricia Glasscock/Michael D. Hall   Flint Institute of Arts   2003

Edris Eckhardt: Visionary and Innovator in American Studio Ceramics and Glass   Henry Adams/Kirk Nelson   Cleveland Artists Foundation   2006

Masterworks   Cleveland Artists Foundation   2009

Against the Grain: Modernism in the Midwest   Christine Shearer/William Robinson   Massillon Museum   2010

Out of the Kokoon   Henry Adams   Cleveland Public Library   2011

Painting in Pure Color: Modern Art in Cleveland before the Armory Show (1908-13)   Henry Adams/ Lawrence Waldman   2013

A Great Joy: The Women's Art Club of Cleveland   Marianne Berardi   Lawrence Waldman/Marianne Berardi   2014

ARTIST CHRONOLOGY

Allen Smith, Jr (1818-1890)

George Clough (1824-1901)

Henry Church (1836-1908)

Archibald Willard (1836-1918)

William Holbrook Beard (1840-1900)

R. Way Smith (1840-1900)

DeScott Evans (1847-1898)

John Semon (1852-1917)

Adam Lehr (1853-1924)

Caroline Williams (1855-1931)

Otto Bacher (1856-1909)

John Kavanagh (1857-1898)

Frederick Gottwald (1858-1941)

Ora Coltman (1860-1940)

Herman Matzen (1861-1938)

May Ames (1863-1946)

Henry Turner Bailey (1865-1931)

Charles DeKlyn (1865-1958)

Louis Loeb (1866-1909)

William Sommer (1867-1949)

Max Bohm (1868-1923)

Nina Waldeck (1868-1943)

William Edmondson (1868-1966)

Henry Keller (1869-1949)

Louis Rorimer (1872-1939)

Horace Potter (1873-1948)

Grace Kelly (1877-1950)

Julia Severance (1877-1972)

Frank Jirouch (1878-1970)

George Adomeit (1879-1967)

Anna Pfenninger (1880-1950)

Mary Susan Collins (1880-1967)

Mary Hortense Webster (1881-1964)

Clara Deike (1881-1964)

Walter Sinz (1881-1966)

Julia McCune Flory (1882-1971)

William Donahey (1883-1953)

Abel Warshawsky (1883-1962)

Mildred Watkins (1883-1968)

Allen Cole (1883-1970)

Rudolph Ruzicka (1883-1978)

R. Guy Cowan (1884-1957)

Hugo Robus (1884-1964)

Orville Peets (1884-1968)

August Biehle (1885-1979)

Norris Rahming (1886-1959)

Alexander Warshawsky (1887-1945)

Sandor Vago (1887-1946)

Frank Wilcox (1887-1964)

Carl Binder (1887-1968)

William Eastman (1888-1950)

Otto Ege (1888-1951)

I. V. Volper (1888-1985)

Belle Hoffman (1889-1961)

William Zorach (1889-1966)

Clara McClean (1889-1972)

Walter Brough (1890-1978)

Max Kalish (1891-1945)

George Ault (1891-1948)

Elsa Vick Shaw (1891-1974)

Paul Travis (1891-1975)

Florence Bard Wilcox (1891-1977)

Glenn Shaw (1891-1981)

Carl Broemel (1891-1984)

Rolf Stoll (1892-1978)

Charles Burchfield (1893-1967)

Paul Ulen (1893-1976)

Alexander Blazys (1894-1963)

Cora Millet Holden (1895-1938)

William Grauer (1895-1985)

Hugh Seaver (1896-1959)

Louise Morris (1896-1971)

Wray Manning (1896-1976)

John Csosz (1897-1969)

Paul Shively (1897-1987)

Carl Gaertner (1898-1952)

Manuel Silberger (1898-1968)

Sara Mattson Anliot (1898-1991)

Jolan Gross-Bettelheim (1900-1972)

Antimo Beneduce (1900-1975)

Jean Ulen (1900-1988)

Norbert Lenz (1900-1992)

Joseph Jicha (1901-1960)

Kae Dorn Cass (1901-1971)

Willard Combes (1901-1984)

Marion Bryson (1902-1987)

Lawrence Blazey (1902-1999)

Thelma Frazier Winter (1903-1977)

Florence Sampson (1903-1978)

Mabel Hewit (1903-1984)

Margaret Bourke-White (1904-1971)

Russell Limbach (1904-1971)

Milton Fox (1904-1971)

Kenneth Bates (1904-1994)

Alfred Wands (1904-1998)

Clarence Carter (1904-2000)

Thelma Frazier Winter (1905-1977)

Stanley Clough (1905-1977)

Louis Bosa (1905-1981)

Charles Campbell (1905-1985)

William McVey (1905-1995)

Edris Eckhardt (1905-1998)

Edwin Kaufman (1906-1939)

Joseph Egan (1906-1962)

Kalman Kubinyi (1906-1973)

William Gisch (1906-1989)

Viktor Schreckengost (1906-2008)

Leza McVey (1907-1984)

Dorothy Rutka Porter (1907-1985)

Sheffield Kagy (1907-1989)

Claude Conover (1907-1994)

Stevan Dohanos (1907-1994)

Doris Hall Kubinyi (1907-2000)

Honore Guilbeau (1907-2006)

H. Edward Winter (1908-1976)

Elmer Brown (1909-1971)

LeRoy Flint (1909-1991)

Elmer Novotny (1909-1997)

Russell B. Aitken (1910-2002)

Raphael Gleitsmann (1910-1995)

Samuel Bookatz (1910-2009)

John Teyral (1912-1999)

Peter Paul Dubaniewicz (1913-2003)

Charles Sallee (1913-2006)

William E. Smith (1913-1997)

Hughie Lee-Smith (1915-1999)

Martin Linsey (1915-2010)

Hazel Janicki (1918-1976)

OWNERSHIP AND ILLUSTRATION CREDITS

All works in this book are from the collections and individuals below. Photographs of illustrations in this book may not be reproduced without permission from the owners and/or artists.

Fig. 1   Horses in Field, 1940's. Paul Ulen. Watercolor. 20x28 in. Courtesy of WGS Productions (William G. Scheele)

Fig. 2   Wash Day, 1930's. Jean Ulen. Aquatint etching. 8x11 in. Courtesy of WGS Productions

Fig. 3   The Dreamer, 1919. Frederick Gottwald. Oil on canvas. 40x28 in. Courtesy of ARTneo

Fig. 4   View of The Cleveland Museum of Art, 1916. Frederick Gottwald (American, 1860-1941). Oil on canvas; framed: 78.2 x 67.4 x 8.9 cm (30 3/4 x 26 1/2 x 3 1/2 in.); unframed: 61 x 50.8 cm (24 x 20 in.). The Cleveland Museum of Art, Bequest of Virginia Hubbell 1997.310

Fig. 5   Hillside in Berlin Heights, 1921-22. August Biehle. Gouache watercolor. 18x24 in. Courtesy of ARTneo

Fig. 6   Springtime, French Countryside. Abel Warshawsky. Oil on canvas. 18x22 in. Courtesy of Cynthia Maciejewski/ Aspire Auctions, Inc.

Fig. 7   Church Bells Ringing, Rainy Winter Night, 1917. Charles Burchfield (American, 1893-1967). Watercolor and gouache over graphite; sheet: 77.2 x 50 cm (30 3/8 x 19 5/8 in.); secondary support: 77.5 x 50 cm (30 1/2 x 19 5/8 in.). The Cleveland Museum of Art, Gift of Mrs. Louise M. Dunn in memory of Henry G. Keller 1949.544 Reproduced with permission from the Charles E. Burchfield Foundation

Fig. 8   Wisdom and Destiny, 1913. Henry Keller (American, 1869-1949). Oil on canvas; framed: 94.6 x 120 x 5.8 cm (37 3/16 x 47 3/16 x 2 1/4 in.); unframed: 76.5 x 101.9 cm (30 1/16 x 40 1/16 in.). The Cleveland Museum of Art, Gift of Mrs. Henry A. Everett for the Dorothy Burnham Everett Memorial Collection 1928.580

Fig. 9   Bal Masque Invitation, 1925. Joseph Jicha. Commercial lithograph. 38x25 in. Courtesy of Cynthia Maciejewski/Aspire Auctions, Inc.

Fig. 10   Otis Litho Ad, 1924. William Sommer. Commercial lithograph. 9x6 in. Courtesy of WGS Productions.

Fig. 11   Bal Masque Invitation-Midas, 1927. Joseph Jicha. Commercial lithograph. 38x25 in. Courtesy of Cynthia Maciejewski/Aspire Auctions, Inc.

Fig. 12   The Pool (recto); Landscape (verso), c. 1916-1919. William Sommer. Oil on panel; framed: 99.7 x 79.4 x 6.4 cm (39 1/4 x 31 1/4 x 2 1/2 in.); unframed: 80.7 x 60 cm (31 3/4 x 23 9/16 in.). The Cleveland Museum of Art, Silver Jubilee Treasure Fund 1945.46

Fig. 13   Rhythmic Movement, 1956. Clara L. Deike (American, 1881-1964). Oil on board; unframed: 60.4 x 50 cm (23 3/4 x 19 5/8 in.). The Cleveland Museum of Art, Cleveland Traveling Exhibitions Fund 1957.176

Fig. 14   Contemplation, 1946. Hazel Janicki. Casein on board. 14.5 x 23.5 in. Courtesy of WGS Productions.

Fig. 15   Riding the Crane, c. 1926. Max Kalish. Bronze; overall: 51.4 x 32.4 x 15.3 cm (20 3/16 x 12 3/4 x 6 in.). The Cleveland Museum of Art, Gift of Friends of the Artist 1946.434

Fig. 16   The Furnace, 1924. Carl Gaertner (American, 1898-1952). Oil on canvas; framed: 110.5 x 110.8 cm (43 1/2 x 43 9/16 in.); unframed: 88.9 x 104.8 cm (35 x 41 1/4 in.). The Cleveland Museum of Art, Gift of The Huntington National Bank 2013.66

Fig. 17   Terminal Tower 6, 1927-32. Louis Rosenberg. Drypoint etching. 7.5x11.5 in. Courtesy of WGS Productions

Fig. 18   Farm Scene in Hills, 1930's. William Grauer. Watercolor. 14x20 in. Courtesy of Cynthia Maciejewski/Aspire Auctions, Inc.

Fig. 19   Farm on the Northfield Road. William Sommer. Watercolor; The Cleveland Museum of Art, Gift of Dr. and Mrs. Theodor W. Braasch 1963.616

Fig. 20   Milliken at the Century of Progress, Chicago, 1940. Clarence Holbrook Carter. Oil on canvas; framed: 90.2 x 125 x 9 cm (35 1/2 x 49 3/16 x 3 1/2 in.); unframed: 74 x 109.5 cm (29 1/8 x 43 1/16 in.). The Cleveland Museum of Art, Mr. and Mrs. William H. Marlatt Fund 1992.6

Fig. 21   My First View of the Congo Forest, 1930. Paul B. Travis (American, 1891-1975). Oil on canvas; unframed: 76.9 x 101.9 cm (30 1/4 x 40 1/16 in.). The Cleveland Museum of Art, Hinman B. Hurlbut Collection 2083.1930 © Estate of Elisabeth Travis Dreyfuss

Fig. 22   Tiger & Bullock, 1951. Paul B. Travis. Watercolor. 21x29 in. Courtesy of ARTneo

Fig. 23   The Old Market, Cleveland, 1920. Frank Wilcox (American, 1887-1964). Gouache; overall: 73 x 57.8 cm (28 11/16 x 22 3/4 in.). The Cleveland Museum of Art, Purchased with funds given by friends of the May Show 1920.279 © Wilcox Family Collection LLC

Fig. 24   The Ohio Canals, 1969. Frank Wilcox. Illustrated book. 9x11.5 in. Courtesy of WGS Productions

Fig. 25   Ohio Indian Trails, 1970. Frank Wilcox. Illustrated book. 9x 11.5 in. Courtesy of WGS Productions.

Fig. 26   Cocktails and Cigarettes Punch Bowl, 1931. Viktor Schreckengost (American, 1906-2008), Cowan Pottery Studio (American, 1921-31). Glazed earthenware with engobe, sgraffito; diameter: 42.8 cm (16 13/16 in.); overall: 23.5 cm (9 1/4 in.). The Cleveland Museum of Art, Gift of Elizabeth Mather McMillan 2000.128

Fig. 27   Female Bust. Walter Sinz. Red Earthenware. 6" H. Courtesy of Rachel Davis Fine Arts

Fig. 28   Ol' Peckerwood, 1939. Elmer William Brown (American, 1909-1971). Linoleum cut; The Cleveland Museum of Art, Gift of The Print Club of Cleveland 1939.240

Fig. 29   Old Grizzly, 1934. William McVey. Limestone sculpture. 48" H. Courtesy of The Cleveland Museum of Natural History.

Fig. 30   Soldiers and Sailors Monument, 1930's. Samuel Popkins. Etching. 6x8 in. Courtesy of WGS Productions.

Fig. 31   Prehistoric Animals, 1950's. William E. Scheele. Illustrated book. 12x9 in. Courtesy of WGS Productions.

Fig. 34   Devonian Incident, 1993. William E. Scheele. Acrylic on board. 48x72 in. Courtesy of The Cleveland Museum of Natural History.

Fig. 35   Winter Birds, 1960's. William E. Scheele. Watercolor. 10x9 in. Courtesy of WGS Productions.

Fig. 36   Escape to Sky, 2017. Elizabeth Emery. Plaster, silicone, thread. 10x7.5x7 in. Copyright Elizabeth Emery. Photo Credit: Jerry Birchfield

Fig. 37   Horrible that ate Cleveland, 2004. Derek Hess. Pen and acrylic. 14x24 in. Copyright Derek Hess

Fig. 38   Harvey P. As Sisyphus, 2008. Gary and Laura Dumm. Markers and ink. 10x16 in. Copyright Gary and Laura Dumm

Fig. 39   Our Love Letter to Cleveland, 2013. Gary and Laura Dumm.   Copyright Gary and Laura Dumm

Fig. 40   Cedar Center Hardware, 2016. Chuck Mintz. Photograph. 32x40 in.   Copyright Chuch Mintz

Fig. 41   CLE, 2016. Pam Spremulli. Graphic illustration. 37x19 in.   Copyright Pam Spremulli.

Fig. 42   Cleveland, 2014. Pam Spremulli. Graphic illustration. 32x32 in.   Copyright Pam Spremulli

Fig. 43 Under the Stadium, 2015. Lori Kella. 30x40 in. Copyright Lori Kella

Fig. 44   Looking for Artificial Reef, 2015. Lori Kella. 22.5x30 in. Copyright Lori Kella

Fig. 45 Mr. Jingeling, 2017. Aaron Lange. Ink on bristol. 1x11 in. Copyright Aaron Lange

Fig. 46 Peter Laughner, 2017. Aaron Lange. Ink on bristol. 11x17 in. Copyright Aaron Lange

Fig. 47 Cleveland 1988, 2017. Jason Z. Pott. Pen, ink, marker. 16x20 in. Copyright Jason Z. Pott

Fig. 48   Photograph. Copyright Jeremy Umanski

Fig. 49 Totally Spent, 2013. Liz Maugans. Found object/neon. Copyright Liz Maugans

Fig. 50 ISG/ Mittal Steel's head safety officer Tom Krizman, 2003. Herb Ascherman. Black and white photograph. Copyright Herb Asherman.

Fig. 51, 52, 53 and 54   Spark, 1997. Stash Kowalski, Super-Host, The Ghoul, 2016. Ron Hill. Watercolor. Copyright Ron Hill

Fig. 55a, 55b   The Chief, 2015. Leslie Edwards Humez. Porcelain/cellulose clay, baseball, acrylic paint. 6 1/16 x 9 1/16 x 11 1/4 in. Copyright Leslie Edwards Humez

Fig. 56   Book Lovers Map, 2016. Karen Sandstrom. Adobe illustrator. 16x20 in. Copyright Karen Sandstrom.

Fig. 57   Summer at the Rock Hall, 2014. George Kocar. Acrylic on canvas. 16x20 in. Copyright George Kocar.

Fig. 58   Blue Water Still (The Sirens Series).   Sarah Curry. Charcoal and watercolor on panel. 48x24 in. Copyright Sarah Curry

Fig. 59 and 60   Forest City 1 and Forest City 2, 2016. Mary Jo Bole. Gouache, coffee, photo retouch paint. 18x24 in. Copyright Mary Jo Bole.

Fig. 61 Arctic Blast, 2016. Frank Oblak. Acrylic on watercolor paper. 19 1/2 x 19 1/2 in. Copyright Frank Oblak

Fig. 62   Steel Mills, Quigley Road. Steve Cagan. Black and white photograph. 19x12 1/4 in. Copyright Steve Cagan

Fig. 63   Steggie the Road Mender, 2017. Scott Kraynak. Colored pencil. 20x30 in. Copyright Scott Kraynak

Fig. 64   Mykos, 2016. Scott Kraynak. Colored pencil. 20x30 in. Copyright Scott Kraynak

Fig. 65   The Monster That Ate Cleveland, 2017. John D. Morton. Giclee print assembled from watercolor paintings. Copyright John D. Morton.

Fig. 66 Hulett Ore Unloaders, 2018. Nina Vivian Huryn. Leather, tooled, painted, and dyed on wood. With assorted nails, brads, tacks and found objects. 24x19 in. Copyright Nina Vivian Huryn.

Fig. 67 Moonlit. Evie Zimmer. Copyright Evie Zimmer

Fig. 68   Doan brook slowly got buried over 200 years but it pops out here and there, around Superior, up to Coventry (it smells in the Summer), 2015. Corrie Slawson. Screen print, paper lithography, acrylic, Sumi ink, spray paint and pencil on paper. 96x47 in. Copyright Corrie Slawson

Fig. 69   A Wet Spring. Brinsley Tyrrell. Glass enamel fused onto steel. 36x48 in. Copyright Brinsley Tyrrell

Fig. 70   Wind in Winter. Brinsley Tyrrell. Glass enamel fused onto steel. 36x48 in. Copyright Brinsley Tyrrell

Fig. 71   Naji's World. Judy Takacs. Oil on canvas. 24x48 in. Copyright Judy Takacs

Fig. 72   Cleveland Industry #2. Chris Deighan.   Copyright Chris Deighan

Fig. 73   Shine. Judy Brandon. Ink, charcoal and pastel on Incised printmaking paper. 42x29.5 in. Copyright Judy Brandon.

Fig. 74   Lead the Way, 2018. Rich Cihlar and Bob Peck. Acrylic and spray paint. Copyright Rich Cihlar and Bob Peck.

Fig. 75   A Place to Stay, A Place to Pray, and Creeping Pollution. Moses Pearl. Oil on canvas. Copyright Moses Pearl and The Artists Archives of the Western Reserve

Fig. 76   Innerbelt Bridge Demolition. Stuart Allen Pearl. Photograph. Copyright Stuart Allen Pearl

Fig. 77   Under the Lake, 2018. David Cintron. Acrylic on canvas. 48x24 in. Copyright David Cintron.

Fig. 78   Reflections, 2017. Christina Sadowski. Photograph. Copyright Christina Sadowski

Fig. 79   Black Walnut, 2011. Hilary Gent. Oil on canvas. 72x48 in. Copyright Hilary Gent.

Fig. 80 and 81. 2018. Photographs. Copyright Courtney Bonning.

Fig. 82   Valley of Revelations, 2018. John W. Carlson. Oil and charcoal on canvas. 24x30 in. Copyright John W. Carlson

Fig. 83   On the Rocks, 2018. Mark Brabant. Digital illustration. 18x24 in.   Copyright Mark Brabant

Fig. 84   Satchel Paige, 2018. James Quarles. Copyright James Quarles

Fig. 85   Julie. Ryan Kacsandy. Copyright Ryan Kacsandy.

Fig. 86   Star, 2017. Timothy Callaghan. Gouache on paper. 35x35 in. Copyright Timothy Callaghan.

Fig. 87   Planar Study, pink, 2018. Rebecca Cross. Dyes on silk. 27x33 in. Copyright Rebecca Cross.

Fig. 88   My Home Town, 1998. Michelangelo Lovelace (American, 1960-). Acrylic on canvas; unframed: 139.7 x 243.8 cm (55 x 95 15/16 in.). The Cleveland Museum of Art, Gift of the Artist, Michelangelo Lovelace, Sr. 2015.83

Fig. 89   The Community, 2016. Michelangelo Lovelace. Acrylic on canvas. 39x42 in. Copyright Michelangelo Lovelace.

Fig. 90   Cleveland Fixed Again, 2018. Glenn Baskin. Ink on paper. Copyright Glenn Baskin.

Fig. 91 and 92   Cuyahoga, 2018. Michael Greenwald. Spray enamel, gold and silver leaf and epoxy resin on wood. 12x24 in. each. Copyright Michael Greenwald.

Fig. 93   All Over Town, 2015. Michael Gill. Color wood block print. 8x8 in.   Copyright Michael Gill.

Fig. 94   He Wanted to Finish the Job, 2015. Michael Gill. Color wood block print. 8x8 in. Copyright Michael Gill.

Fig. 95   Untitled, 2018. Diane Zizka. Watercolor and charcoal pastel on paper. 21x17 in. Copyright Diane Zizka

Fig. 96, 96b, 96c Loci of Potential/Sites of Transition, 2016. Laila Voss. Installation with Core Sample Silo. 2016. Corrugated polycarbonate, steel, taconite, plaster, limestone, coke, sand, clay, soil, concrete, resin. 7'x 3.3'D and preliminary studies. Copyright Laila Voss.

Fig. 97   Sunset Bridge, 2018. Nick Taylor. Acrylic on panel. 6x6 in. Copyright Nick Taylor

Fig. 98   Red, 2018. Frank Oriti. Oil on panel. 10x8 in. Copyright Frank Oriti

Fig. 99   CLE Feeds Me. Claudio Orso-Giacone.   Copyright Claudio Orso-Giacone.

Fig. 100   Terminal Spin, 2011. Mike Nekic. Photograpy. 11x14 in. Copyright Mike Nekic

Fig. 101 and 102   Hayden and Shaw, Corner of Plato, Mural on East 152nd St. Douglas Max Utter. Both acrylic and pencil on canvas. Both 24x24 in. Copyright Douglas Max Utter.

Fig. 103   Rusted Heart #6, 2018. Tim Lachina and Ray McNeice. Mixed media. 12x12 in. Copyright Tim Lachina and Ray McNeice.

Fig. 104   Columbus Road Lift Bridge. Michael Prunty. Courtesy Michael Prunty and WGS Productions.

Fig. 105   Hogsback Lane 1, 2018. Eileen Dorsey. Oil on canvas. 30x30 in. Copyright Eileen Dorsey.

Fig. 106   Untitled. Billy Nainiger. Mixed media. 32x36 in. Copyright Billy Nainiger

Fig. 107   Untitled. Jonathon Sawyer. Marker on paper. Copyright Jonathon Sawyer

Fig. 108   Promethian Web #2., 2008. Randall Tiedman. Acrylic and oil on paper. 33x49 in. Courtesy of Wges Porducitons.